Rugby–The ART of SCRUMMAGING

RUGBY
THE **ART** OF
SCRUMMAGING
Enrique TOPO Rodríguez

Meyer & Meyer Sport

British Library Cataloguing in Publication Data

A catalogue record for this book is available from the British Library

Rugby–The Art os Scrummaging

Maidenhead: Meyer & Meyer Sport (UK) Ltd., 2014

ISBN: 978-1-78255-059-4

© 2015 by Meyer & Meyer Sport (UK) Ltd.

Aachen, Auckland, Beirut, Cairo, Cape Town, Dubai, Hägendorf, Hong Kong,

Indianapolis, Manila, New Delhi, Singapore, Sydney, Tehran, Vienna

Member of the World Sport Publishers' Association (WSPA)

Manufacturing: Print Consult GmbH, Munich, Germany

ISBN: 978-1-78255-059-4

E-Mail: info@m-m-sports.com

www.m-m-sports.com

Table of Contents

CHAPTER

1

First section

FIRST SECTION

TOPO's introduction and explanation

Rugby—The ART of SCRUMMAGING was originally published in Sydney in August 2012 and quite obviously didn't cover the new scrum engagement sequence changes that were introduced in 2013.

One of the most significant characteristics of those changes was the elimination of the noxious and dangerous hit on engagement, prior to the put-in of the ball. The introduction of the pre-bind engagement by the IRB took place in early April 2013 during a South Pacific competition and trial matches played between teams of Australia, Fiji, New Zealand, Samoa and Tonga. These new changes and modifications were adopted for official trial in September 2013 for the Rugby Championship (Southern Hemisphere) and soon after in the European Premier Rugby Championships.

The amazing thing with the hit was that neither the law book nor the coaching manuals ever refer to such a maneuver or tactic. This means that it developed on its own out of competitiveness at the high international levels as a way of circumventing the law or other restrictions imposed by referees.

This is not new as the scrum has been adapting and morphing through hundreds of years whether the referees like it or not. I will weigh in on over-officiating which on one hand may prevent accidents but on the other are killing fun, initiative and creativity. Today we are no longer watching just a sport; we are watching a business, an entertainment and lastly, a sport.

In my opinion the priorities, particularly on the part of rugby management, have dramatically changed and are affecting the final product we receive in the stands on the field or at home on TV.

Therefore *Rugby—The ART of SCRUMMAGING* will cover the developments regarding the rugby scrum and its law since late 2012 onwards. Plenty of controversy, myths and contradictions have already developed, so I will endeavor to cover those points as much as possible in *Rugby—The ART of SCRUMMAGING*.

Disclaimer

Rugby—The ART of SCRUMMAGING (RTAOS) may serve as a scrummaging instructional guidelines document provided for general information. Information contained in RTAOS is provided without any warranty, and no guarantee is given in relation to the accuracy or currency of any information. Care has been taken in the formulation, preparation and presentation of this technical knowledge for the benefit of rugby followers and the general public, however, the author does not claim that RTAOS is an authority on the subject. RTAOS must not be used or relied upon as a substitute for professional supervision or professional advice, particularly in reference to sports medicine practices. Before undertaking any scrummaging training exercises or scrummaging programs, you should consider consulting a qualified fitness adviser or qualified rugby coach to ensure the activity or regime is suitable for you and is in accordance with the official guidelines of your country of residence.

In any case, it would be wise and strongly recommended to consult with your own doctor in case you have or may have developed a medical condition or are taking medication, or have any other concern that may interfere with your health.

We discourage anyone from undertaking any exercise or sporting program without appropriate professional or qualified supervision/advice. The author cannot be held responsible for any injuries, loss or damage which may occur as a result of following RTAOS or related activity.

The author is not responsible for any other published material referred to in RTAOS, nor does it endorse any commercial product or service referred to in RTAOS. Should you feel that any of the information contained in *Rugby—The ART of SCRUMMAGING* is erroneous, incomplete or incorrect, we request you contact us as soon as possible to assist us in rectifying it.

Copyrights reserved

Acknowledgements

Crossing over to psychology in a book about scrummaging has raised a few eyebrows. However, I've always been a firm believer of mind over matter. Many thanks to Michael N. Fox, Steve D. Mellalieu, and Peter C. Terry for sharing your invaluable insights and helping rugby people to improve their scrummaging regardless of position or area of responsibility. The selfless contribution and artistry of my daughter, Victoria I. Rodriguez, that has made this book so much easier for everyone to read—whether neophytes, aficionados, or professionals—can never be underestimated. Thank you, Victoria.

The original version of *The ART of SCRUMMAGING* published in August 2012 could never have been undertaken without the professional expertise of my consultant and writer R.J.P. Marks, my editor Peter Fenton, OAM, and my coordinator R.V. Turnbull. All have a lifetime involvement in rugby and have provided their time and skills with the desire of improving the game that they value so much. The same applies to the many expert collaborators who, with their personal comments, have added invaluable insights to the final chapter.

My message to family and friends

I would like to give a special thank you to my father, Enrique Nuri Rodriguez, and my mother, Lidia Josefa Basi, not only for bringing me into this crazy world but also for never showing me the easy shortcuts of life.

Throughout the last 50 years or so I have gathered many friends, both in Argentina and Australia. I can't begin naming you all because I may either unjustly forget some of you or even run out of space. Many have been guiding beacons to follow and others have been much cherished emotional company. Some, as mentioned throughout chapter 1 definitely have been and continue to be a source of inspiration and motivation in both good and bad times for me. Life after rugby has been a colourful rollercoaster ride at best, a bit rough, lean and disheartening at times, but definitely invigorating and worth sticking around for. Through good times and bad I've always received the support of sincere and generous friends. You know well who you are, and I am indebted to you forever!

I learned not so long ago that when I receive any form of help, I chain up my ego; I accept whatever help is offered; and I pay it forward and, if possible, increase it two-fold! I have learned that those three steps are a very important part of the universal circle of gratitude.

In a household of five siblings we were quite often told: "It has to be done" and "It is up to you." We had to find our own way. A sense of responsibility was ever present in the air and any sense of indulgence or complacency seemed to have been stamped out (perhaps at birth). Although during our infancy and adolescence we rarely went without a meal or clothes, everything was measured and we had to endure several tough financial times.

Our family started in Concordia, Entre Rios (Argentina) with Liliana Maria, Enrique Edgardo, Silvina Iris, and Eugenio Daniel. Around 1960, we moved to Cordoba in Cordoba Province where Melisa Nuria was born completing the Rodriguez quintet.

A big thank you goes to all of you because each one contributed in different measures and areas in my formative years and to the development of this rare clan sense. We all had to pull together in order to get through, and so we did.

To my family and friends, and so to all of you, I extend my eternal gratitude from the bottom of my heart and I ask providence for the health to continue producing whatever

I can produce; a good dose of perseverance to continue assisting people in whichever way possible.

Thank You!

Enrique TOPO Rodriguez

New life in Sydney

After arriving in Sydney in 1984 with my ex-wife Ines and children Victoria and Ignacio, the four of us practiced teamwork, helping each other at all times, and we made things work.

As immigrants, we had to make tremendous efforts to adjust to a new country with many new things and to demonstrate that we are worthy candidates for anything. And so we did! Victoria and Ignacio are two wonderful professionals, gainfully employed and contributing to this wonderful country. This was our number one reason for coming to Australia back in 1984!

And another new story begins

In 1982 in Cordoba I started to wonder about the pros and cons of playing a season or two in France. However, the conditions weren't right for the four of us so we decided to wait until a better opportunity came. A year after, during the Argentine Pumas' tour of Australia in the winter of 1983, I came to appreciate this country , its people, and its climate and saw the enormous potential for a growing family We soon decided it was a good time to move to Sydney just for a season or two as we never contemplated full migration. Thanks to Warringah RC I had the opportunity to play for them for seven years and our family lived happily in Newport, Mona Vale and Cromer. Contrary to popular belief, I came to Australia without a job, without a contract and without any money being paid to me to play! Those were very different times compared with today's rugby.

We were very happy with our permanent resident visa status and the one-way ticket to Sydney both of which were organized by the club. Mind you it took us four full days to travel: Buenos Aires – Iguazu Falls – Rio de Janeiro – Miami – Los Angeles – Tokyo – Sydney. By the end of 1984 and having played eight tests with the Wallabies, my fate was more or less sealed with the Ockers.

My original reason for writing this book was always to share experiences and knowledge acquired as a player and coach and through time spent studying the scrummaging subject. This process has invariably involved the contribution of many teammates and coaches through the years. We must remember that scrummaging involves teamwork at its best, something which I am immensely grateful for and very proud of too.

Sharing the contents of *Rugby–The ART of SCRUMMAGING* with other players, coaches and aficionados will also help me avoid taking these secrets to my grave. I sincerely hope that the collection of opinions expressed by this book will receive the full attention of the rugby world, and that they are accepted as a small contribution toward the big discussion currently taking place which aims to solve the global conundrum the scrum has faced for the past eight years. It is also my desire to become involved in an active semi-retirement capacity spreading the gospel where needed.

To my own family, even though circumstances changed through life, since our arrival to Australia, it is very important for me to acknowledge the part you all have played in my life and the realization of *Rugby–The ART of SCRUMMAGING*, 17 years in the making.

The good oil

By Peter Fenton OAM—INTRODUCTION by TOPO

Blokes' bloke, rugby man extraordinaire, scrum and sports poet, editor, and collaborator, Peter 'Fab' Fenton has coached Parramatta R.C. (Sydney) to a First Grade premiership victory, as well as the Sydney representative team to wins over several international sides. In my 30 years in Australia I've been blessed with his friendship and companionship whether as a coach or even a luncheon companion and have shared many belly laughs over his jokes and anecdotes. Having him as an editor and advisor to *Rugby–The ART of SCRUMMAGING* was a great asset and wonderful experience. His comments, opinions and insights have invariably thrown the proverbial light into quite a few tricky situations. Fab, my full gratitude to you.

Let's hear it from Fab

One thing that is extremely clear to me is that a very large number of people have become progressively disenchanted with the modern scrum despite how much time is taken trying to perfect it. I am sure we all know avid supporters who feel this way along with those who no longer attend top level games as they once did. To deny this is folly. Yes, it is convenient to watch on a big flat screen with a bottle of red, but large TVs are not new, nor is red wine. The magic of being at the game, feeling the excitement created by a boisterous crowd, and being part of the ambience of a thrilling sporting contest is not as appealing as it was.

There are too many stoppages, too many occasions where the ball is not cleared and result in melee behind where it was set. There are too many collapsed scrums, too many penalties. Worst of all, however, there are too many penalties for reasons neither seen nor understood by the spectators. If you go to a motion picture and don't understand the plot, an all-star cast will not save the film. This is what we have at scrum time in rugby matches continually around the world.

Positive, not negative, play should always be rewarded. The laws should encourage this. Remember a few seasons back when half backs constantly baulked to pass from the base of the scrum or ruck in order to get an offside penalty? How much better off did we become immediately when we decided to penalise the baulker? Now nobody baulks and the game goes on. I also believe the leniency given defending half backs while harassing the opposite number has increased alarmingly. Defending half backs are literally climbing into the opposing pack.

TOPO's insistence that a positive attitude from players themselves is essential and must be encouraged by coaches is spot on. Of course this positive play should be legal. Allowing crooked feeds because they allow the game to flow is a cop-out that leads to more problems as so many point out. One thing often mentioned is that the art of hooking has been lost. How could you disagree with that?

If the ball was thrown along the middle line and the defending team had a chance of snaring the occasional tight head, it would soon reappear and a natural depowering of the scrum would come with it. One astute contributor suggests the hooker should now be termed the thrower as he does actually throw in and no longer hooks. Promises made that referees would clamp down on crooked scrum feeds during the recent World Cup did not eventuate.

The fact that collaborators share differing views adds considerably to this book's merit. There are many possibilities in tactics and techniques that are dependent on the level of competition, together with the physical makeup and capabilities of the players and adventurous coaches.

Where do we go from here? Hopefully neither lawmakers nor referees will misunderstand the purpose of this book. Mind you, since referees have had so much input into the scrum there have never been so many problems. England and British and Irish Lions captain Martin Johnson's comment after a recent Six Nations game cannot be ignored: "What we had at Murrayfield was a game of rugby trying to break out between scrums." If this quote had come from David Campese we might have understood his frustration, but not from Johnson.

Both the writers and collaborators agree the players must be given, and must take, more responsibility for the safe setting of the scrum. Yes, safety is paramount, a fact realised and fully appreciated by the writers. Yet the groundswell of opinion doubting the safety of crouch-touch-pause-engage is so strong that it surely cannot be dismissed out of hand. If this much maligned engagement sequence is not making things safer, it is impossible to understand why it has any value at all.

The scrum is recognised by many as the single most important part of the game. It sets the scene for so much that follows. Without it there is no rugby as we know it, and there is a real fear that some are in favour of its elimination. We must treasure it, respect it, practise it and fix it. I was asked to write some simple verse to open this book and another one at the end. In this book version you have both together. Enjoy it!

Two very unique scrum poems

"The rugby scrum is quite unique,
depending not on pure physique.
Here courage, strength and rare technique,
produce a world of grand mystique.
Its artisans might justly claim,
the rugby scrum defines the game."

"If you've never been in a rugby scrum
You've played in a band without a drum
You've been on the hunt but fired no shot
You've ridden a ferry but never a yacht.
You lift your weights but you just don't sweat
You live by the course but don't have a bet
You eat your steak without red wine
You've never quite got to the front of the line.
But to those who revere this wonderful craft
You're in the top bar with the host's best draught."

CHAPTER 2

Foreword

FOREWORD

By Phil Keith-Roach

Congratulations TOPO, another masterpiece to follow your original version of The Art of Scrummaging (published 2012).

Whether for players, coaches, referees, spectators, or law makers, your work gives a special insight into the world of the scrummager.

TOPO was an outstanding Argentine/Australian loose head prop who has also played the other two positions in the front row. In this book he not only covers techniques, scrummaging styles, and preparation but he also gives some significant suggestions and recommendations as to where the law makers could go next, should the ongoing dissatisfaction with the elite scrum continue through the Rugby World Cup 2015. In his 40-year career as prop, coach, and now author TOPO has never lost his focus on: i) organized and disciplined scrummaging; and ii) professional preparation, which is so vital these days.

Our paths crossed a few times in our rugby careers; in 1978 he was part of the Argentine Pumas team that played London Division at Twickenham. Then, after immigrating to Australia with his family in 1984, TOPO was selected for the 8th Wallabies who toured the UK and Ireland. It was then that Coach Alan Jones opted to trial our Rhino Powerhouse scrum machine for the duration of the tour. We followed their 18 match Grand Slam tour to every training venue with the giant roller machine. And the Australian success at scrum time proved to be the bedrock of their unparalleled playing achievement.

TOPO was already a renowned international scrummager prior to his arrival in Australia with unique inside knowledge of the famous Argentine coordinated shove system tradition, equivalent to the 8 men shove also known as 'la bajadita' (Spanish for lowering the scrum). With his experience, age, and wisdom he quickly became the natural leader of an otherwise youthful Wallaby scrum which developed into perhaps the most efficient and powerful unit the Australians have ever fielded. Moreover, this forward domination greatly helped their very talented backline which enjoyed front-foot-possession most of the time, thus allowing them to display their brilliance as we got to see then.

TOPO brought timing and discipline to this particular band of men particularly in the scrum. His efforts paid off and how fortunate we are he's still here today dispensing his invaluable words of wisdom in his latest publication. Maybe this time World Rugby and the ARU will take note.

Curriculum Vitae

FULL NAME:	Philip Keith-Roach
BORN:	11/08/1943
EDUCATED:	St Luke's College Exeter and Pembroke College Cambridge
TEACHING:	Trinity School Croydon (1966-1968) and Dulwich College (1973-1996)
RUGBY PLAYER:	Hooker (1962-1984) Cambridge University, Gloucester Rosslyn Park London Division, England Reserve Hooker
PROFESSIONAL COACHING:	Scrummaging Coach – Wasps RFC (1996-2000) England Scrum Coach (1996-2007 Sale Sharks (2005-2010) Russia RU(2011) Stade Francais (2013 onwards)
TEAM ACHIEVEMENTS:	England 2003 Rugby World Cup Champions 2003, 2001, 2000, 1996 Five Nations Champions Sale Sharks Premiership Champions 2006. Wasps RFC Tetley Bitter Cup winners 1997 and 1998 Premiership Champions 1996 and 2000

***

CHAPTER 3

Prologue

PROLOGUE BY RAY WILLIAMS, OBE

The famous front row for Pontypool and Wales in the 1970s (left to right) Graham Price, Bobby Windsor, Charly Faulkner and Ray Williams providing key instructions, 1976.

It was Dick Marks, the former and first director of coaching of the Australian Rugby Union and a long-time friend of mine who told me that a paper was being prepared in Australia on scrummaging subsequently to be delivered to World Rugby for scrutiny and possible law changes. He asked whether I would be interested in making a contribution or at least casting an eye over the paper and offering some observations. Initially I was somewhat sceptical because over the past decade the Wallabies, despite their success, have not been renowned for their scrummaging, and in view of this I wondered how much credibility such a paper would have.

Then I became aware of some of the people involved in this exercise: Enrique TOPO Rodriguez (a prop for Argentina and Australia), Dick Marks (Australian centre and serious student of the game), Ross Turnbull (former International Rugby Football Board member and Wallaby prop). My scepticism disappeared! I well remember the 1984 Wallaby XV, of which TOPO was a much-valued member, scoring a push-over try against Wales—something that had never been done before, at least not in my memory! Eventually I received a copy of TOPO's monumental piece. Let me state that this is the most in-depth study of the scrum that I have ever read and I congratulate those responsible for its production. It will provide an authoritative discussion paper when the laws are reviewed after the 2011 Rugby World Cup. I wondered how best I could make a contribution to the *Rugby—The ART of SCRUMMAGING* and then I realised that the words philosophy and attitude figure strongly in the text. I felt, therefore, that it might be more productive if I set out some general principles rather than being specific by discussing mechanics or foot positioning, as there are others who have operated at the coal-face and are far better qualified than I to comment in this regard.

Rugby consists of a series of contests of which the scrum is one. What is my scrum philosophy? I am going to quote from my book *Skillful Rugby* (1976): "The scrum is the most important single platform in the game. It makes such physical demands that it affects one's ability in the lines-out, in the rucks and mauls, in supporting attacks and in covering in defence. In other words it affects a team's overall performance." I now use another quote from the same source: "Attitude as in all facets of the game looms large! Players must believe that good scrummaging is important. They must be prepared to scrummage for the whole game. Many packs begin a game with a rush of enthusiasm and scrummage well for the first 20 minutes, then they lose their concentration and the will to dominate. This is precisely where the side with the right attitude developed through concentrated practice can reap the benefit."

I still believe that what I wrote all those years ago is pertinent today which, in a sense, brings me to the current situation. The perception of most followers of the game is that the modern scrum is a shambles, a view that is strengthened by the number of times the scrum has to be reset. Furthermore, when the ball is put in, it is rarely straight and, even worse, referees allow it. My opinion is that the scrum has become over-regulated and consequently over-refereed. There is an urgent need to get back to a situation where players themselves take a more active part in self-regulating the formation and take control of the scrum. At the moment the referee often insists on players adopting positions which are uncomfortable and sometimes downright dangerous; so many of them try to manage situations that they do not understand. Much more attention must be paid in referees' courses to understanding the mechanics of the scrum and not merely learning the laws that govern it.

As to the crooked feed, I find it difficult to appreciate how World Rugby can issue an edict that says referees must insist the ball be put in straight and penalize the player responsible if it is not, when it is so plainly ignored. If the ball were put in straight it would restore the partnership between the scrum-half and the hooker, a relationship that I regard as just as important as that between the thrower in at the lineout and the jumper. I realise that I have not really said anything new in my comments, but this is because *Rugby—The ART of SCRUMMAGING* is so comprehensive that it is difficult to think of an area that has not been covered in some detail.

However, maybe my thoughts will strengthen those that TOPO and his colleagues have so expertly expressed. The scrum is a unique feature of rugby and if the treatise contributes to this continued position it will have served its purpose well.

Career CV

PLAYING CAREER:
Loughborough College, London Welsh, Northampton, Moseley, East Midlands, North Midlands, North Wales, Final Welsh Trial

PROFESSIONAL POSITIONS:
Senior Technical Officer – Central Council of Physical Recreation 1956/67 Coaching Organiser – Welsh Rugby Union 1967/79 Deputy Secretary/Centenary Officer Welsh Rugby Union 1979/81 Secretary – Welsh Rugby Union 1981/88 Tournament Director – Rugby World Cup 1991

HONORARY APPOINTMENTS:
Churchill Fellow 1970 Chairman, British Association of National Coaches 1971/73 & 1975/77 President, National Association of Sports Coaches 1979/90 WRU Committee 1993/97 – Vice Chairman 1995/97

Represented WRU on International Rugby Board 1993/97. Chairman, IRB Tours & Tournaments Committee 1995/97. Represented WRU on Five Nations Committee & Committee of Home Unions 1993/97. Chairman, Lions Committee 1995/97. President, Mid Glamorgan District Rugby Union 1999/2009

PUBLICATIONS:
RFU Guide for Coaches 1967. WRU Wall Charts 1973. Rugby for Beginners (Souvenir Press) 1973. Skilful Rugby (Souvenir Press) 1976

FILMS & TV:
RFU Filmlets 1964. HTV Coaching Series – Skillful Rugby 1971. This is Mini-Rugby 1973. BBC Coaching Series – Play Rugby 1974. Co-Producer BBC Wales – WRU Centenary Film 1980, "A Touch of Glory"

OVERSEAS ASSIGNMENTS:

Coaching assignments in Argentina, Australia, Bahamas, Canada, Fiji, Italy, New Zealand, Spain, Sri Lanka & USA. Advising Hungary, Latvia & Lithuania

HONOURS:

Fellow, National Association of Sports Coaches 1989. Appointed OBE 1995. Elected UK Coaching Hall of Fame 2002. Awarded Hon. BSc Loughborough University 2009. Elected Hon. Rotarian by Rotary Club of Haverfordwest 2010

TOPO's Tribute to Ray Williams, OBE

Since 1976 I have heard many stories about your deeds and achievements with the Welsh Scrum and your connection with Carlos "Veco" Villegas. You both spoke similar language when it came to scrums and rugby. In 2011 I got to know first-hand that you were a very special rugby man. Unfortunately during 2014 your health started to decline and around December we lost you. I'm forever indebted to you for your support and encouragement to continue writing *Rugby—The ART of SCRUMMAGING* no matter what. Your contribution to rugby, sense of justice and contagious joie de vivre are worth remembering and imitating. VALE Boyo Ray!

CHAPTER 4

The assignment

THE ASSIGNMENT

The object of this exercise is simply to make the scrum a safer part of the rugby game. It will be argued that the current approach has already made an improvement in this area, but it can be made even safer with a number of highly significant collateral benefits.

Safety and spectacle

In recent Super 15 games we have seen scrums collapse with multiple resets following. In the major Australian local derby between New South Wales and Queensland we had five resets for one scrum, and in another game involving Waikato one scrum took seven minutes before it was resolved with a penalty try. With so many collapses this cannot be safe and if it continues, there will be a very serious injury at the highest level.

This book is dedicated to finding a solution to the problem. The basis of the safety factor lies in the theme of togetherness and tightness.

In the scrum the safety of the individual is in the collective eight providing that protection. If they are tight and pushing in the right direction, no one player is left exposed and vulnerable to potentially damaging forces. The ancillary benefits are in the production of a spectacle free of such annoying stoppages. The celebrated Lions and Rugby World Cup winning captain, Martin Johnson said some time ago: "What we had at Murrayfield was a game of rugby trying to break out in between scrums." "The game was brought to a standstill and decided by the scrum and its interpretations."

This situation can do only harm to the game and our efforts are directed at rectifying this as well. After looking at the YouTube video 'Modern Rugby Scrum' taken from a 2011 Super 15 match, most rugby enthusiasts would regard this sequence as an all too familiar sight and one that is blight on the game.

For the last four years we have witnessed these complications with the poor execution and at times incomplete scrums. And they have been too many and too often. It is generally agreed that SAFETY is a priority No 1 for all involved. Furthermore, the reduction of wasted TIME should be priority No 2. Because any long winded engagement sequence increases player fatigue and loss of concentration. This invariably generates additional risks and spectator dissatisfaction. Thus, let's aim for more CONTINUITY of proceedings (as opposed to a plodding stop-start).

The former Argentinean and Australian great front rower, Enrique TOPO Rodríguez delves into the problem and lays down his ideas in this book. By no means does he claim to provide any definitive solutions, intending rather to start a discussion with his peers and other informed experts on the scrum. The most important part of the assignment is for them to build on TOPO's work for the purpose of producing a collective view on ways to improve the rugby scrum. (Peter 'Fab' Fenton)

Proactivity and Positivity

To preserve its identity the scrum needs to be retained in the form of a robust contest. There are so many infringements proscribed in the scrum law that compliance is very difficult and penalties can be applied at will. It is the belief of the author that many problems in this area can be overcome with the application of a proactivity which allows a scrum to be executed successfully through legal means.

He promotes the idea that you can be successful in scrummaging by entering the contests with a positive attitude. A negative attitude is going in to cheat. A positive attitude is to go in so the opposition can't cheat. Part of the assignment is to promote the latter.

CHAPTER 5

Introduction

INTRODUCTION

Problem solving has always been an important factor in good scrummaging. How do you deal with an effective opposition tactic? I always enjoyed helping to devise successful counters in an individual scrum, but I now face the much bigger problem of solving the challenge we face today. We now have difficulty, not with an opposition scrum tactic, but with the scrum itself and its once revered place in the game.

Some might suggest that the scrum has an ailment, but the illness is of a more serious nature, and I think malady is a more accurate description. It is collapsing in more than one sense. I never tried to effect individual scrum cures on my own, and in tackling this issue I shall be co-opting expertise from others who share my concern. I do not mind taking the lead, however, and my process involves setting out the factors and the mechanics of a safe, effective scrum, and then opening a strong discussion on what might be the cause of the illness. After that my peers will become involved, but at the end of it all I am sure coaches will have a better idea of sound scrummaging technique and that the cause of the collapsing will be found. This should then lead to a self-evident cure.

My first writings weren't put down with this in mind but the scrummaging events of recent years have expanded my focus and determination. I started writing in 1997 and over the last 18 years I've updated my work several times in the hope of attracting the attention of a sponsor, or someone who would be interested in disseminating material that would assist coaches, players, referees and other interested people in further educating themselves on scrummaging. I am still very keen to publish it to all the rugby playing nations. This time, however, I'm doing some things differently!

I'd love to combine my knowledge and experience with that of other ex-international front-rowers and coaches to make it more relevant, topical and wide ranging. I achieved success my way but others accomplished their goals with different techniques and approaches. The fact is that the scrum is a human machine that can be tuned in a number of ways, just like a car engine. The mechanical principles are the same, but the assembly of the parts has its own nuances, and I want this work to include them all.

I want this to be a scrum manual for all, for those at the highest level, for those at the base of the pyramid and for all those frustrated supporters of the game who for too long have had to put up with the painful and boring sight of collapsed and reset scrums. I also want it to help referees who have been put in the invidious position of having to manage and to adjudicate on something they don't know much about. After they read this they may help me in my campaign to bring about change to their situation. This rather ambitious scrum manual contains personal insights, philosophical views and specific technical information collected through many years of playing and coaching experience, but it is also greatly enhanced by the contributions of experts who have done it all before. In a nutshell it contains a complete overview of all the fundamental aspects of the rugby union scrum.

It is ambitious in the sense that it is meant to provide not only an instructional reference, but also to become an instrument for further progress. You can't have a good scrum under the current laws and the way that they are applied. It is my intention, therefore, that this paper will play its part in a changing of the scrum law that makes compliance possible, that removes any incentive to collapse, that recognizes the competitiveness of the contest and that partially reduces the involvement of the referee.

With that in mind this treatise will deal with the history of the scrum, the technical aspects of it and the surrounding issues, and conclude with a philosophical approach to the laws and some ideas on how they might be improved.

This last section contains some strong comments from me concerning necessary changes, but there are equally robust recommendations from my scrummaging colleagues. Whatever form the post-2011 Rugby World Cup scrum review takes, I would hope its scope is wide enough to consider all the ideas in this book. I venture to say that there aren't many proposals that haven't been canvassed in later chapters.

I hope this information helps to achieve one more thing, and that is to restore the integrity of the scrum. It is plainly wrong that it has been allowed to fall into its current state of disrepute. The importance of the scrum is encapsulated under the following headings:

UNIQUE. No other sport contains this sort of contest.

DIVERSITY OF SKILLS AND PHYSIQUES. The front-rowers, hookers, second-rowers, number eights, blindside flankers and open side flankers have special physical and mental attributes and tend to be shaped differently. Reduce the influence of scrummaging in the game and many of those players would suffer selection consequences. In junior and schools rugby we already see coaches picking flankers instead of props to achieve more speed to the breakdown.

ATTACKING PLATFORM. This is the one occasion where all forwards are forced to assemble and to leave the backs in a one-on-one situation which is conducive to open, innovative and clever combinational work. Furthermore, the method of delivery from the scrum itself can enhance the options of the backlines.

COLLATERAL BENEFITS. Scrummaging is the most tiring part of the game and good scrummagers require a strength and endurance that will be of immense benefit to them, not only in defence, but also in other contests such as rucking and mauling. If the front row is unable or ill-equipped to push, then the back five have to work extra hard, and are likely to suffer serious consequences when contesting the breakdown. Already we are seeing a downgrading in endurance and I say that because one of the qualities of rugby players was being able to play intensely for 80 minutes. With the use of seven reserves as impact players, many players no longer have to work for 80 minutes. Reduce scrummaging any further and this great quality of endurance will be diminished accordingly.

CONCENTRATION AND COMBINATION. A good scrum requires a disciplined group effort that cannot be attained without a high degree of concentration and mental toughness, which again enriches the diversity of the game itself.

The lawmakers have already eliminated a lot of scrums in favour of kicking and the unit is currently being demonised to the point that this trend is likely to continue. There is even some radical thought that the scrum should be converted to a non-pushing contest or even eliminated altogether. There is no doubt that the scrum has lost popularity through the wasted time associated with it. During its better days the packs would go down, the ball would go in and the scrum half would clear it by passing, running or kicking; it was quick and it was clean.

I believe I can help to rectify the situation with the assistance of a band of expert collaborators who share my apprehension and I'll start sowing the seeds of change in our later section on law. Without wishing to lift scrummaging to a religious level, I would like this chronicle to be regarded as an ecumenical document meant for the entire rugby family.

This treatise may seem Australia-centric or in some instances Argentina-centric, but I beg you to keep in mind that is only because it is in those countries where I had my opportunities to play and learn. I would like to think that, while people interested in this subject from those two countries will benefit from this publication, this knowledge is universal. Anything that I can relay now is from a schooling that involved the many players and coaches with whom I have played and under whom I have worked. It was with their support and tutelage that I was able to play in excess of 500 games in 21 years from my beginnings in 1971 at the grassroots level playing with Universidad Nacional RC and later from 1978 with Tala RC (Cordoba, Argentina) until 1984 when I moved to Australia to join Warringah RC in Sydney until 1992.

Some history to consider

Although not an essential part of a book like this, an historical background on various aspects of the scrum not only enlightens us as to its evolving place in the rugby game, but also explains what a key part of the game it has been.

International Account

Its origin is very much based in the early days of rugby when the game consisted of everyone just diving onto the ball wherever it was and hacking anyone that was in the way—one giant amorphous scrum, so to speak.

Those who didn't approve of the hacking of players broke into a separate game that eventually became football, or soccer as it is called in some countries.

Eventually the original form of the game was refined by reducing the number of participants to 20 players per side, but you could still pile in to get at the ball and the indiscriminate kicking of players that got in the way remained. In 1871 the International Rugby Board was formed and the first game it sanctioned was between England and Scotland with 20 players per team.

Around 1886 it was decided that the game should involve the hands as well as the feet, so players were empowered to pick up the ball and run with it, as well as being able to transfer it to other players in their team. So began another of the game's identities—passing.

Around this same time, Harry Vassall, the very inventive captain of the Oxford University team, theorised that half of the team should go forward into the contest to get the ball and that the other half should be designated as passing specialists and remain back. This is where we derive the terminology of forwards and backs. In this formation he then determined that one player should be a half forward and one a half back. That explains another piece of terminology, although in most countries the half back is now called the scrum half.

Once the idea of a half back had been established, Harry found names for the other backs. Those a bit further away became known as the three quarters and those on the wings, or side extremities, were called just that. The player between the half back (4/8ths) and the three quarters (6/8ths), of course, became known as the five eighth. The last player who was out of the backline and right at the back was appropriately called the full back. All very logical you might say!

While on the subject of terminology the disputation process needs to be recalled. In the event of a dispute it was the two captains who would determine the outcome. Where there was no agreement the matter was referred to a third party who, not surprisingly, became known as the referee.

It was in the late 1880s that the scrum developed. It was formed by those members of the team that played in the forward division but, although it was the forwards who took part, it wasn't in the ordered structure that we have today. The packing down took place in the order of arrival with the first group going in, the second lot in next and the last arrivals joining at the back. That's how the current names of front row, second row and back row came into being. By this stage it became the practice to have eight forwards in the contest with three players in the front row.

Enter the Originals, the All Blacks on their 1905 tour of the UK, Ireland, France and North America who smashed everyone except Wales, who beat them at Cardiff Arms Park by the gigantic margin of three points to nil. Therein lies the great rivalry that was to exist for many years between New Zealand and Wales. It was significant that Wales achieved its success by copying the opposition with the installation of a rover.

In their treatment of the scrum these Originals also swapped players around but only used seven players in the scrum. Of these only two went into the front row and the eighth, who happened to be the captain Dave Gallagher, played as a rover who ran around getting in everyone's way. Apart from giving the All Blacks an extra back, this two-man front row was able to grab the loose head no matter whose put-in, and this greatly advantaged them in the hooking contest. Later on its players specialised in their positions and the inward pressure exerted by the two props on the opposing hooker more than compensated for the weight of eight opponents driving straight ahead.

From the late 1890s until 1931 the scrum formation varied both among countries and within countries. The structure was not very detailed in terms of the law, and a number of the changes occurred after tours when one country saw first-hand what another was doing. During this period the battle for the loose head played a big role where the two-man front row, a specialty of New Zealand, continued to have an advantage. The stupidity of this battle was highlighted when, out of frustration, Wales put six men in the front row during a 1906 test against South Africa.

With this freedom we saw international teams using all sorts of combinations, some with designated players and others still working on the first-there basis. Those variations included 2:3:2, 2:3:3, 3:2:3 and 3:4:1, the modern day configuration. It appears that the South Africans settled on a three-man front row fairly early which is significant as, for the first half of the 20th century, they built their game on the scrum.

The South Africans had the incredible record of never being beaten in a series from 1893 until 1956 when they lost against the All Blacks in New Zealand. That supremacy was founded on an incredibly powerful scrum accentuated by the 'kick out on the full' law, and until 1949 being able to take the option of a scrum when the ball was put out by the opposition. Many historians rate the 1937 Springboks as the greatest team ever.

After two tests and with one to play in 1937 it was one all when the Springbok team captain, Philip Nel, received a telegram from the President of the South African Rugby Union which consisted of three words: SCRUM, SCRUM, SCRUM. They did and they won. As a matter of interest that team contained such greats as Danie Craven and Boy Louw.

Moving on in 1930 the British Lions toured New Zealand, with a short stopover in Australia, and interestingly enough had no players listed as hookers. That particular tour was the catalyst that saw the demise of the 2:3:2 scrum. The manager James Baxter started a crusade against the host's habit of fielding a two-man front row with a wing forward deployed outside the confines of the scrum. He condemned the rover outright as a cheat and Baxter's mission ultimately led to a change in the laws and the outlawing of this practice.

Some would argue that the 2:3:2, or diamond, scrum was on the way out during the first All Blacks tour of South Africa in 1928. The nemesis struck in the form of the South African 3:4:1 scrummage. By driving inwards rather than straight ahead, the South Africans put the two-man New Zealand front row under intolerable pressure.

The All Blacks managed to square the series after copying the three-man front row, but reverted to 2:3:2 against Australia in 1929 and lost all three tests. The old formation had its final fling against the 1930 Lions and the rest is history.

I should conclude this brief account by saying that the scrum has produced some quite extraordinary practices. The six-man front row has already been mentioned above, but here are excerpts from two old articles. The first is by A.C. Parker from the Cape Argus in South Africa: "Realising the futility of their two-man front row they [the All Blacks] came up with a clever counter in the second test at Johannesburg. As soon as a scrummage was formed, the rover, Ron Stewart (who had replaced Scrimshaw), packed down as a third hooker on the side on which the ball was being put in. Eventually Daunce Pretorius, the South African scrum half, waited for Stewart to pack down before throwing the ball to Nic Pretorius, the flanker on the opposite side, to put in."

How can we let a piece of rugby with such a distinctive and colourful history continue to be the bane which it now is?

The second article was written by William 'Offside Mac' McKenzie who played for the All Blacks from 1893 to 1897 and is credited with developing the wing forward into a specialist position.

"Our front-rankers [the two hookers in the front row] get possession by a half-circular sweep of each outside leg so soon as the ball is thrown in to the scrum. Constant practice engenders machine-like precision, but it is always advisable to wear shin guards – you may trust in Providence, still, wearing bullet-proof protections will give a cast-iron confidence. The ball passes from the front-rankers to the 'pivot' or lock who, if his side is pressed essays a 'screw', or he may 'screw' when his team is in its opponent's 25, just to mystify them. Remember the golden rules of rugby football are – Condition, Common Sense, Combination, and to do that which the enemy does not expect. As Mullineux [see *] states that screwing is in its infancy in the Commonwealth, the Maoriland modus operandi may be of use to the novice.

When the ball is passed to him, the pivot (who has one arm just above each of his two front comrades' outside hips) picks it up with his knees, then the hands give notice by a tighter grip and push, and the two front-rankers turn half round, the opposing scrum is swung one way, and the pivot and his four comrades – the front-rankers cannot join in – attended by the two wing forwards, who have dropped to the back of the scrum, career, a phalanx of muscle and activity, on to the unfortunate backs.

The only way to defeat this screw is for the opposing scrum, when it finds that it is swerving, to fall down. Having nothing to push against, the other side also falls. However, players are not advised to fall down, as to do so is distinctly against the rules."

*Matthew Mullineux (8 August 1867 – 13 February 1945) was an English rugby union scrum half who, although not capped for England, was selected for two British Lions tours. He gained one cap during the 1896 tour to South Africa and captained the 1899 tour of Australia. An Anglican minister, he would later become a chaplain in the British Army, and was awarded the Military Cross for his actions during World War I.

TOPO's Argentine Perspective

"A lot has been said, through the years, about the powerful Argentinean scrum and its techniques. There have been some amusing folklore interpretations. Many Argentine teams have come to Australia and many players have shown different sets of skills. It is amazing that to date no one has replicated or copied that technique, that approach or those philosophies, except when it worked for the Wallabies between 1984 and 1986. To the best of my knowledge and with the intention of explaining some of the myths and beliefs I will touch on the subject briefly."

THE WORD THAT STILL RESONATES MOST IN MY MIND WITH REGARD TO SCRUMMAGING IS ATTITUDE. Even today "you may or may not have the put-in, you may win the ball or not, but if you want to, you can win the scrum without getting the ball." Those are the words of engineer Carlos A. (Veco) Villegas, the renowned coach of San Isidro Club from Buenos Aires, Argentina. From the 1970s to the 1990s he designed the template for that club to produce one of the most dominant scrums of the modern era in international rugby. San Isidro Club has out-scrummed many international packs for more than 30 years both overseas and at home, including countries like Wales in 1972 and 1980; France in 1974, 1985 and 1988; South Africa in 1972, 1973 and 1980; Australia in 1979 and 1987; England in 1981; Fiji in 1980 and Romania in 1973.

Carlos (Veco) Villegas was a disciple of Francisco (Catamarca) Ocampo, a great rugby coach from 1930 to 1970 in Argentina. Ocampo was a very studious and astute man who developed his technique from the All Blacks' 1904-1905 model, a seven-man scrum with a 2-3-2 formation. Additionally he embraced some ideas and techniques from the Junior Springboks team tour of Argentina in 1932. Villegas began to write a book on the famous Argentine Coordinated Push, the forerunner to the eight-man shove subsequently adopted by other countries. Unfortunately, he was unable to finish his book before his death in a plane crash in 1988.

The Argentine coordinated shove system

"A perspective on the background of the father of the coordinated push" By Marcos J. Ocampo

In order to give a clear understanding of this system which I will be explaining here, it is essential to make a brief reference to the background of the person who created and developed it over a period of 40 years, my late father Sr. Francisco G. Ocampo, who was born in the north western province of Catamarca in 1902 and died in Buenos Aires in 1970.

Catamarca is a province situated eight hundred miles away from Buenos Aires, the capital of Argentina, where in 1921 my father was sent to the Agricultural College. He was expected to obtain a university degree and then return to Catamarca to take up the family business. He eventually gave up his Agronomy studies, settling in Buenos Aires where he married Sra. Susana Thwaites. Sra. Susana would always be involved in the after match discussions, quite capable of holding her own on any of the rugby subjects.

When he attended his first rugby match in Buenos Aires around 1923, Sr. Ocampo´s first comments were: "What I've just seen is what most reminds me of the hard duties of country life in my province." He took up rugby and became known by close friends and fellow players by his nickname "Catamarca." He played rugby from 1924 to 1934 as wing forward and occasionally as stand-off.

During those years he became a scholar of the game. He read practically every book and article that had been written in English at that time. Two books had a profound impact on Francisco Ocampo´s knowledge and ideas of the game. These were Rugger by Lord W. W. Wakefield and The Complete Rugby Footballer by Dave Gallaher and J. W. Stead. This resulted in Sr. Ocampo's vast knowledge of the game. He studied the scrum in greater detail as he thought that it was the best expression of teamwork, which confirms the assertion that the whole is greater than the sum of the parts.

In 1927 Sr. Ocampo saw the strong England XV that visited Buenos Aires and won every match. The same occurred with the Junior Springboks in 1932. Sr. Ocampo resented the lack of interest shown by the local authorities in improving the preparation of the local teams.

From 1936 to 1938 he coached the famous Old Georgian team, champions of the league during those years. In 1938 he also coached the Club Atletico San Isidro (CASI)

so there was an overlap as he was simultaneously coaching two teams playing in the First Division League. He was very successful with both teams.

In the 1940s Sr. Ocampo withdrew for several years before taking up Olivos RC, San Fernando RC plus other Second and Third Division teams in 1949. In 1954 and 1955 he returned to coach CASI who won the championship both years. Besides a narrow loss (0-6) against France, who visited Argentina in 1954, CASI won every match they played.

Meanwhile he continued to develop his ideas. He read and thought through his ideas by trial and error, which led to success as well as frustration. However, scrum was always a strong point in all the teams that he coached.

Sr. Ocampo followed another principle clearly expressed in *Why the Whistle Went* (published by The Rugby Football Union, in 1948, page 6). *"There are a lot of rules about the proper way of putting a ball into a scrum – and getting it out again – but they all come down to this: that the team whose forwards can shove the other lot off the ball ought to get it. Possession of the ball is meant to be a result of a good honest shove, not of some bit of 'cleverness' by a scrum half or forward."*

For many years he coached Liceo Militar RC (the Military Academy High School), guiding the club through its early years, and in the early 1960s, it became a club to compete with in senior rugby.

At the end of 1968 he was invited by the board of San Isidro Club (SIC) to coach their first fifteen. In previous years SIC's performance had been below expectations when considering the very high standard of its players. SIC was seen as a bohemian group of players who lacked discipline and commitment.

However, Sr. Ocampo found a group of players who were prepared for strict discipline and ready to learn and practise new tactics. By the end of the 1969 season, SIC was in fourth place, a significant progress from previous years.

Their scrum as well as the team progressed very fast with strong commitment from the players, all of which resulted in a surprise for the rugby community at large. In 1970 SIC shared the championship title with Club Universitario Buenos Aires (CUBA) and since then, they have won the championship 21 times, including in 2010 and 2011.

Strict discipline, scrummaging and improvement in all skills and, obviously, the players' commitment have been the key to their success. Sr. Francisco Ocampo died in April 1970 and SIC decided to continue in the new era inviting Sr. Ocampo´s best disciple, Carlos 'Veco' Villegas, by then in Liceo Militar, to carry on. Villegas, who was only 24, did an excellent job as head coach, assisted by SIC´s experienced coaches who enthusiastically adhered to the new ideas.

SIC's success in 1971, 1972 and 1973 was the reason that practically all clubs in Argentina decided to improve their scrums. When Villegas, together with Emilio 'Gringo' Perasso, took up the Pumas in 1974 he brought in the coordinated shove. From then on a powerful scrum became a feature of the national team.

A Special Mention of San Isidro Club's Most Important International Achievements

In 1972 SIC drew 13-13 against South Africa's Gazelles dominating and pushing back their much bigger forwards. On 8 June 1974 they lost 10-34 to France, yet they scored a pushover try. This was highly praised by L'Equipe which mentioned that France was for the first time heavily pushed over. They also succeeded in scoring a pushover try against Australia during the 22-22 draw on 10 October 1987.

Principles of the scrum

There is a common belief that the scrum is just a way to restart play after a minor infraction. This idea ignores the hard preparation required to obtain a solid scrum. If that were the case it would be much easier to restart play, such as in rugby league for instance, with a free kick. But, as Ray Williams, OBE (Wales) used to say, "that would become another sport then as the scrum still is a key feature of rugby." The 2011 RWC has demonstrated this clearly. It should be stressed that it is one thing to win the ball, and something completely different 'to win the scrum. If a team wins the ball going backwards the scrum half would be in trouble and the three quarters forced to move off their position thus leading to a disorganised defence. On the other hand a scrum that wins the ball moving forward should have different attacking options as well as being in a stronger position psychologically.

Assuming that we have eight forwards with strict discipline, conviction and commitment we can start with the principles of the scrum.

a) Straighten the back

The back of each forward must be straight and parallel to the ground so it can transmit the force of the other forwards as well as their own through their legs.

b) Coordinated shove

When packing the scrum, the legs of the eight forwards should be crouched so that when the forwards receive the command to shove; all sixteen legs are straightened at the same time, thus enabling a strong shove forward.

c) Correct direction and application of force

Forwards must be firmly bound leaving no gaps. This is one of the reasons why we prefer that the second row bind to the prop's hip joint and not between the legs grabbing the prop's shorts. This way both second row forwards can each use their outside arm to attract the respective prop towards them and with the inside arm hold their colleague in a tighter grip. When talking about correct application of force we are referring to a subject which is commonly overlooked (i.e., the positioning of second row and flankers' shoulders on the props' buttocks).

This is a very important point because if the four forwards in the second row (3-4-1 system) do not apply their shoulders in the correct point (neither above nor below the props' buttocks), strength is completely dissipated and a strong scrum by the opposition can take advantage of that weakness.

d) Feet position

All forwards must try to apply as many studs as possible into the ground, only leaving those of the heel off the ground, in order to allow a good crouch and a further shove. In the case of the props our opinion is different from the one prevailing. We think that the outside foot should be slightly behind the inside one. This generates a better utilisation of the flankers' force and favours the direction of strength towards the centre of the scrum. The hooker's feet are then aligned with the inside foot of each prop. In regards to the second row, their inside foot slightly rearward should favour the number eight's shove. The flankers should bind parallel to the second row, their feet the same as the props' for the reasons mentioned above, bound to the second row with their inside arms. They should press the props' hips with their head and place the outside hand on the ground thus adding to the concentration of force. **Our aim is that none of the power for the shove is dissipated.**

Note that we use the word slight. The reason is that if feet are excessively separated from each other, too much force is wasted because one foot would be supporting the body's weight and the other would not be fully utilising its power when extending the legs at the moment of pushing. This error is very common in wing forwards.

It is also very common that the forwards tend to change the position of their feet to suit their comfort. But this is the moment to remind the players that scrum is teamwork, every forward is one eighth part of a scrum, so each forward should do what is best for the team.

Regarding the push taking the centre of the scrum as target, there was something that Sr. Ocampo always had present in mind and inculcated to his charges:

"... each man pushes so as to get the maximum of his power applied to the blunt point of the wedge as represented by the shoulders of the hookers. In the English system the eight men push forward with a result that inevitably will become a considerable amount of waste."

Furthermore, the shove directed to the centre tends to push the rival props out and as a consequence push the whole opposition pack backwards.

Obstacles

This path to success has not been an easy one. I shall just mention some of the problems that Sr. Ocampo faced when starting up with a new team:

» Usually hookers were the first enemies he found, as players in that position refused to accept they were only the eighth part of the scrum and not the stars. SIC was lucky enough to have the late Osvaldo "Coco" Rocha as hooker and the first forward convinced that they were on the right track.

» Sometimes wing forwards did not like to lose visibility in loose play. But now they had to understand they were forwards above all so their first duty was to pack and shove in the scrum as explained above.

» Referees interpreted the rules against the system.

» Other teams, who were not used to being pushed backward, lobbied against the system (through the media, former senior players, the rugby grapevine, etc).

» People resist change.

» Improvement was slower than expected.

Tips on training the scrum

» As with all skills, in rugby it is always preferable to go for quality rather than quantity (i.e., it is much better to have a short and intense practice with good technique than a strenuous session in which everyone leaves aside technique).

» The scrum machine is useful to teach packing, binding and shoving, but long sessions without making any correction to players pushing the machine do not serve any purpose.

» When a team achieves an effective scrum with experienced players, it is ideal for them to practice with another team whose scrum is on a similar level. If coaches and players are convinced that the practise will be productive for both teams to improve their scrums, it is a win/win situation. Strong discipline is essential. The forwards should always keep in mind that each one is one eighth of the scrum, not looking to remain in their comfort zone but how best to serve the team.

» A scrum half has to be involved in the whole scrum practice; he must be the ninth forward and perfectly understand how the scrum works.

Regarding the rules of the game I am sure that they can be improved upon but there must be a concerted commitment not only from the referees in applying such rules, but also from players and coaches. For instance, if a team practises to collapse the scrum (completely illegal) each time they notice that they are about to lose the ball, they are the ones who spoil the game, not the referee.

The Author

Marcos J. Ocampo was born in Buenos Aires in 1939. He graduated as a lawyer and practised in Buenos Aires until his retirement in 2001. Like his father he has a passion for rugby and has been a keen follower of his father's ideas.

Club de Regatas Bella Vista is his club where he started coaching its junior divisions in 1966 at the time that the club was introducing the practice of rugby. From then on he has coached practically all divisions of the Club including a long period with the first

XV. He was president of the club from 2000 to 2004. The first XV's best performance was in 2002 when they became vice champions losing the final game precisely against San Isidro Club (SIC) 10-16 in a very even match. Marcos has been a member of the council of the Argentine Rugby Union (UAR). As a member of the coaching committee he visited several provinces and provincial clubs. Between 1974 and 1976 he was head coach of the junior Buenos Aires provincial team as well as of the junior national team (Pumitas). In 1999 he was a council member of the Argentine National delegation (Pumas) to the RWC, played in Cardiff.

Acknowledgements

First I want to thank my wife Annie who enthusiastically did all the typing with plenty of patience and suggestions for improvement in the text. Sylvia Lodge did an excellent job in improving the English, reminding me of her time as my secretary. I also wish to thank Emilio C. Perasso, Diego A. Alcorta and Federico Fleitas for their contributions.

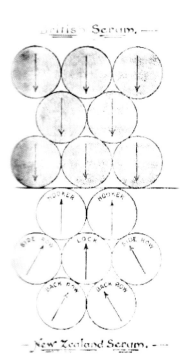

1904/05, D. Gallagher & J.W. Stead's drawing of the eight-men British scrum strategy vs the seven-men NZ scrum strategy.

Carlos 'VECO' Villegas

Testimonial by Ray Williams, OBE

Late 1960's Teacher & Disciple Sr Ocampo & Veco Villegas

The rich tapestry that is the history of Rugby Union Football is littered with famous names of rugby men who have made their own unique contribution to the game. Sadly many of them are long forgotten but from time to time one name stands out as worthy of recall; Carlos Villegas was such a man. Why else would we be commemorating the death of someone who died 20 years ago?

To put matters in perspective it is necessary to understand that during the whole of the 1970s the rugby ties between Argentina and Wales were extremely close. Unfortunately, the business in the Falklands/Malvinas in 1982 put a halt to such cooperation, but before this time many club teams from Argentina visited Wales to play games and to improve their rugby experience and knowledge.

Wales, during this period, set new standards in quality of play and, even more significantly, appointed the world's first professional coaching director, a position I had the privilege and honour to serve in for more than 12 years. These developments intrigued Carlos Villegas and he set out to ascertain what was happening on the Welsh rugby scene.

The first thing he did, in 1972, was to bring his club team to Wales and when he was here we spent many hours together discussing the game and the pursuit of excellence. It was no surprise for me to hear that Carlos had been appointed coach to the Pumas and that in 1976 he, along with Carlos Contepomi as manager, was to bring the Pumas on tour to Wales. What a tour it was! The Pumas in the test match gave Wales the fright of our lives; only a last minute penalty goal by Phil Bennett saved our blushes.

The match was advertised as A Wales VX v Argentina but this was the strongest team that Wales could field; a team that was on the verge of four Triple Crowns in succession. On that day we were outplayed by the Pumas and the astute planning of Carlos Villegas.

I well recollect speaking to Carlos after that game and trying to console him because he was very upset; a condition I could understand because in the same circumstances I would have felt exactly the same, outplaying the opposition but losing the match. However, life goes on and it was some years before Carlos and I had contact again. As part of the Welsh Rugby Union Centenary celebrations in 1980-1981 it was decided to organise the world's first International Conference for Coaches and Referees. The plan was to invite coaches and referees from all over the world to come and share their rugby knowledge and experience. One of the first names on the team sheet was that of Carlos Villegas. He gave a fascinating insight into the mechanics of scrummaging by way of theory and practical field work and showed that the coach needs much more than a sound background in the game. He needs to be a thinker, a motivator and a man manager. Carlos Villegas had all these qualities and what is more he was prepared to share them with others. He was a true rugby man.

Tragically his life was cut short at a relatively early age and apart from the immense loss to his family, his death was a huge loss to Argentina rugby. In 1989, shortly after his death, I was privileged to lead some coaching seminars in Argentina to honour his contribution to the game. Initially they were due to be confined to Buenos Aires, but such was the respect and regard in which he was held that we had to travel the five rugby provinces to satisfy the demand.

The interest made me aware of this man's rare qualities; he was an exceptional person and I finally understood that Argentina and rugby had lost a very good man.

Cordoba, Argentina

National University of Cordoba RC

Between the 1960s and 1970s Argentina had a number of followers and disciples of Francisco (Catamarca) Ocampo's and Carlos (Veco) Villegas' doctrines on the Argentine Coordinated Shove System. Amongst them Dr Carlos Bassani, Coach of the National University RC of Cordoba (Centre of Argentina). This is the club where I initiated my rugby as wing in second division. Bassani was a very keen observer and studious of all those developments in Argentinean scrummaging and forward play. He refined a technique for the Empuje Coordinado (Coordinated Push) and his own training methods. This was later popularised and known as the Eight-Man Shove in the English-speaking world and its influence through the years also trickled down to France and Italy, today's powerhouses of scrummaging.

National University of Cordoba RC - 1977 Championship Winning Team

Bassani coached several clubs through the 1970s, 1980s and 1990s, such as Universidad Nacional of Cordoba RC, La Tablada RC, Tala Rugby Club and Palermo Bajo RC. Almost invariably those packs were totally committed and single-minded scrummagers. Tala RC (my second club) dominated rugby in Cordoba during the same time period, going on to win the provincial championship from 1979 to 1985. This was done through uncompromising scrummaging complemented with dedication and commitment to teamwork of a good backline.

From 1986 to 1997 Tala RC was on top of the competition ladder, but now shares success with other clubs that have learnt those principles and how to apply them. The seeds of Dr Bassani's work, and the many hours of dedicated effort have given this strong little club and its individuals the basis for many achievements in life. An old friend and rugby rival Alejandro Oviedo, a disciple of Bassani, successfully coached Tala RC and Cordoba provincial selection for several years. Additionally the representative team of Cordoba Rugby Union won the National Championship two years running (1996-1997).

Many of the things that I know today with regard to scrummaging, forward play, training, weight conditioning, rugby in general, and life, I owe to my old friend, teacher and coach, Dr. Carlos Bassani, who today is an eminent and highly respected cardiologist in Argentina. Just as the discipline in learning Latin is a good training ground in general scholarship, so it is with the art, or should I say science, of scrummaging!

The Wallabies 1984-1987

I cannot let pass this opportunity to make mention of an extraordinary team with a sensational scrum that took the resurgence of Australian rugby to a new level in becoming a world power. The 8th Wallabies of 1984, full of extraordinary people, were coached by Alan Jones and Alec Evans (a wonderful partnership), both great leaders of people.

Above his attention to detail as a micro and macro manager Jones kept an eye on the big picture, ensuring all men were totally focused and attuned to the objectives of the team, the pursuit of excellence and to maximising every minute of our productive lives while on tour. Alan set the bar very high when it came to performance and often referred to the perfect 10 which Nadia Comaneci had scored in gymnastics at the Montreal Olympics in 1976. He introduced a No Mistakes continuity drill that had to be executed perfectly before we were allowed off the training paddock. This drill made more enemies than Attila.

One thing we learnt from our coach was how to be single-minded in our approach to training. I was quite okay because I was brought up under the Bassani regime, where I learnt a lot about discipline, toughness and character moulding, as well as the professional mentality of work ethics.

However, in a team of 30 players you can imagine we had a rainbow of upbringings and some would not stomach the strict discipline instilled by Alan. During the Grand Slam tour we had a few lost-temper incidents that luckily didn't escalate thanks to the intervention of some senior players and the ubiquitous Charles Wilson and his famous disciplinarian whisky sessions. Charles 'Chilla' Wilson was our tour manager, former Wallaby flanker and captain who complemented Alan and balanced things perfectly with his laid-back style.

The interesting thing was that the hard training was compounded by all positions being literally open. Of course, this created a lot of physicality and a bit of animosity in training. Mark Ella had to train very hard because at a moment's hesitation Michael Lynagh or even Michael Hawker could have been selected in front of him. Stan Pilecki and Cameron Lillicrap were always a threat to me. The competition in the back row was fearsome with David Codey, Chris Roche, Simon Poidevin, Steve Tuynman, Ross Reynolds and Bill Calcraft all touch and go. So it was on for young and old and the tension was very creative.

Jones also regularly provided the platform for senior players' input into training and sometimes into selection too. Nevertheless, when it came to the intricate world of forward play, he had a very astute and able assistant in Alec Evans, who had vast experience with Wests RC (Brisbane), and had coached the Australian U21s team. Subsequently Evans has coached Cardiff RC, Wales and many other teams like the Queensland Reds in the last couple of years. His keen eye complemented the contribution of senior players during scrummaging sessions, but his experience and knowledge of other aspects of the game proved invaluable in getting the team to perform to its capability. The ultimate reward for all the scrummaging effort came with the pushover try against Wales in 1984, because at that time in rugby history the Welsh scrum was the benchmark. With the confidence that came from that along with the individual talent that we had in the side, the crew obtained the Grand Slam for the first time and went on to capture the Bledisloe Cup in an historic winning series in New Zealand.

Everything was done around a very dominant pack of forwards that provided a platform for an effective backline. Alan Jones instituted for himself and the whole team, a set of values and principles, indoctrinating us single-mindedly every day on tour or during regular training sessions at home. We were always aiming for a top fitness level, very sound technique, total pursuit of excellence, proactive organization, preparation, positive thinking, attitude and high levels of awareness.

Jones would often say to us on tour, "You are training while you are resting," just to give you an idea that hard work can be complemented by smart work! But as I mentioned before, the internal competition was tough, so nobody thought of resting or doing less. Only injured players took time off.

Everything counted. We could say that it was a new, totally professional preparation, without today's money (what a pity!). Many of the members of that team are today very successful professionals and businessmen highly respected in the community.

I may summarise by saying that every successful team in which I played, both in Argentina and Australia, owed much of its success to its top scrummaging ability.

A rare incursion into Sevens Rugby 1979 at Cordoba Athletic Club, TOPO handling the ball

61

RUGBY : CUADRANGULAR INTERPROVINCIAL : TUCUMAN LAWN TENIS - EL TALA DE CORDOBA - MENDO-ZA RUGBY CLUB - LOS TORDOS : MZA. 15-3-80

Cordoba Province Champion 1981 - Tala Rugby Club

TALA Rugby Club logo

Mendoza, Argentina Interprovincial Championship - Tala Rugby Club

The Australian account

By Norman Tasker

The leading Australian rugby journalist of his time and a successful first grade Sydney club coach.

In Australia and in fact around the world scrummaging provokes questions that rugby supporters and spectators seem to ask over and over. They have done it for half a century but more particularly in the last 15 years since the inception of professionalism. Apart from some notable high points in our Wallaby rugby history which include a Grand Slam, a Bledisloe Cup and two World Cups amongst other trophies in the last 3 decades, attention and concentration on the scrum have waned critically, and we have suffered as a consequence.

Concord, Sydney, 1987, 1st Rugby World Cup

These days the question is a much wider one. What can we do to save the scrum itself, given the current ills of repeated collapse, unfathomable penalties and significant imbalance in technique and ability that distort the contest? The certain thing, though, is that knowing how to scrum, working at it and developing its national good health through all levels of the game is vital to any rugby country seeking to compete. In this sense, it has to be said, Australia has missed out.

As a young rugby writer the most emphatic lesson I learned of the scrum's value, and our ignorance of it, was on the Wallaby tour of South Africa in 1969. At an early scrum of the first Test, the massive Springbok front row took their comparatively lightweight Australian opponents so low that the hooker Bruce Taafe was forced to reach for the ball with his nose. As a mighty roar went around the ground, the Wallaby dirt-trackers in the stands scoured the crowd. They figured there must have been a fight somewhere. What else could the crowd be getting so excited about?

They were, of course, merely appreciative of great scrummaging. Australians, bred on the popular face of rugby league and its press saturation, had always looked upon rugby as a running game. We were pretty good at that, and the concentration that other nations gave to the scrum and forward play generally never much happened for us. We tried to change things after that tour. Scrums then were generally higher and less powerful than they are now, but we figured we needed power at least, and bigger men to lead the charge. They tried to do that, rather disastrously as it turned out.

When the Springboks came to Australia in 1971 selectors switched the heavyweight second-rower Reg Smith into the front-row to solve the bulk and power problem. Unfortunately, he had never played there, and as a novice was treated mercilessly by the technicians in the South African front row. Technique, for Australians, was something that came later.

In 1967 Ray Williams was appointed Wales' coaching organiser and with Clive Rowlands as coach, John Dawes as captain and a privileged crop of wonderfully talented players, such as Barry John, Gareth Edwards, J.P.R. Williams, Mervyn Davies, John Taylor, Gerald Davies and many others commenced the Golden Era of Welsh rugby (1969-1980).

At about that time coach Carwyn James and the Lions front-rowers Ray McLoughlin and Ian 'Mighty Mouse' McLachlan, started to work on scrum mechanics as a modern day science. Angles, application of power, timing, foot position, body height and the rest were refined to the point that their scrum led a revolution in New Zealand, and for the first time they won a series against the All Blacks. Meanwhile in Australia, bad results through 1972 and 1973 led to the formation of the National Coaching Panel under the astute and meticulous guidance of the 1960s Wallaby centre Dick Marks.

A 1975 trip to Wales by Marks and the chairman of the National Coaching Panel, Peter Crittle, ensued with revelations and revolution following as Marks and his cohorts sought out best practice from around the world and began educating Australian coaches everywhere. The scrum became a matter of importance, a weapon with which to attack opponents, rather than merely a means of re-starting the game. We got pretty good at it and things started to turn. Australia had big wins against England, Wales and the All Blacks, and the Bledisloe Cup returned to Australia for the first time in 30 years.

Revolutions, however, don't seem to last. In the afterglow of professionalism in the mid-1990s, marketing and spin seemed to overtake the measured structures which had served so well. Marks lost his job. The coaching structures dissipated. Momentum was lost.

It is an undeniable fact that Australian rugby has done well when a good scrum was in place. We recovered from 1984 when the Argentine powerhouse Enrique 'TOPO' Rodriguez joined the Wallabies and, combined with the talent picked by Alan Jones and selectors, helped to trigger the first ever British Grand Slam and, the cream on the top, a pushover try against Wales.

Australia drew together another good scrum when they won the 1991 World Cup, and again in 1999 when they won another World Cup. But the momentum, the continuum, never really came back in the waves needed.

One of the problems was the perceived need to depower the scrum at the Under-19 level and below. This was considered a safety issue, and clearly there was some need to look to the protection of young players. But it had some effects from which scrummaging as an art form has never recovered.

Pot-hunting coaches at elite school and junior levels realised that a front row made up of tearaway flankers was always going to be more profitable if survival at the scrum was no longer an issue. Soft scrums made for soft props, and the production line dried up. These days we get pushed around more than we should. The scrum generally is a blight on the game. Legislators have over-controlled it; coaches have given up on it; referees just don't know how to handle it. In many ways, we have simply lost the plot.

TOPO is making an effort to fix that. It is an enormous task. But if anybody can analyse the Australian scrum, identify its deficiencies, offer some solutions and teach some hard lessons it is TOPO. We can only wish him luck.

2004 Reunion 1984 Grand Slam Wallabies
Sydney Convention Centre (from left to right) Front row Chris Roche, Ian Williams, Enrique TOPO Rodriguez, Steve Williams (vc), Andrew Slack (c), Alan Jones AO, The Hon John Howard, Alec Evans, Charles Wilson, Mark McBain. middle row Simon Poidevin, Stan Pilecki, Tom Lawton, Brendan Moon, Andrew McIntyre, Nick Farr-Jones, Nigel Holt, Michael Hawker, Ross Hanley. back row James Black, Matthew Burke, Greg Burrows, Bill Calcraft, Bill Campbell, David Codey, Roger Gould, Peter Grigg, Phil Cox.

Preamble

The need for expertise in this complex collective art is as great today as at any time in my memory. Since 2007 we have seen the ups and downs of many teams in this department including the Wallabies. The exceptions are those countries that have dedicated a lot of time, energy, money and human resources to getting it right.

Coaching its responsibilities, guiding and mentoring roles

The role of the coach has evolved from a state of non-existence in many foundational IRB countries to one of very high profile, particularly in the professional leagues. A good coach is a valuable asset to a team in its preparation and in the formulation of its playing strategies and tactics.

Nowadays, the role of the coach or head coaches has become one which is more that of a human resources manager, coordinating all the technicians and helpers. They have three teams to deal with: one on the field, the reserves, and the team of specialist assistants. So the job has changed greatly with the priority being to have a group of 45-50 people all going in the same direction and following a common timetable.

Coaching is a good thing but coach dominance can be a bad thing, because when on the field the players have to be able to think for themselves. They must be able to resolve the problems posed by the opposition, the referee and the weather (the three constant variables of every game). They must be able to do on the field what the coach does off the field in the area of problem solving, and to a large extent they should play according to opportunity. It is no good continuing to do something that isn't working or that hasn't gone according to plan A. They must have the capacity to move to a plan B. The coach can prepare them to do all these things and give them guidelines about decision making, but in the end, and in the game, it is up to the players.

Rugby is not only about how to execute skills and ploys; it is also about when to use them. Continuity is lost as much by poor decision making as it is by skill inadequacy. When I started playing, coaches weren't allowed on the field at halftime. Having gained that concession I now see them wired up to the water boys carrying instructions about what to do in the next scrum, and to me that is being coach dominant. A good coach will not endeavour to turn his players into robots.

As far as the scrum goes, "In my scrum the credits and the debits will always go to the eight players on stage."

If it goes well I won't say, "That is because they did what I told them," and if it goes badly I won't say, "That's because the players did not do what I told them."

This manual is only a guide to scrummaging; it is a tool in the process of producing a good scrum. It needs to be in the hands of a supervisor who understands the stated principles and who can carry out the necessary tuition and mentoring work. I shall be dropping coaching hints all throughout the book, but in these preliminary remarks I need to touch on some inner beliefs.

Many things and theories in life are relative and the views and philosophies expressed in this book are no exception. There are three things about rugby coaching that I remember being taught a long time ago and reminded of fairly frequently afterwards:

» **The absolute truth does not exist.** Every different view can have some validity. Every team has to construct its scrum with a different group of players. The scrum that emerges should be designed to exploit their particular strengths and avoid their particular weaknesses while at the same time being based on sound principles. To do this we have a uniform system of analysis and when the characteristics of each member of the unit are applied to it, we produce a scrum that best equips that collection of individuals.

» Many systems are good; **generally the system that works best is the one we commit to and stick to.** How often have we seen teams that read better on paper being beaten by less fancied teams whose players are fully committed? The mental attitude, commitment, X-factor or whatever you may call it, plays a much more dominating role in outcomes than is generally imagined. This applies to any sport but especially in rugby where physicality, toughness and endurance have a prominent place.

» In almost all close contests the winner is the one who makes the least unforced errors. Anyone can falter under extreme pressure. This factor has a big bearing on both performance and results. However, making mistakes under normal circumstances provides a gift to the opposition. That is not a reason for being negative in one's play because ball carriers, in particular, need to make quick decisions and act unhesitatingly. Mistakes are excusable as long as the players responsible do their best to recover from them and as teammates in the form of support players will be on hand to help. The point is that good technique and practice under pressure will produce the skill to reduce unforced errors. When rugby actions are executed without hesitation, mistakes are easier to correct by other players in support.

In general terms I'm talking about the right of dissent and the right to contribute, which we want to uphold above anything else. The authority of the coach as the head of a group and his opinions must be respected, but a good self-assured coach will encourage input as much as possible. The coach will create a structured environment and the forum in which this can happen in an orderly manner. Personally I prefer technical discussions to take place outside of training times and in off-field venues.

In a recent discussion with a former Wallaby teammate, who happened to be a back of some repute, he was commenting on the need for players to outthink and outmanoeuvre thereby surprising the defence. The professional players are prepared with all the necessary programs, technology and support teams at their disposal and go into games with the full range of physical attributes that result from that. That is fine so long as it is not at the expense of their decision-making ability which will atrophy if underemployed. The big danger is to become too dependent on the walkie-talkie-water-bottle message from the stand. Very simply, if the boat is sinking in the middle of the ocean, the players immediately consult with the captain and not with the coach who is back on land.

Training practices

I have devoted a section to the specifics of scrum practice but, in general terms, I can say that it involves lots of the never to be underestimated BHW (bloody hard work) and that it can't happen without determination; scrummaging is as much about mental attitude as it is about size, strength and technique.

The good thing about scrummaging practice is that, unlike some other aspects of the game, it gives you a very good return on effort. Increase the quantity of time and the performance will improve accordingly. Add the quality that I propose to explain in this section and, of course, the dividend will be much higher.

Again in general terms the following need to be understood:

» The closer the practice is to match conditions the more effective it will be.

» Cost-effectiveness is a priority. Quality work beats quantity work every time. Volume is important for fitness (particularly at the beginning of the season) and perfecting technique but it has to be productive.

» Concentrate on perfecting one thing in each session because problems or enhancements need that detailed attention. Remember what the great Green Bay Packers coach, Vince Lombardi said, "Practice does not make perfect. **Only perfect practice makes perfect.**"

Principles and success formulae

Education is the base of human progress, advancement and betterment. I have managed to overcome my mental health problem and the same recipe can be used to enhance a scrum or to fix any problem associated with it. The principles of finding solutions carry over from one discipline to another.

Indeed an understanding of principles will allow you to apply them to many aspects of life and to different sports. If you establish the right principles the processes that follow will work, as long as they conform. This is where some of the lawmaking has gone wrong by not having the correct guidelines.

My Wallaby coach Alan Jones is a good example of being successful because his chain of thinking is based on establishing principles and working down logically from there. He was chosen to be the Australian coach not so much on what he had done in rugby but on the basis that he had achieved success in other areas, including sport. Combined with his intelligence and a good knowledge of rugby at the lower levels, this was a cocktail that had all the ingredients of a winner, particularly as the Argentine ingredient was about to be added!

When Alan Jones attacked his grand mission of trying to win a Grand Slam, he started with a plan which subsequently found its way into the National Coaching Plan and I quote: *"Running a rugby team requires much the same skill as running a business and the more successful coaches are those who adopt the corporate approach* *and use a structured preparation. It is very much a case of man management and establishing a formula for success."*

This process involves three main stages: analysis, articulation and action which cover six well-defined actions, outlined as follows:

ANALYSIS			ARTICULATION	ACTION	
Devise a Plan			Explain the Plan	Implement the Plan	
Collect	Select	Dissect	Sell the plan	Practice	Perform
Establish a data bank	Choose what is good	Package it in a precise logical form	Get the players to understand it and believe in it	Rehearse it until you can do it well	Reproduce it in a match

It should be understood that none of these tasks can be carried out successfully unless the previous ones have been attended to. This is why the old cliché is so true, "proper preparation prevents pretty poor performance."

The skills that distinguish the top coach from the others are the selecting, dissecting and selling. The other functions can be delegated, in many cases to the players themselves. With this approach to coaching we can see that the job comes very close to being a chairman of committees, particularly in the higher echelons of rugby. The better the communication the coach has with the players, the easier this task will become.

This paper should give you a comprehensive data bank on scrummaging and it contains a number of views. It's up to the team coach to choose what he wants, not only from this bank of information but also from his or her own ideas, and then put the rest of the above process into action.

My formula will be delivered when we reach the relevant chapters, but like any project the development of a scrum requires planning, preparation and perseverance. As previously stated, however, the outcome depends on the volume of perspiration: practice, practice, practice and then even more scrums.

Adapting to change

Not being a student of evolutionary biology I have never read Charles Darwin's On the Origin of Species, but I do understand his message: "It is not the strongest of the species that survives, nor the most intelligent, but the one most responsive to change." This is why I still have cockroaches in my house. They have been around for thousands upon thousands of years, always adapting to any pesticides used against them.

We all know that resistance to change is a fact of human nature. Ever since the times of ancient civilisations the human race has hated change and found it difficult to get through.

In fact in some of those earlier civilisations change was accompanied by rituals, often of a brutal nature. This attitude to change can, however, change when it is accompanied by seeing something better in the future. If in our imagination this is the case, then we are more likely to accept change and become willing to cross that bridge. What was seen as something disruptive is now seen as progress.

Rugby, of course, has undergone great change at the elite professional level, but has every part of that change been progress? We don't need to become too semantic in a scrum book, but we can define change as to make different in a particular way; to alter drastically; to undergo a modification. On the other hand we can define progress as gradual betterment; to advance forward in quality. In short, while change requires that whatever is in question become different but not necessarily closer to a goal, progress requires that whatever is in question become different gradually and towards a specific end or goal. Without confusing the issue we can look further ahead at development with the difference that development is a permanent change and progress is like a step to the next level.

At the top end, rugby has evolved from a sport played by amateurs with jobs into a full-time career where playing rugby full time became the job. At this level, the game has progressed to something more than a game and everything in it has to be managed differently with decisions being made within the full context of a business. Mistakes have occurred in the progress made with professionalism, but to maximise the potential of the game's development we need to make a number of modifications to our attitudes, our laws and our systems, and it is ideas on these that I am attempting to outline in this discussion. I see development as the end game and, while we have made great progress with professionalism, the development navigational chart needs some minor resetting as we head toward our end goal.

Returning to the script, law changes in recent years have altered the dynamics of the game in producing fewer scrums but, just as it was in the days of the Australian Coaching Plan, there are some things that have to be done well to perform at your best and the scrum still remains a critical one. Furthermore, being a faster and more intense game, players' fitness has accordingly varied (lots more running involved, lots more matches played, lots more travelling required) All these variables need to be carefully attended to because they could also be a source of frequent injuries and underperformance.

Rugby has two main components, preparation off the field and delivery on the field. In the professional world the preparation has become a lot easier because of the extra human resources, the extra physical aids and the extra facilities, let alone the extra time that is available. That doesn't change the principles at all or the techniques very much, so this reference material should be applicable at all levels of rugby.

Organisation, leadership and teamwork

I learned early in my career that where two opposing teams are rated similarly the deciding factors usually come down to organisation and motivation. They are the pluses that provide the winning edge. Having eight participants in a unit as structured as the scrum requires a lot of organisation, and much of this is provided off the field by the coach or the scrum coach.

On the field it requires a scrum leader not only to organise but also to motivate and to keep the players switched on. The team captain or, more likely, the forwards leader is the person to order scrum tactics. The best placed player to implement them and to supervise the organisation of the scrum is the No. 2 because this player is the only one that is the focal point of all the forces and who can feel if the mechanics are right. Thus, the micromanagement and leadership of the scrum should be the hooker's responsibility. This player needs to be a thinker with initiative and a precisionist temperament, whereas the scrum leader must neither be shy nor over aggressive. Some teams have one of the props fill this role but the person has to be one that the other members of the pack will follow.

The hooker fills this role by getting the prior preparation right, by providing the coordination and by determining the timing. To be the scrum leader the hooker must not only supervise the preparation but must also get this done early so that everything is spot on for the engagement. Too often have I seen packs saunter up, go in at the last moment and wonder why their scrum has been disrupted. The hooker, therefore, needs to be at the assembly point first and to continually remind the cohorts that the scrum is not just something to lean against in between plays. Conversely, this player needs all the help he can get for as long as it is needed from everyone in the pack.

Teamwork promotes efficiency and the preservation of energies needed for the times of heavy demand. If the unit is not working in coordination or in unison, put very simply, it won't work! Worst of all, everybody will rapidly become fatigued.

One of the defining factors of the scrum is the total dedication to common objectives, and the sacrifice of individuality that it requires. In a nutshell, it is the **unselfish giving** of the eight players that produces the ultimate scrum with its control, power and effectiveness. I like to call it **uncompromising generosity**, a quality which is naturally rare but which can be developed.

To me, the scrum is the epitome of teamwork where the eight individuals are performing eight totally different positions and tasks, and all have to come together in unison or in perfect accord at the time the ball comes in. It requires a big sacrifice of individuality to become one eighth of the equation and to make the collective mind a priority.

Many times have I used the analogy and likeness of an orchestra to explain the complexity of the performing scrum. All the instruments are finely tuned to one another, to the one single score and with the one conductor (maybe the half back) directing the actions.

Furthermore, the discipline required for and achieved through scrummaging is one of the foundations of forward play. Those qualities are invariably transferred to lineouts, rucks and mauls. Additionally, we can utilize it as a great educational tool on teamwork for forwards and backs alike.

We also know how destructive the absence of teamwork can be and how the lack of authority translates into a lack of common direction. Forward teamwork starts at the scrum and its influence on the backs is quite astonishing, either in building their confidence and optimism, or in totally annihilating both in the whole team. The positive or negative psychological influence is ever present in all pockets of the team and impacts on game outcomes.

Social loafing

Most of what I have just outlined is fairly well understood, but knowing how important the melding of the mental and the physical are in this unique unit of rugby, I have studied the subject in a little more detail. It is not the purpose of this chapter to unleash a general academic dissertation on psychology, but a summary of the Social Loafing Syndrome will provide a further insight into this very relevant topic. The specifics of scrum psychology are the focus of a later chapter by Michael N. Fox, Steve D. Mellalieu and Peter C. Terry.

The rugby scrum is a formation, a structure where eight players come together covering eight different positions that require, in some cases, a slightly different technique package, but in other positions a completely different technique package. These technique packages are determined by the intricacies and demands of each position.

Almost everyone understands what teamwork is about. Nevertheless, committing to teamwork is a different kettle of fish; it requires absolute uncompromising generosity that has and will be mentioned in other passages. At the end of the day when closing the shop you don't count and take your pay until you have paid all the expenses or the business will not stay alive. To put it another way, when you milk a cow, you have to keep stuffing its mouth with grass to keep the continuity of this cycle happening! It is simple and universal: you give first, you take second; everything in time.

The scrum is like a stage in the rugby theatre, where some players stand up and perform while others with secondary roles can hide behind or next to a fellow forward. The scrum after engagement may last for five or ten seconds and this is the time where the participating players sacrifice their own individuality to become a collective eight. After those ten seconds everyone then has a job to do BUT NOT BEFORE.

When players in a defensive scrum are thinking about the next tackle they are going to make, or, in attack, are thinking about the hole through which they will run, they are over-anticipating the play and getting ahead of themselves, and this lack of concentration on the current phase can be categorised as social loafing.

It is quite difficult to synchronise the movements of eight bodies and the concentration of eight brains required for the job. Furthermore, not all brains think alike, so coaching and motivation may play a big part in finding that unison. Even the best orchestras in the world get their timing wrong from time to time. Scrummaging is more an art than an exact science, but we try as much as possible to get players to conform to a pattern, shape, togetherness, timing, responsiveness, etc.

When we don't get that harmony there will be some consequences. For example, if the No. 7 is absent-minded or too forward thinking, then No. 3 will suffer from the lack of support and have to put in an extra effort to compensate for the deficiency. Also No. 5 has to add more pressure and if we have already compromised the pushing positions of three players it doesn't end there. I can assure you the other five are also feeling the consequences.

So now that we are pedalling backward, the question for No. 7 is: Where is that tackle you were thinking to make? More than likely five metres behind the gain line!

The chain reaction goes even further. If the pack needs to go to the next ruck or maul to contest possession and territory, the back row might get there quicker due to its lack of effort in the scrum, but the trade-off is that the tight five will be slower than normal to get to it and less effective than normal while there. It's even possible that these five players will be chastised by a coach who has seen the symptom without recognising the cause. The events are interlocked.

So if we are to stop the opposition team and send them backward, we better start from up front with the eight forwards, going forward being the most important principle of rugby. The more we do that, the closer we get to their ingoal where the tries are scored! One of the consequences of social loafing is to go backward, either at a slow pace or at a fast pace (in 'my book' this is called going in the wrong direction). A bad habit will soon become a cancer. It needs to be removed and the sooner the better. Passing the buck for effort to the heavy brigade is not acceptable and must not be tolerated, particularly in representative teams. The collective drum that I keep beating is both physical and mental. Without both the scrum is gone!

Some research studies by Latane, Williams and Harkinsin (1979) on the behaviour of individuals working in groups and individually, argued that when their output is not recognised because they are part of one big group, their output diminishes. When they were merited singularly for their efforts, their output increased. It was they who invented the term and who came up with the solution of individual evaluation. Their experimentation was conducted over trivial activities such as pulling a rope or engaging in shouting or pumping air. I wonder how much more revealing it might have been in a scrum where a flanker can look like he's pushing but is pushing only like a feather.

Representative players are selected to play for their country or province; they already are mentally engaged with the activity and in a general way they are committed.

If they don't understand the laws of the game or the strategies of the team, good coaches will tune them by clarifying goals and objectives and the kind of effort that is expected. It is the sum of the individual efforts that counts.

Too many coaches concentrate on group coaching which of course is essential in developing unit and team skills. Having said that, far too little time is spent on individual player improvement. It is my contention that if you can improve each player by five percent that will have a greater impact on team success than anything else. Coaches tend to shy away from this responsibility because they feel they don't have the micro knowledge to do it. Well, they just have to seek help from others, but a lot can be achieved through film.

The best way to evaluate players is to track them on film throughout an entire game. The exercise not only tells the coach a lot but it is an exercise in self-coaching as well.

When the players see what they do for 80 minutes they can tell where their weaknesses are and when they are loafing. One way to improve your swing in golf is to have it filmed and then compare it to a pro's swing on film. The same can work in rugby.

Players need to know what their jobs are and then play one phase at a time, all the time! For the coaches, please do not be reticent with player evaluations and use criticism and praise whenever it is justified. Evaluations provide the ideal opportunity to get to know your players more, to see what makes them tick and to see how competitive they are. That will help you to identify where some extra motivation and work may be needed. After all communication is the glue that keeps groups of people together.

Stakeholder responsibility

There is an extra dimension to teamwork in my report. Just as one player in a scrum cannot fix a problem within the structure, no one person nor one group can fix the systemic problem that we now have with the scrum in the modern game. The administrators have recognised this and foreshadowed changes after the 2011 Rugby World Cup; the players and coaches don't enjoy collapsing or having to reset scrums and, of course, the referees will need to reconsider their role.

The serious injury focus has shifted from the scrum to the tackle, but referees must still harbour an apprehension regarding the potential for spinal injuries which can carry the implications of permanent disability and legal action. That uneasiness will vary according to their experience. Ironically, on the one hand this can cause a psychological pressure born out of an unwanted outcome that produces the very physical pressure that can cause the same accident.

I am referring to the universal law: If in doubt, don't. Referees would then slow and stop scrummaging until they feel safe. In the meantime the players ready to engage are subject to enormous pressures in the whole body (cramps and fatigue being some of the symptoms that will weaken the players, particularly in the front row). We are well aware that referees are under a lot of other psychological pressure from their evaluating peers. A bad performance may signify the end of a career. They need to conform to a template of a game pre-established by the collegiate group of referees.

This has destroyed individuality, it has devalued the hugely important man-management skills, and it has focused referees on to the process instead of on the outcome. This so often gives us the 'Stop, start' game instead of the 'Let's get on with it' one that we all like.

Nobody doubts the difficulty facing referees, particularly with the expectations of their being partly responsible for the show. The show looks after itself if the players, coaches and referees are all trying to do the right thing. It is hard to criticise referees for not doing this without their being unshackled and being allowed to apply all of the laws in a sometimes slightly discretionary manner. Too often they are pressured to be nitpickers when it comes to some laws, while being encouraged to be oblivious to others. In the professional ranks this makes it difficult for them to contribute to the overall display.

The role of the referee has changed since the game has become part of the mass entertainment industry because the chief officiator has moved much closer to the centre of attention on this new stage. Big games being watched by large television audiences are now being presented in show business fashion and the money involved with all the stakeholders certainly makes the game a business. In other words we have a game, a show and a business angle to the events, and all of the people under the lights should have a vested interest in maintaining a high standard in these three facets of rugby. When I use the acronym GSB, this is what I am referring to.

Applying discretion

Discretion is a great thing in every part of a justice system or a law system because it is impossible to legislate for every circumstance. At the end of any policy there must always be a discretionary clause that allows for the introduction of common sense. Some unkind critics of referees might say that such discretion could influence the outcome of some games. This, however, is much more likely to be the case now with referees being able to find an easy penalty in almost any phase of the match.

There have been attempts to standardise discretion but that is an oxymoron. Discretion is a freedom to decide which can't be bound by rules.

There is no such thing as a template for the scrum or even the actual game, because such a notion ignores the difference between elite competitions and other standard competitions as they go down the scale. I simply cannot comprehend the idea and concept of referees moulding a game of rugby to look like this or look like that! That is the job of the lawmakers, the players and their coaches, but NEVER the referees. The referee is there to administer the laws and if one match produces twice the number of penalties on scrums than another, then so be it. If one referee is consistently out of whack with averages over a long period then it begs questions, but it is entirely wrong for a referee to act in accordance with a predetermined set of figures.

Rugby is a collective physical and mental creative expression of a group of 30 different individuals, 30 different brains that need to explore the opportunities and threats presented by the opposition and the conditions.

The worst thing we can do is to manipulate those expressions! Furthermore, I'm sure that spectators do not want to pay to see a mechanised robotic spectacle that needs to conform to a bureaucratically designed model. Variety and unpredictability are and should always be the spice of rugby life and templates have no place in this game.

In the case of the scrum this mechanistic approach disregards the fact that each scrum comprises different players of all shapes and sizes and that the conditions vary between one game and another.

A qualified referee with good interpersonal skills and a sense of presence can supervise an attractive contest under almost any set of laws if given some flexibility; but that does not mean that some changes in the current laws could not make everyone's job a lot easier, including the spectators who should be able to detect most infringements from any good vantage point.

Referees keeping up

In the last 20 years the speed and intensity of the game have increased by approximately 30 percent. Professional referees' fitness may have increased accordingly but I doubt that this applies to their speed. Some seem to struggle with the quick reactions and quick decisions that are required in avoiding the inexplicable blunder that the unforgiving television replay sometimes reveals. The presence of the TMO (the begrudged Television Match Official), sometimes a necessary intrusion into the match, has taken a fair bit of responsibility away from the match referee. Other codes have countered this by having one referee for each half, but would that be an expensive overkill?

Onto some personal benchmarks

Having played rugby for 21 years, coached for another 15 years at all different levels including Australian U21s (1995), I must have packed down no less than 100,000 scrums (maybe a bit less!) in all front row positions and for two highly ranked countries in Argentina and Australia. Yes, I know this subject backward and forward; I have also put it under the microscope and observed it from the moon down. I must confess that through my playing years I became a bit of a perfectionist and single-minded when it came to my team's objectives and preparation. Nevertheless, I am also very reasonable when somebody puts an argument in front of me and makes me reason and consider other options. I listen well when somebody talks to me, not at me!

The pushover tries

Armed as I am with all the information that I'm about to present to you in this book, it is very important to stress that "The scrum is a means to something, and not an end in itself.".

Very simply, we play a rugby match for 80 minutes (with all its facets) and the scrum is only a portion of it. Through the years there have been teams so obsessed with the scrum that they forgot to play rugby!

In saying that, however, if you ask seasoned coaches, they will say it is a very vital and important part of the structure of any rugby team. Sometimes its importance is underestimated, on other occasions overstated. I will attempt to find a balanced opinion that throws some light on this fascinating and complex subject and how it fits within the 15-a-side game called rugby.

When I came to Australia I remember the National Coaching Plan (NCP) stating that the skills of the game were like the rugby alphabet which allowed a team to express itself on the field, and the better the skills the more scope that expression had. The scrum and the lineout are of course the two set play unit skills and the pillars of possession on which the game is built. The NCP identified the scrum, in particular, as a unit that could influence other areas of contest and that the benefits of a good scrum overflowed into all other aspects of the game (music to my ears!).

I know that the scrum was discussed a lot in Australia at the same time the NCP identified the scrum as the Achilles' heel of many past Wallaby teams. For example, in 1983 I was the tight head prop (3) in the Argentine Pumas team that scored two pushover tries against the Wallabies in its 18-3 victory at Ballymore, Brisbane. This left an indelible mark on both teams but certainly emphasized to the Australians that they still had a way to go in this department.

Incidentally, 12 months later I personally helped to make up that ground and proved it with the famous pushover try against Wales at Cardiff Arms Park. This was the first pushover try scored against the very proud scrummaging Welsh. So finally we could see the results of our hard and uncompromising work of eight weeks starting to pay off.

To keep things in perspective, I must also add that before arriving in the UK we hadn't played in four weeks due to the different rugby seasons and our scrum for the first two

weeks on tour was very shaky. So in speculating a bit, perhaps if we had played Wales in the first test on tour the result may have been different! Yet, Cardiff Arms Park was hushed at the time, an eerie experience that I will never forget.

Springboks vs Jaguars at Wanderers Club, Johannesburg, 1980.

While we are on pushover tries which are not very common amongst the top rugby-playing nations, I'd like to indulge a little bit with another true story. In 1980 I was privileged to be selected for the South America XV to tour South Africa, a tour intended to break the apartheid deadlock. Our team comprised 23 Argentines, a Uruguayan, a Chilean, a Paraguayan and a Brazilian player. The first test against the revered Springboks was played at the famous Wanderers Johannesburg on 26 April 1980. The referee was Welsh Ken Rowlands and the Bok pack was by far the favourite according to all unbiased local media. Somehow, we scored a pushover try to salvage a memorable 23-9 loss. Their front row comprised Johan Strauss (my prop), Dave Frederickson (hooker) and Richard Prentis (loose head), see photo opposite.

The punchline? At the after-match function (as was the tradition in those years), Dr Danie Craven announced the team for the 2nd test, almost unchanged except one position, Daan Du Plessis to replace waltzing Johan Strauss as tight head. Needless to say this was one of the proudest moments of my rugby career. We played seven matches, won four and lost three. This tour was a terrific and invaluable experience for both nations because Argentina and South Africa were craving some international experience.

So how does it happen?

My apologies to those expert coaches and players (the eight forwards need to be interested), but the following detailed explanations are for all and sundry (experts or novices) and I am sure that they could be very beneficial to many of you.

A pushover try always has a special significance for any forward and more so for us front-rowers. In a way it is the seal of approval that at least at that moment of the match you have completely dominated the opposition pack, sending them back beyond their goal line and inflicting on them the ultimate humiliation, in addition to winning the points that come with it.

Curiously the backs as non-participants in this type of feat have not been mentioned, yet when a pushover try takes place it also affects the backs significantly. A pushover try, apart from scoring much needed points, also acts as a psychological motivational boost to the whole attacking team.

This domination gets transmitted to the whole backline because more than likely these players will continue their game on the front foot. This advantage has huge benefits for the forward progressing team, which incites the opposition to hesitancy and noncohesion. It puts those players on the back foot in both attacking and defending situations and this going forward dominating pack always makes things easier for its own backline. Conversely, the opposite happens with the team going backward.

It takes a lot of courage, determination and commitment to counter or neutralise a pack that has just pushed you over the line.

Scrummaging efficiency pre-conditions

A pushover try may occur when a well-trained, determined and very well coordinated pack combines together with:

(a) excellent technique;
(b) above-average fitness (strength, power and flexibility);
(c) mental attitude and aptitude;
(d) the vital timing to pull the trigger in unison; and
(e) a degree of controlled aggression to apply under pressure.

Moreover, all this work may be facilitated by an opposition in disarray due to lack of concentration and cohesion or, quite simply, due to a lack of preparation for such contingencies. In some cases it may eventuate early in the game as a consequence of immediate superiority.

On other occasions it could be a product of a gradual ascendency (also known as a bit of a demolition job) which will yield benefits within the last quarter or so of the game.

Hence patience, discipline and perseverance are important ingredients for a pushover try to be produced.

As I mentioned previously I have participated in scoring several pushover tries, mostly at club level back in the mid to late 1970s, with the National University Rugby Club and Tala Rugby Club in Cordoba, Argentina. Nevertheless, at international level, due to much better preparation, application and mentality, these are very rare. In ending this topic I may be forgiven for reminiscing on those very few proud and glorious moments of my career:

1980 South America XV vs Springboks, Wanderers Cricket Club, Johannesburg
1983 Argentina vs Australia, Ballymore, Brisbane
1984 Australia vs Wales, Cardiff Arms Park, Cardiff

Photos taken and kindly
donated by Adrian Short on
24 November 1984, Australia
vs Wales

CHAPTER 6

The fundamentals and mechanics of the scrum

THE FUNDAMENTALS AND MECHANICS OF THE SCRUM

The Nitty Gritty

Let me explain my basic theory on efficiency and safety in scrummaging; fortunately, they are one and the same. It is appropriate to repeat what I said in The Assignment. In the scrum, the safety of the individual is in the collective eight providing that protection. If they are tight and pushing in the right direction, no one player is left exposed and vulnerable to potentially damaging forces.

Intrinsic qualities to take into account

Even though I will be covering these areas at length, I just want to whet your appetite with some general concepts and qualities of a good competitive scrum. Thus, as a way of brief introduction I'd like to provide you with these snippets of information:

» **Togetherness:** The job of the eight players formed in the three rows we know is to fill in all the gaps with as much compression as possible both horizontally and vertically, like a vacuum extracting the air and space in between bodies. At the assembly all players come from a loose independent position and move to a somewhat regimented technique combining with the other players. Everybody has their own technique to accomplish this which has an element of compromise with the other seven players. Some players use their arms very effectively but forget the gripping with full fists and squeezing to produce that reduction of air and space. For example, if we are boxing, we do not punch our adversary with an open hand, we clench the fist as tight as we can and off we go.

» **Timing:** After we have achieved that ideal position and we are ready to push in the scrum we need to be synchronized in the 16-leg deflection. I refer to timing which for a scrum to be effective and efficient must be spot on! The best way to coach it is to have one common signal, gesture or voice that everyone can follow at the correct time. The necessary timing can't be achieved if the scrum operates in two sections (left side and right side or front three and back five), it has to be the whole eight thinking, acting and reacting as one.

» **Support and stability:** Starting from our feet position to the connection made with the opposition is just as important as that between our own players, so both props must clamp and grip onto them with vice-like grips and maintain a force that is going forward (never down, up or backward).

» **Attitude and temperament:** These are two qualities that will define and differentiate the top contender from the also-ran.
Top international players are born with attitude and temperament but adequate training can help an average player to become a superlative one, particularly in the front where the physicality is a deciding factor. Temperament and attitude are what makes us want something, contest every scrum regardless of the put-in and that is the example or standard to be followed. We must approach every single scrum with an attacking mentality which means that the pack must never go in with the aim of just holding the opposition. Everyone can contest scrum and possession!

» **Simplicity:** The more steps and frills that you add to the basic scrum the more difficult it is to get and to maintain the required balance, synchronization and togetherness. Every player must be self-sufficient. In the scrum there is no room for assistants to do X or Y jobs in helping the other players. Everyone should be busy looking after their position and anticipating what their opposition counterpart is doing or about to do.

So far I have made some conceptual remarks about the scrum, but before looking at the nuts and bolts of the formation it is important to say that it is like a machine, but it is not a machine. A true machine is driven by mechanical factors alone including a mechanical injection of fuel; a scrum is based on mechanics and physics principles but in part its fuel injection comes from the intangible source of the mind or the will. In other words there are interconnected physical and mental factors.

As I have said from the beginning, scrummaging is an art, as it demands personal selection and observation of the coach, personal input of the players and adaptability and flexibility to abnormal circumstances. In playing rugby, the weather, opposition and referee are variables we must deal with—and at times put up with. A win is hardly ever presented on a silver platter, therefore we must go and fight for it.

This is not necessarily a recipe for feeling comfortable but scrummaging was never meant to be comfortable anyhow. However, if we can achieve a relatively comfortable yet strong position, this will lead the player to scrum effectively. In the end it is up to the coach to establish priorities, but I don't think that comfort should come at the expense of efficiency.

A powerful scrum is a very effective weapon that may last for only five to ten seconds at a time. As such it's a matter of intense concentration which is a word and a discipline that I shall repeat often. There is not much time to fix a particular scrum when it's in trouble, so the solution is to be proactive and to get it right to start with.

The scrum is NOT just the restart of the game!

Scrums are the platform from which you start to build your attack or defence. This is where you can dominate the opposition or be dominated by the opposition.

Scrummaging and tackling are two distinctive features of the game because both can exert an enormous influence on other facets of the game. More often than not the scrum is closely tied to the confidence and the success of the team. An average team with a good scrum and good tackling attitude throughout can hold its own against anyone, and at a pinch may even win.

During a conversation with some international players, Ray Williams OBE from Wales was asked which ball he considered the most important one for attacking purposes, the ruck or the maul because of the variety of options, or the line-out. Williams said, "The most important ball is the one coming from the scrum, because this one can influence line-outs, rucks and mauls, and not the other way around."

Roles and positions

Perhaps it is a good idea to define general roles before we delve into too much detail. Whatever the reader's interest in the game might be, it's advisable to understand what the various parts of the engine do and, more importantly, what the function of this machine-like formation is. In simple terms, the collective roles concerning a scrum are to obtain possession (i.e., ball) and position (i.e., territory).

To carry out this function, all 16 players (both packs) must push together and parallel to the ground. It is the players' responsibility to maintain stability of the formation thereby ensuring safety for all involved during scrummaging.

To facilitate the reading and to simplify the identification of the positions, I will use the regular traditional jumper position number to code name each individual in the scrum. The scrum half is included on the basis that this player is involved in the scrum process and the numbers and alternative descriptions are as follows:

Front Row:
No 1 Loose Head Prop (left)
No 2 Hooker
No 3 Tight Head Prop (right)

Second Row:
No 4 Left Second Row/Lock
No 5 Right Second Row/Lock

Back Row:
No 6 Left Flanker/Breakaway (or Left External Second Rower)
No 7 Right Flanker/Breakaway (or Right External Second Rower)
No 8 Centre Back Rower
No 9 Half back (coordinating scrums, ball put in and connecting with the back line)

Let's now assemble the whole 8 forwards, as one single, united and effective pack:

Front row

At the outset perhaps I should give you a light-hearted account of the value of scrum possession and the ones at the forefront of that process. Getting that possession involves hard work that sometimes deserves more acknowledgements from the backs who quite often demand it! Other times tactical kicking takes place and the majority of the backs watch and cover some spot on the field. Of course when there is space and time the backs can exert the surprise factor with clever maneuvers that may outsmart the opposition.

The front row is on from the moment the referee's whistle indicates scrum. Showtime! This is the chance in the game where you can demonstrate or validate why you have been picked. This is the moment for the forwards but more particularly for the front row to perform on stage. There is a widely known scrum script. In it lies a golden opportunity to dominate the crowd and the opposition, and to wrestle the ball from them before carefully presenting it to your back line on a silver platter as if it were the last ball of the game.

Rugby is a game of 15 players that must share the load as much as possible. Scrums are about one third of the game of rugby yet it influences the outcomes of line outs, rucks and mauls, and even the backs are psychologically dependent on the performance of the pack. So, no need to get obsessed with scrums but for the same token let's give it due consideration for the team's health.

Rugby is an interdependent game where the backs must cross the gain line out wide and the forwards must push the opposition pack up front. If the backs go backward, the forwards will lose ground inevitably. If the pack goes backward the backs will have no space or time to operate. So, at the end of the match more than likely, we'll end up with 15 heroes or 15 villains.

Nonetheless, a popular truism states that "out of the 15 positions, front rowers play more time than anybody else." This is because in the set plays they come into contact with the opposition well before the ball is introduced and are jostling for position before the play restarts. Some backs might be reluctant to admit it but this is a simple fact with the numbers 1, 2 and 3, at the head of the pack having the most diverse of tasks and functions:

» Transmitting the power from the back five onto the opposition

» Generating their own power

» Engaging with and combating the opposition, as well as maximising the combined push of the pack (penetration)

» Taking responsibility for scrum tightness, particularly at the front

» Dictating the height of the scrum over the opposition thus maximising effectiveness

As a long-time member, I say the front row is like your parents—when you have them you don't notice them, but when you don't have them, you wish they were there!

Second row/lock

» Numbers 4 and 5, the big power generators, push with both shoulders onto the front row.

» They lock up the scrum to combine power with the front row.

» They need to be tight themselves like conjoined twins.

» The front row and second row comprise what is widely known as the tight five, the guts of the engine or the heart of the scrum.

Back row

From the setting-up of the scrum to when the ball is in the scrum, the flankers must be considered as outside second rowers with full responsibility for pushing until the ball leaves the scrum. Their weight is crucial in the first impact of the engagement and decisive when the forces are evened up.

One important aspect worth noting, and to remind the back rowers about, is that the more they look after the tight five in the scrum, the more the tight five will look after them in the breakdown (the next phases of tackle, ruck or maul). In a good pushing position the flankers can view the ball through the scrum so they are able to get away quickly once the ball is out. No need for relaxing at pushing time, the whole eight must be committed to each scrum.

Packing the number 8 between the flanker and a second rower on either side is still an option but back row moves have been restricted by the law preventing any player from leaving the scrum until the scrum has ended with the ball emerging.

So on the above tactic of moving any of the three back rowers before engagement to a different position, I'd recommend it be done only in attack (or put-in) whereas in defensive situations this could be counterproductive as the opposition can simply pick the ball up and attack the vulnerable side straight away while the scrum is wheeling away from the action.

Something we don't hear enough is that the push of the back rowers is vital not only because it adds their weight and force to the equation but more importantly they provide the tight five with a more solid base to push from. It is very noticeable when the back rowers are not in; then the second rowers rapidly lose effectiveness. This demonstrates the interrelatedness of these positions.

Flankers/breakaway

» Numbers 6 and 7 push with their internal shoulder onto 1 and 3 respectively.

» The weight given by the flankers provides a more solid platform for the props (1 and 3) thereby complementing the work of 4 and 5.

» Besides the forward push, flankers should simultaneously squeeze the props inwards in order to achieve scrum tightness also asked of the props.

» As soon as the ball is out, they are the first line of defence and attack.

» They also support the ball carrier.

» Any flanker that welches on his responsibility to push is letting down the teammate prop in front and inviting the opposition to target and give that player a bad time.

» Furthermore, the over-exertion of a prop will result in late arrival to the breakdown where that flanker will be needing assistance while struggling with the opposition, so the benefits of good support are mutual.

Number Eight

» The number 8 is an integral part of the back row (numbers 6, 7 and 8).

» While numbers 6 and 7 each supports their respective prop, the number 8 provides vital support to numbers 4 and 5.

» Without the number 8, the second rowers' push reduces considerably.

» In addition to providing full forward thrust, the other task of this player is to keep the second rowers pulled together so that power loss is minimised.

N.B. A number 8 cannot push effectively with the head out of the scrum!

» When a pack pushes the opposition 30 to 40 cm off the middle line (i.e., the imaginary line at the centre of the tunnel which extends beyond the scrum to become the advantage line or gain line), the defence is always much easier. Conversely if a pack is conceding any territory, this will make things much easier for the opposition.

Respect for law

We many times have heard expressions like 'there was organised mayhem' or, from Hamlet, "though this be madness, yet there is method in't," and yes, it may be chaotic at times. Nonetheless, if there are sixteen players congregated around the one ball like a medieval demented beast, there must be a law and a referee. And if a law is to exist and prevail, in order to preserve that method and organization and to please and provide enjoyment for the majority of the viewing public and its participants, it must be obeyed by all.

Before I proceed to other topics it is necessary to provide some official definitions and laws to which I shall be referring. Some of these will be repeated as we move through the process and others will be added where required.

Definitions and points of law (2005–2013)

» The purpose of the scrum is to restart play quickly, safely and fairly, after a minor infringement or a stoppage.

» The player of either team who throws the ball into the scrum is the scrum half.

» The middle line is an imaginary line on the ground in the tunnel beneath the line where the shoulders of the two front rows meet.

» A crouched position is the extension of the normal stance by bending the knees sufficiently to move into the engagement without a charge. *The crouched position may vary according to body types and degree of fitness. That being said, all front rowers should aim at having their backs parallel to the ground as much as possible before entering the engagement phase.*

» A front row must not form at a distance from its opponents and rush against them. This is considered charging and is dangerous play.

» Until the ball leaves the scrum half's hands, the scrum must be stationary and the middle line must be parallel to the goal lines or perpendicular to the touch lines. A team must not shove the scrum away from the mark before the ball is thrown in.

» The referee will call "Crouch" then "Touch." The front rows crouch and, using their outside arm, each prop touches the point of the opposing prop's outside shoulder. The props then withdraw their arms. The referee will then call "Pause". Following a pause the referee will then call "Engage".

The front rows may then engage. The engage call is not a command but an indication that the front rows may come together when ready.

We have seen for the last 8 years that this long, drawn-out process creates a crescendo of anxiety in both packs that puts such a focus on the engagement that, when finally untethered, they crash in with only the 'hit' in mind. It's not unlike the tension that bedevils sprinters as they wait to explode out of the blocks at the sound of the gun.

I am devoting considerable space to a specific discussion on law later in this book, but it is appropriate to comment on players' attitudes toward the law as it has an enormous influence on the outcome of games.

I do not want to be accused of promoting illegal play and I shall be careful not to do that even with the fine line that I have to tread. I say a fine line because you can no longer have faith in the law book with the authorities encouraging the referee to ignore some of the laws. No more evident is that than in the way that the ball is allowed to be put into the scrum.

My desire to coach within the law must not stop me, however, from pointing out that in a scrum we must expect to encounter dubious tactics and be ready for the counter. I am all for a robust contest and a battle of the wills which in terms of diversity gives rugby the advantage it has over other football codes.

There is a big difference between taking the law to its limit and cheating. The latter is unsporting and ignores the overall spirit of both the law and the game. On a more pragmatic note, coaching illegalities is cheating the players because while they are concentrating on unfair play and getting results through short cuts, they will never improve their skills, fitness or general play and that is a fact. Of course, the other huge benefit in abiding by the law when coaching means that there will be far fewer costly penalties that so often make the difference, along with a simultaneous reduction in the potential for injuries.

In relation to the scrum in particular, the law is adamant that premature engagements are not in the interests of either fairness or safety. My quarrel with cheating in this case goes beyond the obligations of adhering to the rugby spirit in that it is not practically productive. When you try to go earlier than you are supposed to, you don't do it with full power. It is better to wait and have a strong hit rather than an early tentative one. In the end right does prevail over wrong!

TOPO's guiding lights: The 11 vital beacons

In my preamble I mentioned that principles need to be established before designing the procedures that lead to proficiency and success. In line with this I'll begin with the 11 vital beacons I shall use to navigate our way through the journey to a professionally prepared and efficient scrum.

1. URGENCY

Immediately after the referee has awarded the scrum, players must sprint to the mark arriving before the opposition to put them into scrum readiness mode.

If the scrum collapses or the referee orders it to be reset, or both, your players must jump to their feet and get ready to start again as if nothing happened and without complaints to anyone. Complaints will invariably waste valuable time. More than likely when you are ready before the opposition, your chances of beating them for the ball and for territory are much greater; this is called anticipation, a mental aptitude resulting from mindfulness.

2. ASSEMBLY

Front Row Assembly:
» Correct feet position (determined beforehand by the coach)
» Low body height, ready for engagement
» Hand grips tight and secure
» Mental concentration on correct technique
» Head up at all times
» Ready to execute special calls or tactics

Second Row Assembly:
This includes four players, the **two internal** and **two external** second rowers.

» Correct feet position and no shuffling
» Low body height, maintaining upper body square on
» Strong hand grips
» Head up

» Concentration on technique

» Second row joined with front row.

Number Eight Assembly:

» Weight to second row on engagement

» Second-rowers' hips together

3. STEADY FOOT POSITIONS.

Maintain foot positions after the engagement. Not having to adjust the feet after the engagement precludes any loss of pressure.

4. HEIGHT

» Getting under the opposition front row provides a dominant position.

» The rule is that lower (together) is better than higher (alone). The lower the scrum can work effectively the better its chances are of weakening the opposition effort and undermining its organisation.

5. DIRECTION

The engagement movement must be one of going forward and not downward. The movement has to be parallel to the ground.

6. TIGHTNESS

Hand grips and arms must tighten up during the whole duration of the scrum. The effect of this is too often overlooked, but by bringing the power together it greatly heightens the strength of the unit and its push.

7. SPEED

When actions have been decided upon they must be taken quickly to gain the initiative. Most initiatives in rugby can be countered but not speed. Speed of movement and speed of mind are as important in our game as they are in Sumo or Greco-Roman wrestling. Part of the front row engagement relates to both of these other contact contests. If you want to get into a preferred position, you have to beat the opponents to it by anticipating. Here it is mind over matter and when done collectively it is lethal in its effectiveness!

8. WEIGHT

The weight or pressure must be loaded on to the opposition while ready but without pushing off the mark. When the ball comes in (i.e., when the ball leaves the half back's hands), or when our signal indicates it, everybody springs into an inward and forward pushing action. It's very important to keep the weight on without relaxing as it is the constant forward pressure that makes the difference.

9. COMMUNICATION

We must have a single call or signal for everyone to know when to explode forward. When properly executed the push should be like a tube of toothpaste, the pressure concentrated into one central point (i.e., the opposition's hooker). During scrummaging practices I have come to call this the Colgate effect for reasons just given. The worst thing is to have six players going for a wheel and two going for a shove or vice-versa. You can't all concentrate on the one aim without clear communication which is essential for the unity and the coordination required.

10. TIMING

The timing of the push is paramount. A call to action results in a reaction in unison! This will give your pack the maximum efficiency with the minimum energy spent. The coordinated push of eight men at the same time can produce devastating effects that flow on to the entire opposition. This will also make our backline feel psychologically superior and give it the opportunity to get on the front foot in both attack and defence.

11. ATTITUDE

The catalyst for everything else to work is a positive mental attitude that provides a determination to compete. The mental disposition or mental toughness must never be discounted. All players have to be totally convinced of and committed to what they are doing. There are no shortcuts or easy ways here. Apart from training technique you also need to train the temperament! It's important to understand that putting a scrum together with the correct technique is no different to building a multistory tower. Start from the bottom with the foundations which don't need to be pretty but do need to be solid. Then block by block we go up as we need to.

The preparation

This chapter essentially deals with the pre-engagement phase and covers the assembly of all participants in terms of gripping, binding, body positions, leg extensions and feet positioning. Once this feat of engineering has been carried out orderly and systematically, we are ready to meet the opposition head on.

The objective is to establish a static structure that will produce the tightness and the togetherness to prime a spring that can release its power on the opposition at the pushing moment. If that is an image that the authorities don't like then they are denying the fact that rugby is a power game, a combination of strength and speed. We all know we are competing against an opposition unit but we often forget that we are also competing against a force called gravity. There is a natural tendency for the 16 bodies and 1,700kgs plus of both packs to go downward, whether standing or lying on the ground.

Our main protection from this force is tightness which helps all members of the pack to stay up. I emphasise all members because the lamination has to cover the entire unit to protect it. If you put a tarpaulin over a structure everything is kept dry, but if the shelter covers only three quarters of it, the rain will come in, seep through and damage everything.

Assembly

Being a team game, rugby needs a leader to coordinate and motivate the players to implement tactics and to supervise the organisation and the combination of the players. In a good team the leader has deputies to look after the micromanagement, and the scrum is no exception. Since the platform is formed on the front row which is built around the hooker, the hooker becomes the logical and ideal person to call the shots. As mentioned before this player can't be shy or over-aggressive and may not be the one to call the tactics. The hooker, however, must be involved in the implementation of them by getting the preparation right, providing the coordination and determining the timing.

Front row's distance

The first thing to consider here are the players' needs which involve the following factors:

» the variations of body shapes (anthropometry, or short, medium and tall front rowers)

» the need for "space and time" to fully extend their backs and spines onto strong and safe positions (e.g. squats)

» the need for space to stretch their legs into a strong and safe position after the engagement (e.g. squat position)

» the need to prevent being crunched up by the opposition after being beaten in the enagement.

Pre 2013, in law 20.1 (f) it says, "Before the two front rows come together they must be standing not more than one arm's length apart." That is not feasible but I'll talk about the law later. For now and for all practical purposes these players have to stand far enough away from the middle line so as to meet the opposition at that point with their legs back and bent and their backs straight and parallel to the ground. An arm's length distance between the standing positions just does not enable this.

Feet positioning

In most sports your feet position will determine where you are going (e.g., tennis, golf, football, basketball and boxing). Our feet influence our hips which in turn determine where the body is aiming (sometimes correctly and other times incorrectly).

Good tips for efficient and effective scrummaging

The most effective stance at any age or playing level is shoulder width apart, which is the strongest pushing position.

We must minimise any feet shuffling while in the scrum.* Wanting to have the feet in the same position after the engagement as before it means, of course, that the knees need to be bent sufficiently to not only take the unit forward into the engagement but also to retain sufficient flexion for maximum pushing capacity after the connection.

Toes must point forward. Anatomically some players may differ in their physical constitution and conformation, but splayed feet bring about a weak ankle position. In dry conditions we must use the front of the foot for launching forward; on wet days or on softer grounds we need to use the whole sole. These conditions also call for more studs and a slightly higher scrum to give more support.

These recommendations are for the whole pack and lead to the strongest position. As previously mentioned every scrum is mentally, physically and technically set as an attacking scrum.

* To retain and cement feet positions try the following exercise:

Set up the scrum until the eight are in without moving their feet. Call: FREEZE the whole scrum! Then deconstruct the scrum with the coach calling the players to stand up one by one, while checking their feet position, in the following order from the back: No. 8, No. 6, No. 7, No. 4, No. 5, No. 1, No. 2 and No. 3. Then assemble it again, and so on and so forth! The coach must insist and persist until the correct position and technique are adopted and mastered by the whole pack and reserves too!

Force transmission systems

While still talking about feet positioning there are three different force transmission systems known to me which, in order to work, again need the effort of all players in the pack.

The price of ignorance on coordination and understanding of the system is dear. Without those two assets the scrum becomes ineffective and fatigue sets in earlier than anticipated. Simply put, the pack will prematurely run out of petrol.

As you would expect, all three systems involve pushing forward but the different feet positioning will generate more or less force and push the force in different directions. It is best that the coach decides which one to utilise as this must not be switched to suit individuals. The three systems available are:

A. Straight forward push (for beginners)

TIPS

1. Feet square on
2. Shoulders square on
3. Feet at shoulder width apart

This system is generally recommended and reserved for beginners and intermediate levels. It is highly recommended for school players and involves the adoption of the square-on feet positioning with all front row feet in the same line (parallel to the centre field line). Square shoulders will also assist this approach. This feet positioning is safer, easier to coach and less complicated for players to learn. Once this system is mastered, we can then move to the other two more complex and demanding ones.

B. Outward directed push (for intermediate levels)

TIPS

1. Inside foot back
2. Outside foot forward
3. Outside foot heel and inside foot toe at same level
4. Feet at shoulder width apart

This is a legitimate and popular system and is very easy to achieve. It is not, however, nearly as effective as the inward push. A very important thing we must remember is that the feet positions impact greatly on hip positions and, in turn, body alignment. The results of the biomechanics and physics of the forces generated in the scrum are very powerful when multiplied by eight, and it is very important that everybody is going in the same direction at the same time.

C. Inward directed push (advanced)

TIPS

1. Inside foot forward
2. Outside foot back
3. Outside foot heel and inside foot toe at same level
4. Feet shoulder width apart

The inward push is one of the characteristics of the coordinated push, also known as 'La bajadita', Spanish for lowering. This system directs and concentrates all forces inwards towards the opposition's hooker.

Argentine Rugby Clubs, such as San Isidro Club, Liceo Militar Rugby Club in Buenos Aires and Tala Rugby Club in Cordoba amongst many other clubs have adapted and mastered the coordinated push system with great success and have been the flag bearers of the work and legacy of Sr. Francisco 'Catamarca' Ocampo. San Isidro Club in particular has had many international victories and memorable matches against France, the Springboks, the Wallabies, and many other teams touring Argentina.

Hooking feet

Hookers are in a category of their own. They are fairly independent individuals who certainly derive a huge sense of pride (or failure) when it comes to hooking the ball for their team. Nowadays more teams opt for the pushing tactics and the skills of hookers are somewhat neglected. Similarly, for this reason of preferring to push, the hookers these days are much bigger physically. It is not uncommon to find a front row formed with three props.

TIPS

1. Adopt a square-on position from the beginning of the scrum.
2. Vary the feet positions according to whether the objective is to push or to hook.
3. Use the pushing position to deal with the crooked throw-in because the most effective way to deal with this is for the whole front row just to push and step past the ball.
4. Avoid placing the hooking foot directly below or in front of your centre of gravity or you can be pinned and driven up.
5. In consultation with their cohorts, hookers may want to vary the tactical direction of scrum forces according to field position.

Binding and grips

Front row binding (on each other)

The tightness, togetherness, balance, steadiness and safety of the scrum are highly dependent on the binding and grips. These are of extreme importance in the front row because it is at the point of these players' contact with the opposition that in part the outcome of the contest is decided. Both front rows are responsible for the stability of the scrum.

Here and nowhere else is where the collapsing problems occur and where they can be solved. The front rows can do it but need support from the laws and from the referees. These six players need to have the right attitude if they are to play their part in the overall GSB (Game/Show/Business), but that can be helped if they are given more responsibility.

Even international players under pressure can underestimate or forget the importance of their hand grips. The front rowers do push but operate mainly as transmitters of scrum power. It is, however, the back five that generate most of the power, and for these generators to be very efficient, their grips and binding must be spot on.

The hooker (No. 2) should be the first player to arrive at the referee's mark, raising the arms and slightly bending their knees at the same time (toward the crouched position). The props will bind around the hooker's hips with a shorts-and-jumper grip; this is very important. The No. 2 needs to bind at armpit height, closing the scrum at shoulder height. I recommend that the No. 3 (tight head) binds first, allowing the No. 1 (loose head) to push, and then post-scrum quickly get to the breakdown, almost like a third flanker. Once the second rowers have gone, the No. 1 can go because the action is more accessible to that front rower. I've done this myself many times, mostly at club and state level and surprised a few opposition players with a good tackle or support play. At international level the demands and attention needed for the position are much greater because everything happens about 20-25% faster than at the next level down.

Apart from that, the right side of the scrum needs to be the tightest, heaviest and strongest because the majority of the opposition's force comes through the link of No. 2 and No. 3.

Consistent with the inward push system, the inside shoulders of the props should be tucked under the hooker's armpits. This little detail gives you one of the strongest attacking positions, due to the narrow attacking head of the front row. It is almost like an arrow head. However, if comfort is the object, the shoulders may be popped out in a square-on position. I would strongly recommend the latter for school players and beginners, because it's simpler to accomplish, though less effective. The first system is more difficult to coach and demands a lot more work and dedication from the players and coaches.

Front row binding (on the opposition)

Before I start I am going to mention the bridge, but I shouldn't because as you can see in laws 6, 7 and 8 it is an illegal practice. I do so because I have noticed through the years that a few props do get away with it. The bridge (loose head prop's left hand or forearm supported on his left knee) is used by some players to overcome deficiencies in technique or a lack of strength.

Depending on the strength and technique of the opposite player you may succeed or not with the bridge. I can only say this is an illegal, defensive patch-up solution that most times leads you to more trouble. The left leg moving forward to support your upper body gives you a very weak pushing position, and your arm could easily be brushed aside by the tight head prop coming through to take a grip.

More importantly the grips on the opposition are part of the pack's stability.

My theme all the way through is strength in togetherness and this is an example of where the efficiency of the unit is being sacrificed for the comfort of one member, and this is not acceptable.

N.B.: A number of props use this posture during the crouch in the pre-engagement phase, but it is better to get that hand up in the air and halfway to the destination in early readiness for the next stage.

Later on I'll be talking about position at the engagement but let me say here that getting the grip onto the opponent plays a major part in getting into the right position.

When ready to engage, the outside hands of both props must be cocked in preparation, up and ready to connect and to grab the opposing prop's back in a flash. This is vital for the keeping-up of the scrum, stability and the forward transfer of power.

On engagement the arms must swing instantly toward the opposition prop's back. The engagement, the swing of the arms and the grips must be almost simultaneous. An early and strong grip will guarantee a safe scrum and an optimal pushing position for the particular front rower.

My way was to drive the arms straight through not opening up the chest like a straight right or left in boxing. Failure to do that causes a lot of trouble for the hooker, the prop in question and the whole scrum. What might seem like a small mistake in not securing the grip will create a compounding problem for the whole scrum.

Only a slow tight head will not punish the loose head when his grips have failed. As everything happens very fast, you have virtually no time to fix the problem. Even if you manage to do it, the opposition has the initiative and you are behind the eight ball immediately.

The connection of the three front rowers with the opposition must be simultaneous, one hit only, hard, staying firm, putting pressure forward and sustaining it until the ball is in, hold or push and out. In some cases there may be a call for a double shove or delayed shove and wheel. Whatever this might be, the full attention of the whole eight must be given to the calls and their executions.

It is common practice and a preference of some coaches that the No. 3 should lead in the engagement. This tactic should provide a strong platform on the right side of the scrum. This is very useful to counter the natural pressure on our right side that produces the wheel. It also gives our hooker the distinct advantage of being in front and closer to the ball than the opposition's hooker.

However, my personal preference and strong recommendation is that the engagement must be en bloc (eight together). A preoccupation with seeking advantageous angles carries the risk of fragmenting the unit. Conversely, when the opposition has the put-in, we can also counter or disrupt their scrum, with our loose head leading in and up. Again, however, we must be aware that engaging at different times breaks the tightness of the unit which can lead to a weakening of our own scrum.

I have one word of warning for junior and schools' coaches. The front row does not pack into the spaces; the connection is the sternum. It is better to concentrate on getting the front row close and tight in the preparation and that on the engagement you stay that way without worrying about what is in front of you.

The second row

Before addressing the binds it is recommended to pick the heaviest or the strongest player on the right-hand side to provide more support for the No. 3 (on the right-hand side) and No. 2.

The No. 5 (right-hand side second rower) must bind over No. 4 to provide more power and support to No. 3 and No. 2.

Binding should be just under the armpits, flexing the arms afterwards to provide a very tight unit. Bind first and then both pack down as a unit!

The second row is assembled separately as tightly as possible before engaging with the front row.

Second rowers binding to the front row

There are two main types of binding: around the hips and the crotch bind.

The grip around the hips as recommended in the Under 19s' law is probably the strongest and most effective with regards to the whole unit with the arms in an up position projecting the force forward. The contact on the props needs to be high enough to leave a spot at the very top of the outside leg for the flanker to push on. This is often called nature's niche.

Those coaches and players who prefer the crotch bind say it provides a better sense of tightness to the second row. On the other hand, the around the hips bind may take some getting used to because it demands a higher degree of flexibility at the second rowers' shoulder joint. Quite often this may feel uncomfortable particularly if a player is new to the position. It is, however, my preferred option because it closes the scrum better.

Around the hips bind

- » No. 4 and No. 5 bind tightly while standing up
- » Next, both step in with the inside leg which is bent
- » Outside leg has the knee on the ground
- » Both heads insert into the front row at knee height
- » Push heads up to get in a really vice-like tightness
- » Next the outside arms swing around the props' hips

» The hands grab the shorts and jumper for the firmest grip
» Afterwards, just a second before engagement, the outside knees come off the ground with both legs being ready to push

Advantages: It gives superior tightness to the whole scrum, utilizes maximum leg power and provides more freedom around the legs for the props. It is, of course, relative to the size and shape of both front row and second row.

Disadvantages: The abducted shoulder is not as comfortable or as strong as the closed joint used in the crotch bind and this may apply more to older players who are more than likely less flexible. On the other hand they will, by then, be fairly set in their ways.

The crotch bind

» No. 4 and No. 5 bind tightly while standing up
» Next, both step in with the inside leg which is bent
» Outside leg has the knee on the ground
» Both heads insert into the front row at knee height
» Push heads up to get in a really vice-like tightness
» Outside arm goes through the prop's crotch
» Hand goes across the groin and upwards to a jersey and shorts grip ending in a position close enough to the second rower's ear to feel it

Advantages: No. 4 and No. 5 will feel a tighter link to the front row with the stronger and more compact position of the adducted shoulder, and this may make them feel more locked in to the unit. It leaves more space for the connection of the flankers.

Disadvantages: Props may feel restricted around the legs again depending on the shape and size of all involved. Gripping too far through will round the shoulders and restrict the push. Going straight through and gripping the prop's jersey will put an unwelcome downward force on the prop.

Overall I know that with the crotch bind method the upper body is more engaged than the legs which are the powerhouse. The second rower may feel more compact but invariably less forward thrust is transmitted with this option.

Number eight

This player will usually bind around the hips (similar to the second row), with arms up and pointing forward. Some players prefer the crotch bind but in either case it is vital that the No. 8 is ready in position to contribute total weight to the second row, well before the engagement.

The Flankers

They will bind if possible to the opposite side second rower with the inside arm further tying up the back of the scrum. The outside hand is best on the ground as this will force the flanker to stay as low as possible and to push forward parallel to the ground. This outside hand must never go on the prop's thigh, as this is very annoying and restricts the movement of the prop's legs.

Body position

In scrummaging it is vital to understand the functions and application of the different body parts. This in turn will assist in better coaching, better performance and more accurate evaluation.

» Feet will give us vertical stability, direction and a foundation platform.

» Back will provide support and horizontal stability, balancing the different forces that the opposition will subject us to.

» Legs will provide the drive and continuity of forward movement.

» Head is like a rudder, if we point it down, down we go; the head must be up at all times.

» Hands will provide much needed tightness and in the case of both props the simultaneous grip is fundamental to maintaining front row stability. Second rowers remain tight by merit of their grips and the back row's contribution can never be underestimated.

» Hips (except No. 2 and No. 8) play a strong role with the other six forwards who must push inwards with their hips. This applies unless the coach decides to utilize the outward or straight push methods.

Every player's back must be straight and parallel to the ground and as low as possible, thereby adopting the biomechanically strongest and safest position. Following the laws, shoulders must not be lower than the hips. This does not mean the opposite; shoulders higher than hips is not recommended either, thus the back must be parallel to the ground.

It stands to reason that if the front row in particular engages with the back slanting downwards, then that is the only way it can go when forces start to drive them.

The force should always go forward and this is a push through toward the opposition goal line, which creates optimum efficiency. It is also in accordance with the first of the four principles of rugby (go forward, support, continuity, pressure).

Attention should be given to bodies that become unstable which occurs when a shoulder or a hip is lower than the other. This calls for corrective action to be taken immediately as such instability could stop scrum efficiency, promote injuries and even put lives at risk (e.g., quadriplegia, paraplegia).

To reiterate: The head is akin to a rudder, so if you point it down, down goes the force. If you keep your head up and forward, up and forward goes the force. In the scrum it's a lot easier to redirect upward forces forward than to redirect downward forces forward. The head should be in the neutral position because that is the strongest.

As I said before one of the main functions of the front row is to be able to transmit the forces from the back five in a direction that will put maximum pressure on the opposition and which will take the scrum forward if it moves. Merely holding the weight or going up into a higher position contradicts that principle. The combination of tightness, low body height and aggressive attitude avoids that wastage. The No. 3 is the one subjected to most of the pressure as the forces tend to concentrate between No. 2 and No. 3. That is not to forget that the No. 1 also has a special set of forces to deal with and, if not dealt with effectively, they can certainly be a major source of scrum complications.

Technical leaders nowadays say that the first principle of play is gaining possession. I would expand on this sentiment by saying that I want to go forward with or

without the ball! When the opposition has it what do I do? Watch them doing their thing or knock them backwards? The latter strategy starts in the scrum.

Original possession can be obtained through the scrum, the lineout and the restarts. In between those times it can be regained from a kick or a dropped ball made more likely by pressure, or it can be won in a ruck or a maul which like the scrum is more likely and more useful if we are moving forward. Going forward always facilitates getting over the gain line which is keeping the horse before the cart!

Leg positions and angles

First and foremost any scrummager and more particularly front rowers must understand that the bulk of all the participants' power and drive comes from their legs. Furthermore, they need to transfer forward the weight generated by the back row and second row; straight backs and heads up are paramount for the functioning and efficiency of the scrums.

The heavy work must be done with the legs but too many props don't seem to understand the relevant strength of their muscle anatomy. The abdominal wall combined with the back and neck muscles will keep a solid unit that can resist the forces generated by the opposition's scrum.

The sixteen legs must be bent forming an angle between 100 and 120 degrees which equates to a bit less than a half squat. This is the best angle to maintain a forward push with sustained pressure.

Once we have moved forward by straightening the legs, we must then shuffle the feet forward to the original position to start a secondary push if needed. Conversely, this will help to prevent a possible counter-shove from the opposition.

The hooker has a pushing leg and a hooking leg, if the option of hooking is intended. The hooking action doesn't take more than 1 second, and the remaining time that leg must revert to the normal pushing position. Like everybody else, the No. 2 has two pushing legs that can be used to push over a ball as a substitute for hooking.

Anyone with an extended leg or legs cannot push forward; that's why a holding scrum displays a defensive mental attitude with inherent risks. This is not recommended because if the legs are straight, a forward shunt will create instability that will result in a loss of purchase on the ground. There are two other ramifications:

» If the legs are locked, once you lose your feet positions the opposition will be able to shift your whole pack like a dead weight.

» If you have to withstand a sudden opposition shove while your legs are straight you are in real danger of knee damage because that joint will be subjected to a level of pressure for which it was not designed. Even if going backward, I strongly recommend maintaining the exertion of pressure and making the opposition work for every centimetre that they take. The players in the second row must have the outside knee on the ground before the engagement. This greatly assists in the control of forces extending on to the front row thereby enhancing the safety factor.

Body check list

» Feet firmly planted on the ground
» Adopt feet position as required
» Front row assumes the crouching position
» Backs parallel to the ground
» Lowest body height possible
» Individual and collective correctness

This is the precursor to a good connection with the opposition and one that will provide the maximum and effective transmission of force coming from the back five. The body position must be supported with full concentration and a controlled aggression that readies all to attack the opposition.

The engagement

The laws

Let's begin by again taking a look at some of the laws that relate to this and number them for easy reference. My comments are in italics.

1. Before the two front rows come together they must be standing not more than arm's length apart.

2. The front rows must crouch so that when they meet, each player's head and

shoulders are no lower than the hips.

3. The referee will call "crouch," then "touch". The front rows crouch and, using their outside arm, each prop touches the point of the opposing prop's outside shoulder. The props then withdraw their arms. The referee will then call "pause." Following a pause the referee will then call "engage." The front rows may then engage. The engage call is not a command but an indication that the front rows may come together when ready.

4. A front row must not form at a distance from its opponents and rush against them.

5. A team must not shove the scrum away from the mark before the ball is thrown in.

6. All front row players must bind firmly and continuously from the start to the finish of the scrum.

7. A loose head prop must bind on the opposing tight head prop by placing the left arm inside the right arm of the tight head and gripping the tight head prop's jersey on the back or side. The loose head prop must not grip the chest, arm, sleeve or collar of the opposition tight head prop. The loose head prop must not exert any downward pressure.
    [Interestingly this does not exclude upward pressure but in any event a loose head prop would have everything to lose by taking down the opponent.]

8. A tight head prop must bind on the opposing loose head prop by placing the right arm outside the left upper arm of the opposing loose head prop. The tight head prop must grip the loose head prop's jersey with the right hand only on the back or side. The tight head prop must not grip the chest, arm, sleeve or collar of the opposition loose head prop. The tight head prop must not exert any downward pressure.
    [This does not exclude upward pressure which is not good either.]

9. As soon as the front rows have come together, the scrum half must throw in the ball without delay. The scrum half must throw in the ball when told to do so by the referee. The scrum half must throw in the ball from the side of the scrum first chosen.

10. The scrum half must throw in the ball straight along the middle line, so that it first touches the ground immediately beyond the width of the nearer prop's shoulders.

11. Twisting, dipping or collapsing. Front row players must not twist or lower their bodies, pull opponents, or do anything that is likely to collapse the scrum, either when the ball is being thrown in or afterwards.

    [The scrum can be placed at risk through means other than collapsing. If a front row has been crunched, the hooker is in trouble and the scrum is going backwards, the front row may try to take the scrum down or up. The latter is usually done by the hooker and loose head with an upward surge. Both options are illegal and both are unsafe.]

12. Referees must penalise strictly any intentional collapsing of the scrum.

13. A front row player must not lift an opponent in the air, or force an opponent upward out of the scrum, either when the ball is being thrown in or afterwards.

14. If a scrum is wheeled through more than 90 degrees, so that the middle line has passed beyond a position parallel to the touchline, the referee must stop play and order another scrum.

My footnote to point 11 describes an illegal practice and its inclusion may raise a few eyebrows. My policy is to explain what happens in scrums and the motivation behind some of those actions; it is important to know how to defend your position against those seeking an unfair advantage. With so many technical requirements in the law the referee can't pick up everything, so good scrummagers need to be prepared. Apart from things like point 1 in the above list good scrummaging does not require going outside the law, so it is in everyone's best interest to abide by it.

Distance

In relation to point 1 the rationale of the law is that being too far apart can produce a dangerous charge but the law is too prescriptive about the maximum distance. **I'd recommend a 50 cm (1/2 metre) distance from shoulder to shoulder at crouched position.** Please note at this distance opposite heads would be almost touching. The distance required between the standing positions of the front rows will vary according to the builds of the various players, but for short players like myself **it would be 100 cm (1 metre) between the feet of opposite front rows.** This is quite a safe distance that prevents "charging" and at the same time allows both front rows to stretch out their backs and spines, also bend their legs into a safe position.

Great importance of the engagement

The engagement is vital as it can establish an advantage for one side by giving it a superior stability and a better platform for transmitting. A poor engagement can conversely make it difficult to absorb forces which can cause an accidental collapse that attracts a subsequent penalty. In other words the winner of the engagement is off to a flying start. There is still much work to do for the victor but a huge job lies ahead for the losers. It is common knowledge that one of the options exercised by the team losing the engagement is to collapse the scrum. This practice is fraught with danger for both teams by increasing the risk of spinal and neck injuries. One way of eliminating it would be to reduce the stakes in that area which would lessen the value of such a deliberate action. There is also a notion that if you feel your pack is not ready and likely therefore to lose the engagement, you then revert to tricking the referee into calling for a reset. Sometimes it involves standing up, sometimes it involves collapsing and sometimes it means breaking up and retreating off the mark. All of these represent a totally negative and unacceptable approach that should be severely dealt with if detected. Working into the engagement is not dissimilar to building an 80-story tower; it needs to start from a sound and solid foundation and go up brick by brick.

The clusters strategy and problem solving

I said in my introduction that I want my international colleagues to build on my ideas with alternatives, criticisms or endorsements and I have no doubt that my thoughts on tightness will attract considerable comment and I look forward to it. I do acknowledge that the policy needs to have some flexibility. I'll outline that now with some anecdotal justification, and for the sake of having a reference point I'll call it the clusters strategy.

My strongest recommendation to coaches and players is that any individual reactionary measures rarely work. Get it right at the start because, as I'll keep repeating, you won't have time to fix it.

Everything should happen very fast at the final act of engagement with the ball going in and out in a matter of seconds and leaving little time to think and react. In that regard it's a bit like sumo wrestling.

Nonetheless, proactive action combined with other players close to you (i.e., the cluster) is always more effective and long lasting. The left-hand cluster, for example, is made up of No. 1, No. 2, No. 4 and No. 6 while No. 2, No. 3, No. 5 and No. 7 are part of the right-hand cluster. The No. 8 would help or contribute extra to either side as requested. The best antidote for scrum problems is prevention by applying the adequate technique, suitable tactics and proper previous preparation.

Please don't get confused. The clusters strategy is excellent for working on solutions together, but in no way should the scrum ever be trained in separate sub-units; clustering is a sophisticated nuance based on solidarity and the understanding of other positions' needs and problems.

If I might indulge for a moment I shall recount an actual incident which illustrates how each side of the scrum can be used a little differently when needed.

During the 1984 Grand Slam Tour, we were playing the fourth test against Scotland in Murrayfield, and the match was very, very tough at least up front in the first half. We were experiencing a few problems with Ian Milne (No. 3) that were disrupting our scrum put-in, particularly getting Tom Lawton in an awkward position which was affecting his hooking. Tom asked me during the game a couple of times to lift him; Milne's nickname was the Bear, a very strong, huge fellow (125 kg) and experienced scrummager. How the hell was I going to lift him? Here is what I'm referring to as tapping into the clusters available. At the end of the first half we finished 12-9 up but only just. As soon as the referee blew the whistle for halftime, Tom and I started discussing the problems of our corresponding positions and likely solutions; we kept walking and talking absolutely engrossed in the subject. We agreed to get tighter together for starters and to rally support from Steve Cutler (No. 4) and David Codey (No. 6). After about 20 seconds, we realised that we were so focused on our discussion that we were walking away from the rest of the team. It's actually quite funny, on the video we suddenly did an about turn, kept walking and joined the team. In the second half, as we concentrated a bit more power on my side, we got closer with Tom in the engagement and we knew the Bear would tire with running. In the next ten minutes we turned the tables to a well-fought 37-12 and obtained the famous Grand Slam. It was quite a special feat and a great honour!

Physics and biomechanics

Before moving into the individual challenges that those in the front row face, it is necessary to explain some of the natural forces that are brought into play by the scrum's configuration.

Some coaches do not understand how the forces are distributed in the scrum. Due to the configuration of the front row the No. 3 has both shoulders packed in whereas the No. 1 has only one in contact with the opposition. As a consequence, the forces of the scrum are concentrated on the right side of it which leaves the left side with relatively less pressure. To put it in simple terms, the tight head prop No. 3 has to push harder and absorb more weight than the No. 1.

A side effect of this is that an extra effort is needed by the No. 3, who becomes trapped by the forces and is eventually the last player to break from the scrum and, as a result, is often last to arrive to the next breakdown. This is not, however, an excuse for props to be slow to the following formation or passage. Personally, many times in my career—at all levels—when running from the scrum to the next phase, I've often overtaken second rowers and occasionally back rowers. The levels of energy of rugby forwards vary and fluctuate during the game depending on the level of their commitment, the demands of their position and the degree of involvement in particular passages or phases. This is utterly unpredictable. This goes to explain why I would occasionally overtake a breakaway in the broken play and open running.

Each side of the front row also has its own distinctive dynamics and forces to deal with. The four props on the field are responsible for their own position and for the stability of the whole scrum. But too often they may be responsible for deliberately bringing their opposition prop down or up or out! The best defence a prop has is to get very close to the No. 2 (hooker). In fact both props should almost suffocate their hooker in this preventative action and in 95% of the cases the hooker will love this constriction anyhow. Not only is the front row better protected but the whole pack will function much better this way.

In relation to angles the law has requirements regarding pushing angles off the horizontal plane where shoulders must not be lower than the hips, and I am adamant that the back parallel to the ground is the safest and strongest position in that regard. It does not, however, refer to any pushing direction in particular. If everyone had to push at 90 degrees to the middle line then it would be impossible to limit the wheel so there has to be some pushing on angles. At the moment of the engagement the push will be straight ahead like due north on the compass but just as crosswinds will take an aircraft off north so will the imbalanced forces distort the direction of the scrum and its individuals. The torque will start taking the formation around its axis. In my tightly bound scrum the individual angles will remain the same as that of the unit.

While on the forces, I'd like to dispel a widely accepted myth. When a prop (generally the No. 3) has been popped, this is not entirely caused by the No. 1 from the opposition, but more so by the pressure exerted by the back five.

Attack and counterattack between the front rows

I need to say that through my years of playing, I have found a deeply rooted common belief that scrummaging is just the two props going at each other's throats seeking dominance of territory and possession. This notion completely ignores the complementation of the rest of the pack where every forward contributes their pound of flesh, so to speak, toward the end result. This misconception needs to be addressed by the coach in ensuring every forward has a role to play and a responsibility to uphold.

On the engagement proper, the loose head prop (No. 1), the hooker (No. 2) and the tight head prop (No. 3) share the objective of neutralising and absorbing the opposition power and at the same time exerting pressure onto them. To do this they must work together as a sub-unit. The front row comprises specialists to meet the intrinsic demands of each position, but individual demands are more easily dealt with by having the support of an overall combined strategy of the three. It's one of the cluster strategy solutions.

Through circumstances and teams' needs I had to learn the trades of all three, which is why I can speak from personal experience. It may surprise you that I played hooker (No. 2) for six years with Tala RC from Cordoba and alternated between No. 1 and No. 3 for Argentina.

The following descriptions will prepare your players for what to expect from a wily and experienced opposition in the two situations of our put-in (where we have the loose head) and their put-in (where they have the loose head).

In general terms it would be easy to regard the non-putting-in side as the attackers and the putting-in side as the defenders. That sounds incongruous because normally the team with the ball is called the attacking side and the other one is called the defending side. In the scrum, however, the non-infringer is defending or protecting possession and the infringing side is attacking it. I don't particularly like that terminology though, because I think the putting-in side has the need to be every bit as aggressive as the opponents. You could call them the putter-ins and the putter-offs, but we'll stick with the conventional loose head and tight head scrums.

One general tip that applies to all these players is that the whole pack should be armed with tactical variations to unsettle the opposition. These involve angle changes, double shoves, wheels and so on but with the pack always working as a unit of eight. The surprise factor is hugely important and beneficial in any form of competition as it supplies part of the psychological advantage over the adversary. Using these options will create uncertainty and hesitation in the opposition thereby making it much more difficult for their preparation and their ability to channel and to control the ball.

On the issue of safety it should be pointed out that often the heads of the front rows are placed under the chest of opposition front rowers which restricts their independent movement upwards. From this position, however, the head can exert an enormous pressure, sometimes against the sternums of the opposition players and this is akin to having another, more powerful arm. If the weight from behind drives the shoulders of one player upwards, as well as forward in that situation, then the neck is likely to be hyper-flexed because the head is stuck as mentioned before. This is not only very unpleasant for the prop in question, but also increases the risk of neck injury tenfold.

Any twisting of the neck in this situation results in the dangerous combination of flexion and twisting which could cause a severe spinal injury.

Let's now turn our attention to the packing down of the three front rowers—the contests within a contest.

Before I comment on the loose head, hooker and tight head roles I shall reiterate my mantra which is: Strength in unification. The strength of the whole is more than the sum of the individual parts. Nowhere does this apply more than a strong tightly knit front-row formation. On arrival at the mark the first priority of the props is to get very tight with the hooker and to ensure their second rowers are in a good pushing position with the flankers never too far away. Once set their next concern is the engagement and the opposition props. It is here where the back rowers, particularly the flankers, must commit and be in position before the scrum starts. With power from behind and trusting the No. 8 to direct it, both props should have the confidence to deal with anything.

Ball put-in

This is a huge subject! Even today referees do not referee it properly and nobody knows why. Not even WR knows it—a real mystery of rugby union! I feel like writing a full chapter about this because since I started playing rugby at 19 years of age I remember this being the most common infringement, as well as the most argued about subject that came up about referees after the game.

There was a time, I believe, when our representative referees officially decided to ignore the law and allow the ball to be put into the second row. The other law they took into their own hands was to allow lineout lifting years before the law sanctioned it. This idea of making up their own laws extended into other areas that included clearing out which produces a ridiculous situation where there are two sets of laws. If the authorities don't like a law they should change it and keep the law book sacrosanct.

Why anyone would want to destroy a hooking contest by allowing a cheating put-in is beyond me because it has other ramifications, such as encouraging mischief makers that no longer have any incentive to strike for the ball. I came from a school where we chose not to hook, choosing instead to increase our shoving power without disrupting. We not only respected the option of hooking, but also encouraged it because it suited our chosen scrummaging system.

Our loose head (our put-in)

NO. 1

It is understandable that the first reaction in the scrum is the desire to match aggression with aggression, after all that's what the training is for. The No. 1 has a three-pronged role: protect the hooker; control the opposite prop and stop that player from disrupting the scrum; and promote the unity of the front row, giving commitment to their combined cause.

No amount of individual action will be better for the scrum and for the whole team than a strong, tightly knit front-row formation. In reality that third role serves the purposes of the other two so all are inter-related.

Let's talk about the protective role first. What is being protected? It is an effective position for the No. 2 to hook for the ball and to have a clear ball passage. This requires a solid and stable scrum which the opposition will try to disrupt particularly through its No. 3.

If you want to split a log the operation is best started by driving a wedge into it, and the same applies here where you prevent the opponent from driving in the thin end of the wedge. This basic defence requires the tight bind that offers no opening and if the No. 1 and the hooker (No.2) squeeze in on their troublemaking No. 3, the options of that player will be limited. This tightening should be happening before the problem starts and is what I call proactive management. The other proactive approach is to neutralise No. 3 and the following tactics can be applied.

TACTICS

The most effective counter to a force being exerted on us is to use attack as the best means of defence! Drive the opponents up and out of their pushing platform, then cause those players to lose their straight back weapon and their feet positions (e.g., one pack puts a shove on and the other pack may counter with a double shove, or a similarly aggressive action like a sink and shove). Psychologically speaking the pack that goes backward will rapidly lose heart and grit and give up the pushing contest.

TIMING

There are two components here. One refers to taking the initiative, and this part of the contest is similar to arm wrestling where the first person to apply the pressure will get the drop on the other. The other component refers to the coordinated action of working in unison with the whole eight, both at engagement time and when the emphasis on pushing follows.

LOCATION

It is another advantage for a loose head (No. 1) to meet his opposite number No. 3 slightly on that player's side of the mark. This can be achieved even under a No. 3 leads-in policy. It is a common belief that the No. 3 will lead, thus creating an angle that favours the hooking. My preference is that if we create this angle, it has to be with the three front rowers hitting en bloc with the simultaneous support of the back five.

GRIPS

The key to the grips is to very rapidly get the outside arm well over the opponent's back and to grip as much of the back of the jersey as possible. When you do this, No. 3s will pull themselves down if they try to pull you down. Moreover, a bind of this nature doesn't give the opponent much on which to apply any compensating leverage.

For the loose head there is the alternative short grip which is started with the left arm out and parallel to the ground and a bent elbow aiming at the armpit. You then grab a fistful of jersey on the side of the opponent's garment and twist your hand as if you were wrapping it with the jumper. You must flex your arm, closing your biceps to prevent the opposition No. 3 from leveraging you down. This very firm grip on the opponent has the potential to considerably restrict this player's destructiveness.

The short grip may or may not work for you; it is a case of trial and error, mostly dependent on shoulder and scapula strength, either yours or the opposition No. 3's. If this doesn't work go back to the traditional straight arm grip.

DE-POWERING THE SCRUM

This is an interesting term because lawmakers often say they have de-powered the scrum, which they can't claim without limiting the push. All they have done is to empower the referee to manage the engagement. If anything, they have increased the power by forcing all eight to stay in the scrum. Let us return, however, to the players who can restrict the shove. After driving the opponent up, the No. 1 will often press his inside shoulder down on the No. 3's head in an attempt to bend his back which is the transmitter of power.

Another action by the No.1 may be to exert pressure on the oppositions' necks with their right shoulders, and simultaneously push upwards with their necks against the opposition's sternums. This effectively pins those players to a point that limits their combative options. A manoeuvre such as this must be done quickly because the window of opportunity is there for a split second only. This action is generally premeditated and executed as an initiative rather than as a reaction.

The NO. 1's main stability comes from the stance:
» Feet shoulder width apart
» Right heel which must be in the same line of the left toe
» Bent legs in a pushing position

The other requirements include tightness with the hooker (No. 2) and the second row No. 4 and a transfer of power from behind.

OUTCOMES

The result of all this is that the No. 1 has won the initiative with the opponent thanks to the assistance of his other forwards. When everyone sticks to their script the result is efficiency and effectiveness. Therefore the No. 1 doesn't need to go any further alone; the job has been done and there is no real purpose in wasting any more energy—just stay tight and ready with the front row and advance together. Trying to then prove to be the strongest person on the field is only inviting a retaliation which could rebound on the instigator leaving that tough guy coming off second best.

NO. 1

No. 1 will defend this process as a subtle neutralising action not in conflict with law 20.8 (g) which refers to twisting, dipping, pulling and collapsing. There is no collapsing, there is no dipping where the body can be lowered by the legs only, there is no pulling with the hands and arms and there is no twisting which involves turning around the hips. The synchronised work of the whole pack doesn't allow for anyone to be singled out.

NO. 2

The aim is to properly organise the scrum and secure a positive engagement, then get in a better striking position than the opposition hooker. The loose head (No. 2) already is a good 20 to 25 cm closer to the ball than the opponent, but the advantage varies according to the length of legs, flexibility and the timing of both hookers.

THE STEPS ARE:

(a) On the referee's whistle No. 2 sprints to the mark and raises both arms to indicate the start of the formation to the rest of the forwards.

(b) The hooker takes the first bind on the No. 3 and then on the No. 1, both binds being very tight with the props' shoulders tucked under the armpit. The tighter these binds are the better and the narrower the point of contact the better.

(c) Some hookers then like to pull the outside shoulder in front of the No 1, but I wouldn't recommend this because effectiveness comes before comfort.

I'd like to stress that the link between No. 2 and No. 3 is the heart of the scrum, so it should be the strongest; those two must be like conjoined twins.

If hooking, after the engagement the sequence is to:

(a) Secure a very tight and steady front row throughout

(b) Shift the weight onto the left leg

(c) Swing the hips and free the right leg to either sweep for the ball or to use any other hooking action.

Tightness will guarantee a shunt forward which will help in striking for the ball. If the opposition chooses to get into a hooking competition, there is an offensive option which involves having the whole front row tight and ready; when the opposition hooker tries to lift the hooking leg this is the best signal to start pushing, which will be quite an uncomfortable experience for both hooker and pack. Often the success of this tactic will be easier to achieve than it seems. The opposition will have only seven players pushing who will be, I dare say, not very well organised because they are banking on pinching the ball.

With human nature being to relax while somebody else is working, they will tend to have two conflicting or contradictory objectives.

NO. 3

In this situation the No. 3 has to be a rock because if this player goes, the scrum goes. If the player opposite crushes the pillar, the whole group falls. The most important thing is to have a very solid link with No. 2 and for the whole front row to be fastened firmly in place. After that it's a matter of timing where all must hit at once as they go for a favourable position. And don't forget that the grip is the key to winning the engagement and stabilising the scrum. You get the right grip first and you're almost there.

I am a strong believer and advocate of the benefits of the simultaneous and synchronised engagement. When you are doing a demolition job you want a medium-sized ball to hit the walls and to concentrate all hits at one point. Let's relate this theory to a hypothetical case:

» We have 900 kg in our pack, more or less three vertical columns of 300 kg each.
» If the No. 3 leads and hits first, he will project 300 kg onto the opposition.
» Then half a second later No. 2 hits with his 300 kg column.
» Finally in another half-second No. 1 arrives with his 300 kg column.

If we have the 900 kg available and ready from the beginning, why not apply a simultaneous and synchronised engagement every time? Let's apply everything we have when the law and the referee allows us to!

You have heard of the tactics where the No. 1 gets under the No. 3 and lifts the opponent. Even though the No. 1 may apply all his energy and strength, this event of lifting the No. 3 (or popping) can only happen when sufficient force comes from the back five.

To counter this upward thrust the tight head generally uses his bind to lower the connection, using the legs to apply forward pressure on either the hooker or prop's chest and sternum.

This extra dimensional pressure generates a destabilising force into the opposition No. 1 and can be accentuated by twisting the whole torso outwards (a clockwise action).

Apart from that, the No. 3 just needs to set an example by sticking to the general guidelines:

» In countering any of these front row ploys, a tight bind will always make it more difficult for the opposition to disrupt you. This is the best form of prevention.

» The important thing is not to let them gain the initiative, so be ready and don't let the loose head enter the engagement on your side of the mark. Work with the whole front row as a block.

» The hooker (No. 2) is responsible for grips at underarm height of both props. Props must bind at hip height (shorts and jumpers). This will prevent a loose engagement, not giving gaps to the opposition to attack. Having tight grips everywhere is the best preventative action.

» Make sure that after the engagement you don't have to move your feet, because that could weaken your initiative and provide an opportunity for the opponent to exploit your adjustments. The whole body has to be braced and compact, and as such the neck should also be ready for action. Over-tightening your muscles too early is counterproductive but being lax doesn't help either.

» Keep the chin up and back straight—an arch should be formed on top of the player's lower back)—abdominal, back and neck strength are absolutely essential here. They provide our core which protects our neck and spine and structurally maintains our skeleton in top shape. A weak abdominal wall will invariably cause a weak lower back and will also compromise our endurance and resistance. Our lower body is connected to our upper body through the solar plexus (abdominal wall) which is why it's so important to have a strong mid-section. This will cater for all scrummaging demands, as well as the necessary endurance to run for 80 minutes.

» Needless to say during scrummaging we utilise our whole body in a series of movements that requires a lot of strength and flexibility. All major muscles are engaged in this strenuous activity: legs, gluteus, chest, arms, shoulders, lower back and abdominals. This is one of the main reasons why strength training is an ideal complement to the general rugby training conducted on the field.

Our tight head (opposition's put-in)

NO. 1

This player's fundamental aim is to be part of one solid and tight unit: his own front row (No. 1, No. 2, and No. 3) backed by the power base (No. 4 and No. 6). The focus can then shift to giving the opposition hooker a bad striking angle. This means getting the right-hand side of the scrum up in a forward sense, and not in terms of height. This is where binding, arms, and body position, along with the support from behind through the No. 4 and the No. 6, all play their part. Refer back to the clusters strategy where a group works on the one initiative.

No scrum is ever perfectly square-on so you might as well be the beneficiary of this. It should also be noted that the shorter props have an advantage in being able to get under and through in their pursuit of this advantage. Nonetheless, selection is not a lesser art than coaching. All players must be assessed on all the qualities they offer, as well as their adaptability to the demands of each position. A lot of the assessment can be done on the scrum machine but observations in a game are better.

For example, if armed with the ability to control the downwards pressure of the opposition's No. 3, a short prop can fit the bill. Alternatively the short prop could play No. 3 for that same reason provided there is no feeling of constriction or a sense of being trapped by the forces impacting on this position.

With the taller prop you'll have very similar dilemmas, so trial and error within a safe environment seems the best way to identify the front row talent. Alternatively, if you have an honest hooker he or she could write the report sheet for every prop colleague. This sheet could also be a very good point of reference for coaching, not just selecting!

NO. 2

The aim is to properly organise the scrum and secure a positive engagement. There are two options here:

1. If so desired, strike for the ball. Props will need to be prepared for this action, otherwise the hooker lashing out with his leg could be a destabilising force. The opposition will have the advantage of being 20 to 25 cm closer to the ball, but better timing and concentration may overcome this.

2.   The alternative is to exert as much pressure as possible, attacking and disrupting the put-in through a variety of tactical manoeuvres. The sequence in the organisation is as follows:

   (a)   First and foremost the hooker should set an example by sprinting to the mark, because this player's attitude and body language speak volumes to the other seven forwards.

   (b)   Once on the mark and with arms raised in the air, this is the moment to use tactics by calling numbers or another type of code. Remember that soon the second rowers will be in and won't hear any voices clearly. This can involve the barking of commands to those not quite ready.

   (c)   Listening to the referee for clues about the opposition or even your own scrum is vital.

   (d)   The tight head hooker will try to position the right shoulder above the neck of the other No. 2 and then apply forward and downward pressure. The downward component is just enough to cause inefficiency or discomfort (i.e. an element of distraction as opposed to inducing a collapse).

If the law is being properly applied with the ball being put in correctly, the No. 2 may choose to attempt to win the strike against the head. In this case the No. 1 can put his inside foot further up and push his hooker closer to the tunnel entrance. The No. 1 will be able to do this only against an inferior opponent.

NO. 3

The greatest asset a front row has for transmitting force is its tightness. A set of shoulders level and parallel with the ground and the back straight and parallel to the ground is what the doctor recommended and the coach is blessed with. If any of the opposition can interfere and upset that then they have created an advantage for their team in going forward and the No. 3 is ideally placed to achieve this. The most common tactic is for the No. 3 to drive inward toward the hooker (No. 2) and, if it's done powerfully enough, it will split the bind of the opposition loose head prop (No. 1) and hooker (No. 2). This creates the double bonus of not only de-powering their unit but also making their hooking task more difficult.

I used this tactic myself very effectively in 1983 during the Argentina v Australia test at Ballymore. We were rewarded with two push-over tries for a final score line of 18-3; this was Argentina's first big win overseas against one of the top eight IRB countries.

The further through the tight head (No. 3) can get, the less effective their No. 1 will be. At engagement the No. 3 has to try to find the gap. Conversely the opposition No. 1 will try to get in first to stop the No. 3 getting through the gap. The tight head's outside grip will vary, but it is usually along the side of the opponent's back or a short grip around No. 1's armpit.

The body position and adjustments

With the all-important body position there are two essential factors to take into account—the law and the position that generates the maximum power. The law states that at the time the two front rows meet, the shoulders must not be lower than the hips. That presents no problems at all for the front row, because if a prop engages with the shoulders below the hips that player is finished before the start. It's an open invitation to the opposition to bend down the head of that player, which prevents him having the straight back which is so necessary for generating and transmitting power.

There is no doubt in my mind and by common practice that the back parallel to the ground is the ideal position for all eight pushing participants. Additionally, after the engagement, a prop that is overpowered by either a single force or a combined one is likely to end up in an illegal position with shoulders lower than the hips.

The back five have slightly more choice in reaching that parallel position. I prefer to keep it as simple as possible which gives us less margin for human error, facilitates a quick readiness for action and makes synchronisation much easier. When coaching I refer to a dining table to exemplify the required straightness of all backs. This means that, from the No. 8 to the hooker, all backs should be levelled like a dining table. This promotes economy and efficiency, concentrating the transmission of all forces in the same direction: the opposition's hooker!

We have extolled the virtues of being in the strongest position immediately on engagement. That doesn't mean that there won't be some settling of the station. Elsewhere I have likened the situation to a golfer's stance where, after addressing the ball, the shot maker will bed everything down before swinging into the stroke. There are other occasions where a distinct foot adjustment is necessary.

Edging manoeuvring

Edging is the practice of accentuating or exaggerating the exertion of pressure after making contact on a selected side. This is the equivalent to gradually mounting the pressure on one side of the opposition scrum to destabilize the pack, particularly the front row.

At all costs you should avoid having to adjust your feet backward which can be necessary if you lose the engagement. Edging forward is a tactic designed to capitalise on an engagement across the mark; it is securing or shoring up the ground that has been won by adjusting and keeping the ideal leg pushing angle.

The original object is to be able to engage with the feet back and the knees suitably flexed, but if the opposition is slow on the uptake and you advance further than anticipated, the front row then needs to bring their feet up accordingly which requires a technique all of its own. It is fairly axiomatic that the power is generated by the leg push which comes from the purchase extracted from the feet on the ground.

As a consequence, maximum power comes when all the feet are properly positioned and in contact with the ground. If feet positions have to be changed, then the loss of power can be limited by doing it quickly and minimizing the time the feet are off the ground. Because of this simple set of physics, the adjustment must be done with a rapid short-shift staccato shuffle. This is hard to explain, but it is all to do with quick feet and very short steps so you don't lose your footing or your position of strength; that is what edging is all about.

The tightness of the eight, which is achieved during setup, must be maintained after the hit, particularly in the front row where hips must stay together, grips at the top well secured, feet solid and stable and the outside arms of both props locked in good position from the engagement. If either prop has a tendency to adopt a different angle, this must be corrected from the outset. Any angle that is to be adopted must apply to the whole eight, and not just to some individuals.

Whether they result from positive tactics or adjustments caused by the opposition, any changes to the angles, shoulders or head positions of the props after the engagement should not compromise the togetherness of the unit. It is, of course, much more preferable to get the engagement right at the start so that no countering adjustments are necessary.

Remember that while you are preoccupied with adjusting your feet positions, you are not able to pay much attention to the opposition, which is crucial if you are to gain the initiative. A good opposition will seize any opportunity to gain an advantage, and in scrummaging there are a number of tactics used to cause a distraction. Make sure you do not get sucked in!

These days we are playing with the new pre-bind engagement law (2013) which expressly prohibits any movements off the mark. I have left this section on edging on purpose to show newcomers and others, the types of strategies and tactics that went on and were the norm in recent times. These creative initiatives and subterfuge generated a fair bit of confusion with the public in particular. Some were not necessarily problem-solving action-reactions. Quite often they were exactly the opposite, a way of diverting the attention, confusing the opposition and denying them the time to obtain and play the ball.

Props' outside leg foot position

The outside leg of both props has only three positions or options:

(a) Same level as the other leg
(b) Slightly back (toe to the line of the heel of the inside leg)
(c) Slightly forward, foot in front of the inside leg (This is not recommended as it is not biomechanically suitable for transmitting back forces, or for generating your own.)

When the No. 1 placed the left hand or forearm on the left knee or thigh, the practice used to be called the bridge. Today this is illegal because it compromises the stability of both front rows to a point where it could cause the scrum to collapse. Any time a prop moves the outside leg up to support the upper body, it considerably weakens the position of that player who becomes very vulnerable to a sudden thrust of the opposition. With my old team of Tala RC we timed it to perfection; when we saw a leg coming up (hooker included) that was the signal for us to explode forward. It is much more difficult for a lineout thrower to put the ball down the middle of a lineout than it is for a scrum half to put the ball in along the middle line of a scrum. However, referees will police the lineout with some rigour while ignoring the law affecting the scrum put-in. This is an inconsistency that I cannot explain!

Hooking or pushing?

The option of whether to hook or to push is a tactical one and lies in the domain of the coaches and players.

The scrum is a unique contest which offers many challenges to eight players in each team. It is an encounter that involves physicality, mental toughness, discipline, technique, guile, speed and anticipation. Allowing illegal put-ins reduces not only the options, but also the guile, speed, value and anticipation of a good hooker supported by his pillars, the props and those behind. If we keep on going down the rugby league track we will end up with 15 similarly built human tanks playing a game of running, tackling, passing and kicking only and a game that becomes predictable and lacking in diversity.

I have a special section in this paper that relates to law philosophy, as getting the scrum right partly depends on getting the law right. The referees' role will be dealt with further in that section.

Pushing and timing

Nobody has permission to stop pushing because that is the essence of the scrum. There was a time in Australia when the flankers were called breakaways because as soon as the ball went in, their job was to break away from the scrum to become a defender in case the ball was lost. This must not be tolerated in the modern power scrum or you will be deserting your colleagues and setting them up for physical and mental humiliation.

As far as I know, there are some universal truths that must be respected. Since the 1970s when Wales had a formidable scrum, it has been well understood that superior pushing power allows you to move the opposition backwards, which provided the following:

» A better quality ball for the back line and a poorer quality one for the opposition
» A better chance to determine both the nature of the breakdown (e.g. lineout, ruck, maul) and the position of it (e.g., in close, out wide, up field, left, or right)
» An opportunity to put the opposition under pressure from the word go
» Easier defense

On this last point they realised that the scrum is the only platform where pressure and confrontation may be applied in an organised manner to an opposition that is not in possession of the ball. That is why it can be the most exhausting contest in the game.

The three most important macro-elements in the pushing department are:
» pack togetherness,
» coordinating and synchronising the forces towards one common point, and
» transferring the push directly forward on a plane close to parallel with the ground.

Other variations are discussed elsewhere in the cut and thrust of things.

To generate and transmit power most effectively, the members must appreciate the need to apply force in the right direction at the right time, and in unison. This involves a lot of coordination and timing executed through the snap shove which, generally speaking, is used to make an opposition scrum retreat. The most powerful shoves come from an explosive thrust and the starting position for producing such a push originates from:

» feet about shoulder width apart for balance and up on the balls of your feet (before engagement);
» bent forming an angle of about 120 degrees (after the engagement);
» back and neck straight (throughout); and
» grips and hips very tight (throughout).

The most effective engagement sequence is quite simple:
» Raise the heels and get up on your toes. The C-T-P-E sequence has made this step very difficult, if not impossible, because this ideal starting position cannot be held over the prolonged period involved.
» Keep your heels close to the ground as you drop your knees.
» Push off the toes and straighten the knees with an explosive action.

The principles of the scrum push are the same. The recommended actions bring into play other important muscles, such as the hips, thighs, calves and ankles, but it all starts with a solid base projecting your weight towards the toes.

The timing relates to the signals, but when you have the loose head you should bring these into play early before the opposition can organise its offensive. The signal of readiness will be given by the hooker and the return signal for the put-in will be delivered by the scrum half.

On the opposition tight head's ball, the snap shove is called by the tight head prop (No. 3), or flanker (No. 7), or even by our half back (No. 9) who is the closest player to the scrum and ought to know when the scrum is ready or when the opposition is about to put the ball in. Conversely, on the loose head side the ball will be called by No.1, No.6 or No. 9.

The technique of hooking

The previous concept is very relevant here for managing the movements of a diverse group of individuals, such as a rugby pack. To achieve a coordinated and effective action, we need one voice for preparation and another voice for execution! On the signal everybody explodes in an inward and forward pushing action as the ball is being introduced to the scrum.

If referees continue to allow second row feeds then the defending scrum might as well concentrate on the snap shove or the double and triple shoves. There is nothing fair about this contest for possession. I used to believe that fairness and equality were part of the spirit of rugby, but that no longer seems to apply. Consequently, as it stands at the moment, you can be forgiven for forgetting possession and going for territory in this scrummaging situation.

As you watch the modern scrum you would be excused for thinking the ball must travel along the same channel to the No. 8's feet from where the half back retrieves it with some difficulty, or the No. 8 simply picks it up himself. This need not be so if the scrum is allowed to work correctly.

The hooking technique has changed substantially in the last 40 years with the advent of the power scrum (e.g., pushing scrum, eight-man shoves, etc.). No. 2s used to be fairly free-moving in the front row, ready to strike left or right no matter whose put-in it was. There was a time when scrums were used pretty much to restart the game, were packed down about 20 to 30 cm higher than today, and the pushing was not so intense.

Nowadays, however, with different techniques, better conditioning and intense strength training, scrums are packed much lower than in those days. Standards are different too, and hookers are practically restricted to hooking with their fourth leg only (i.e., right foot in their own put-in and left foot in the opposition's put-in). This is necessary to preserve the stability and power of their scrum, as well as maintaining the pushing position required by the law. Any other options are exercised at your own peril.

The hooker's responsibility is to:

1. Organise the front row first then the scrum, coordinating and orchestrating the chosen outcome or tactic.

2. Ensure a solid and controlled aggressive engagement (as much as permitted by the law and refereeing).

3. Shift weight onto the non-hooking leg which is essential during preparation.

4. Stay prepared to strike when the ball comes in.

5. Continue pushing immediately after the strike until the scrum is over. Sometimes territory gains occur after the ball is gone.

As we can appreciate this is a very complex position with multi-tasking required in a very short space of time. The reality is that, in order to succeed in hooking, the hooker must attend carefully to all those steps. Unlike the props the hooker's hands and arms do not make contact with the opposition. However, the head could accidentally do so and the struggle for supremacy is no less intense. In looking at the most common hooking techniques I am assuming that most readers understand that when I refer to our put-in, the ball approaches from the hooker's left-hand side.

It is as well to remember some aspects of law when discussing hooking techniques.

Hooker in a position to hook

Until the ball is thrown in, the hooker must be in a position to hook the ball. The hookers must have both feet on the ground, with their weight firmly on at least one foot. A hooker's foremost foot must not be in front of the foremost foot of that team's props.

Striking after the put-in

Once the ball touches the ground in the tunnel, any front row player may use either foot to try to win possession of the ball, but I should say that I cannot remember the last time I saw a prop being trained to hook for the ball. Yes, it used to happen when the hooker blocked it and the prop guided it back, but losing that weight today would be insufferable. A front row player must not strike for the ball with both feet.

The following were popular hooking options but have not been relevant in recent years without the incentive of hooking the ball from an unfair and illegal put-in. The techniques are included on the basis that this practice will no longer be condoned and that contested hooking will be allowed to return.

Own put-in

Glance

This is done by using the right foot (also called fourth leg of the front row), striking out and simultaneously drawing the toe back toward the back of the scrum and trapping the ball in the action. This option is safer; it controls the ball better, but can also be slower. If the coordination with the half back is not perfect, this method helps in securing the ball. It is easier to control the ball and it doesn't require great coordination between No. 9 and No. 2.

Block and Push

This combines the action of first stopping the ball and then nudging it back as your pack steps over the ball. This depends on your pack having a reactive push or being dominant.

This method exerts even more pressure onto the opposition pack and, although the ball will be slower, gaining forward movement will be easier.

Opposition's put-in

Sweeping

This employs the full sole of the foot which is made available by bending the toe down. This makes for a quick ball. Hooking the opposition's ball is a surprise action.

Heeling

This is a very quick strike out, utilising the heel to push the ball back. This ball could be channelled between No. 1's legs; or between No. 1 and No. 2. The timing between No. 9 and No. 2 must be impeccable. This ball is very fast but is much more difficult to control.

Near Foot or Reverse Sweep

This should only be attempted with a short, very flexible hooker and a very strong and tall tight head prop.

When to use these hooking options

No two scrums are the same. Perhaps I'd recommend it as a surprise factor to vary your game and to give you options so the opposition doesn't get conditioned to one style only. It's a function of the coach to equip the players with the ability to read the play; identify the problems; and select the tools/tactics to fix them.

This process could at times be trial and error because sometimes the most unusual thing will confuse the opposition and thwart a successful tactic for no apparent reason.

Finally, hookers need to be very strong and supple, with a high degree of awareness, quick reactions, and a capacity for leadership. Physically there can be two types; at the top level selectors these days seem to go for the heavy option which adds weight to the push, but they still need to be good scrum organisers. They may also select a third prop. Because hooking is no longer a striking contest, the alternative is to choose an athlete with the qualities of another back rower. To some degree your choice of hooker will enable the other side to make predictions and will influence its scrum tactics.

This is a highly specialised position that doesn't lend itself to improvisation. Knowing and feeling the scrum requires a lot of experience and just being the strongest guy in the team won't cut it! In this position we need to have a player who has the feel for it, who is happy to be in the middle of it and is eager to confront the opposition. The hooker has to be with you until the 85th minute but more importantly needs to be a thinker.

Furthermore, by the virtue of scrum architecture the hooker is player surrounded by more bodies than any other position. Thus, they have the best feel for the way the scrum behaves and reacts. There is no choice or chance; we must pick a seasoned specialist to safely and successfully cover this position.

The channelling

It is fairly well-recognised by players and coaches that there are three channels of choice, with one being short and the other two going on the longer route out the back of the scrum.

CHANNEL 1

Channel 1 runs through the No. 1's feet between the No. 4 and No. 6. This is a very quick ball but could be uncontrolled and unprotected if it bounces around. This ball is ideal for when we're attacking from right to left.

CHANNEL 2

Channel 2 runs through the No. 2's feet, back between the feet of the second rowers and through to the No. 8's feet. The No. 2 changes the angle of foot to reach this channel. The No. 2 also may choose to channel it through the No. 1's feet, in which case the left-side second rower may have to use the outside foot to guide the ball along its path.

Where such assistance is necessary, the second rower should avoid rushing or reaching for the ball as altering the pushing position will result in the loss of too much power. This channel usually supplies a slower ball but a better controlled one.

CHANNEL 3

Channel 3 runs through the No. 2's feet, to the No. 5 and to the left No. 7's feet. Again the No. 2 changes foot angle in order to reach channel three. As in channel two, there are a number of variables and all players should be alert to adapt to them. The ball comes out between No. 8 and No. 7. Again the second row might need to nudge it along the way, but the beauty of this ball is that it is completely protected from the defending scrum half as it emerges on the opposite side of the scrum. The best thing that can happen to a No. 2 is that the scrum moves forward 30 cm every time the ball enters the tunnel. In any case hooking is not a substitute for pushing or vice versa; it is a single temporary action of the No. 2.

As I said at the beginning, no matter whose put-in it is, all players must always push in the scrum. The scrum might be a way to restart the game but by no mean is it a place to rest or switch off.

A quick revision

The success or failure of a scrum is determined in general by three important points:

*The collective understanding and knowledge of team objectives.
*The collective understanding of tactics which may vary from scrum to scrum.
*Awareness, preparation and approach for each particular scrum.

In any close competitive situation the two factors that will decide the winner are organisation and attitude. On the organisational side each individual needs knowledge, preparation and a commitment, not only to his own task, but also to making the total unit work. As far as attitude is concerned, in a contact sport that is surrounded by adversity then a winning, positive approach, especially from the front row, gives a boost like oxygen.

CHAPTER

7

Tactics – traps – troubleshooting

TACTICS – TRAPS – TROUBLESHOOTING

Tactics

A very important recommendation to all coaches: Before you enter the field of tactics you must get your fundamentals right, the ones we have covered in the previous sections under preparation and engagement.

You must start with the ability to set a firm and square scrum which will provide you with a solid platform and a clean enough ball with which to attack. Only when you and your pack have mastered this simple but very necessary group skill can you then dedicate some time to tactics and variations.

On the subject of tactics, a good coach and captain will set a strategy that includes tactics to make the overall plan successful. It is reasonable to expect the players to adhere to those tactics in a macro sense, but they must also have the freedom of choice in a micro sense. Coaches can't predict each passage of play in terms of either opportunity or constraint and to some extent you must react to what the opposition has done.

At the practice session the coach can put the team in predictable situations and work on the best tactic to deal with them. On the field the captain may find that it does not work as planned and be required to change the method of dealing with some circumstances. If the opposition is lax on one occasion or applies extra pressure on another, then the player has to choose an option accordingly.

The players and the units within the team can be given guidelines but they can't be pre-programmed completely.

In the game of rugby, players need to know how to do things but they also need to know when to do these things. It is very much a game of decision making and there are as many mistakes caused by bad decisions as there are by poor execution of skills. The point is that the coach can only give options to the players, the units and, indeed, the team. This is why I do not like the walkie-talkie water-carrier message; only the players know the real conditions to which they are subjected on the field.

Finally, variety and surprise have proven through many years to be the best tactical allies. Furthermore, the organ that is not utilized will soon become atrophied and, if one is not careful, extirpated. Keep the players' rugby brains sharp!

Options

Let's begin with a series of questions which relate to the various outcomes we might be seeking.

(a) Is the objective of scrummaging merely to win your own ball?

Some coaches and players believe exactly that. They say the scrum restarts the game and also helps to concentrate the forwards in one place, which allows the backs to confront each other one on one. In my view this is very narrow thinking.

What needs to be understood is that the scrum is there for both teams to push and this is done by a pack pushing with 15 or 16 legs. You may contest the ball or not, but contesting the scrum is not optional; it is mandatory. We must also remember the two important things that are at play here: possession and position. Having possession in a bad field position is not conducive to scoring points. On the other hand, being in a good position even without possession places us well to use opportunities the moment we get possession.

What also needs to be seriously considered is that in a rugby team we have 15 players all built differently, with different skillsets and with different jobs to do, yet sharing the common goal of combining to score and to prevent scoring. This means sharing different types of workloads, but making the same contribution to the team's four principals: going forward, providing support, maintaining continuity and applying pressure.

(b) Is the objective of scrummaging to push the other pack off their put-in?

Yes, this may be one of the tactical outcomes. Anticipation and surprise are two very important elements in any sport. When the opposition players think they will secure the ball easily, this is when they are vulnerable and open to surprise! Thus, we can capitalise on their surprise, shock and lack of foresight in terms of both position and possession!

(c) Is the objective of scrummaging to wheel the opposition to the left or right?

This can be one of the tactical moves to disrupt them, to push them against the touch line or to put their back row defenders further from our attacking line which, with a wheel to the right close to their line, provides an ideal try scoring opportunity.

(d) Is the objective of scrummaging to reduce the risk of a penalty from a collapse?

Negative thinking should be completely eradicated from the scrummaging mindset. Nobody should take the field thinking that their scrum will collapse at all. Collapsing doesn't help any team that wants to press forward and it exposes both teams to the risk of a penalty because most referees can only guess as to which pack is the culprit. The risk of a penalty is one thing, but the risk of a serious spinal injury is a much more important factor.

(e) Is the objective of scrummaging to set the platform for a field goal?

According to the scores and to the time left in a game the attempt at a field goal can be a very attractive option, especially when you have a good drop kicker like Hugo Porta, Barry John, Grant Fox, Michael Lynagh, Jonny Wilkinson or Dan Carter just to name a few.

A good solid scrum moving forward gives the kicker an ideal platform to launch the attempt for what can be an easy three points and sometimes the winning points. Early in the game the decision is more difficult because a good position and platform for a field goal are also good for scoring tries, and a missed field goal always gives the opposition respite and encouragement, particularly after a prolonged effort in defence. As a forward, I've been there and it is a real downer—a lost opportunity after all the effort and energy put in to the scrum by the majority of the team to secure that ball.

(f) Is the objective of scrummaging to score a push-over try?

Yes, this is also a tactical option. If our pack is on top of the other, then why not? It is another legitimate way of scoring points, it is teamwork, it is a collective skill and apart from withstanding the push, there is no counter to it. Psychologically the 15 players from the team that scores the push-over try will gain a confidence boosting feeling of superiority which is doubled by the demotivation felt by the opposition.

Scrummaging and tackling are both means by which a team can physically and mentally dominate and demoralize an opposition.

Variations

The basics and fundamentals mentioned in the first paragraph of this section extend further and, once you are competent at the following, the tactical nuances open up:

» Early and fast preparation (setting up)
» Steadiness and solidness
» Togetherness (full understanding of the objectives and commitment)
» Tightness (utilising and maximising every single kilogram we have)
» Timing of execution (synchronisation)
» Mental concentration, mental toughness, controlled aggression
» Sound technique and sound execution

We can build our scrum and our team for long-term results going from simple and solid to complex and fanciful moves, but not without a sound foundation. Several variations exist with regard to the execution of scrums. Employing different combinations and tactics you may be able to unsettle the opposition's scrum.

Accepting that the range of tactics will vary according to the competency of the opposition I give you the following ploys, but against worthwhile opposition most of them can be eliminated.

» Shove
» Double shove
» Left wheel
» Right wheel
» Shove and wheel
» Half wheel and shove

» Crabbing (shifting sideways; some referees may not take kindly to this one)
» Bunching (closing the gap)
» Holding (I do not recommend this because it promotes a defensive mentality)
» Delayed shove and wheel

Coaches and scrum leaders might come up with other practical permutations and combinations, but whatever they are you must practise until you can execute them to perfection, otherwise they could prove quite counterproductive. In putting safety first, you must assess the capabilities and fitness of your players before you choose a particular manoeuvre, and you mustn't let egos get in the way of a sensible choice. Obviously the players will need a series of cues that tell them what option to take.

Two standard tactics

There are many of these but while on the mechanics I'll talk a little about the two most common.

Quick Engagement, Quick Scrum

When in a troubled situation due to lacking size, strength or technique, or due to poor selections that result in insufficient power to hold our own in the scrum, a good option is the quick engagement and a quick put-in scrum. This stratagem of introducing the ball quickly as we engage either exploits an unpreparedness in the opposition or reduces their opportunity to build superior pressure. Generally speaking the side putting in the ball tends to favour a quick scrum anyway—go down, get it in and get it out. Delivering the ball quickly takes advantage of the fact that the law prohibits either team from pushing before the ball is put in. This action could be compressed into an engage, hook and pass operation with a very brief push and hold.

Occasionally a dominant scrummaging pack may want to take advantage of this situation, keeping the ball in for a longer time to wear down the opposition. Furthermore, this tactic has an enormous psychologically demotivating effect on the whole opposition 15.

The Wheel

In relation to the pushing angles, the law does not refer to any pushing direction in particular. That would be difficult in any case because it is impossible to eliminate some turning of the scrum, which naturally wheels in a clockwise direction due to the forces and architecture of the scrum.

The forces of the scrum have been described as the coupling. In physics, two systems are coupled if they interact with each other. The fact that each pack is an independent and interactive system produces a very interesting outcome. Referring to the dynamics and biomechanics of the scrum as described above, it can be said that these forces adopt an accidental clockwise direction. That's why almost 90% of the time the scrum wheels to the right-hand side.

Commencing from a forward push then gyrating clockwise, the wheel could take us backwards if not properly countered. There are tactics to counter these natural movements but not many teams manage to master them. The physical characteristics of all players (particularly in the front row) may also contribute to favour or counter this collection of variable forces, so full consideration should be given to the anthropometry (varying physical make-ups) of players when analysing the whys and the why nots.

Of all the tactics the most difficult, but most valuable, is being able to affect the right wheel on your own put-in particularly close to the opposition's goal line, because it virtually puts the defending back row out of play in an attack on the more vulnerable right-hand side.

Back row options

With both back lines being required to stand back five metres at the scrum, the use of the No. 8 in picking up the ball at the back and charging forward is an attractive variation. This ball carrier should be able to get across the advantage line thereby allowing the rest of the pack to run on to the next phase which will start from a going forward platform.

Packing the No. 8 between the flanker and a second rower on either side is still an option, but back-row moves have been restricted by the law which prevents any player from leaving the scrum until the scrum has ended with the ball emerging.

So on the above tactic of moving any of the three back rowers to a different position before engagement, I'd recommend this be done only in attack (our put-in), whereas in defensive situations this could be counterproductive as the opposition could pick up the ball and attack our vulnerable side straight away while the scrum is wheeling away from the action.

Traps

Props popping

Some opposition props will try to force the opponent up and out of the scrum—popping. Apart from inducing a penalty scrum, popping is of no value (the real business is to move forward and not upward). It may be an ego-boosting exercise for some props, but it is detrimental to teamwork as the scrum stops going forward. In any event, the prop should not be given all the credit for causing the scrum to pop, as it occurs when the prop redirects the force of the back five onto the opposition in an upward direction. Going forward must always remain the common objective of the pack.

Collapsing

In saying that popping is illegal, it is worth noting that any attempt to collapse the scrum is also punishable. Essentially these practices relate to front rowers twisting or lowering their bodies or pulling opponents. None of these practices are helpful in out-scrummaging the opposition. That is not to say that the front row in particular doesn't have opportunities to take the initiative; it does. It's all about concentration, preparation, anticipation, and speed of execution!

Milking penalties

The above explanations are relative because a smart and experienced prop could fabricate a role reversal between victim and villain, by making it look as if the player opposite has caused the problem. There have been many occasions where penalties were milked. How often have you seen a front row under pressure just stand up which infers that the opposition has caused the problem? It is not hard to fake being popped: tuck your head under you, bow your back and your feet will come off the ground. This sort of thing remains one of the referees' biggest challenges, but the referee should be guided strongly by possible motives.

We shouldn't be too alarmed by this as the courts of law spend many hours trying to prove intent, so it will be just as hard to prove whether the scrum was collapsed wittingly or unwittingly. This is a good point for referees to remember before they feel obliged to find a culprit.

Another simple ruse is to back pedal on engagement giving the impression that the opposition has pushed you off the mark before the put-in. The offending side is not going to run the risk of the penalty going the other way unless there is much to be gained, so rarely would a side putting in the ball want to collapse a scrum. If they're close to their own line they'd want to win the ball and kick it out and, if they were up the other end, they'd want to secure the ball and score a try, pushover or otherwise. The most common deliberate collapse is in a scrum near your own goal line where the other side is going for a pushover on their put-in.

Ultimately, entrapment is so negative that this kind of attitude will restrict the development of a scrum and the team's capacity for continuity. A good referee will detect a bad attitude, where a team is playing negatively and using spoiling tactics, and this is likely to attract a scrutiny that is not going to help the team concerned.

Troubleshooting guidelines

Thus far, by definition and by application it is quite apparent and fairly obvious that front rowers have a dual-functionality of roles, alternating between being the builders at times and other times the destroyers. This slight contradiction doesn't leave much room to be the repairers, particularly when the problems are happening; there is no time to fix them. However, with a proactive mentality and an armory of skills and tools, plenty can be done to prevent the same problems from happening in the future.

The following scenarios are aimed at assisting coaches in preparing adequate and effective solutions for their players. The scrum is a complex phase of play with many little parts involved in the exacting assembly. Furthermore, this is an area that doesn't allow much time for thinking or even reacting, so to be forewarned is to be forearmed.

1.   There is a sudden problem, you are being intimidated. How do you react?
The intimidation exerted by an effective and dominant pack involves physical, psychological and territorial factors. Therefore, it is important to be prepared to neutralise the opposition scrum with a view to recapturing the initiative and even taking control.

In a single scrum there is very little time to fix problems when things go wrong. We can only stay put and take stock of the problem, think of a quick solution and apply it in the next scrum! Generally speaking a good solution involves a group effort; hardly ever can it be done alone no matter how strong any single forward might be!

As soon as a problem is detected, the best action is to immediately:

» stay low,
» stay tight, and
» remain together in formation no matter what.

When the analysis has provided an explanation, a solution should be devised and applied to the next scrum in a proactive, and preventative manner. If possible, take the first opportunity to mention it to one or two from your cluster to ensure future combined action.

2. Your scrum is overpowered by the opposition. What do you do?
Togetherness and tightness are the areas to work on:

» Work on steady feet position.
» Check the tightness of grips and bodies.
» Aim for a lower body position in the front row and the second row.

Early initiative may be lacking in your pack, as may the necessary mental toughness. If you have achieved the above points and still are suffering from the same problem, additional work is needed on fitness and strength.

Good solid scrummaging sessions on a decent scrum machine should help you to iron out those problems and improve your pack fitness, strength and technique.

Temperament and resolve can also be developed at training. Jack Gibson, a famous Australian rugby league coach, once said, "Winning starts on Monday!"

3. You are being wheeled to the left too easily. How to counter it?
On the left-hand side the No. 1, No. 4 and No. 6 push inward to the centre of the scrum and hold back a little. On the right-hand side the No. 3, No. 5 and No. 7 should push inward and forward to counter the force coming from the front.

It is also important that, when you are wheeled to either side, your No. 8 punishes the opposition by picking up the ball and running in favour of the wheel; their back row will be out of play momentarily. You only need to gain five or ten metres to capitalise on this temporary advantage and build on it.

If your pack is wheeled to the right (this happens a lot less often), the right side of the scrum (i.e., the No. 3, No. 5 and No. 7) should push inward and hold back a little. Conversely, the left side of the scrum (i.e., the No. 1, No. 4 and No. 6) must push inward and forward to counter the force coming through their side.

4. A player in the tight five has the hips higher than the shoulders causing inadequate transfer of force and other problems.

Corrective actions are to:

(a) Bend the knees, aiming to be at between five and ten cm from the ground.

(b) Shift the feet back as much as possible until the back is parallel to the ground. This is the strongest pushing position.

(c) Keep the head up. Remember that the head is like a rudder; if it is pointing down your body goes down and the scrum is likely to collapse.

(d) Remember that your feet must be adjusted with very quick short steps. Big steps reduce the combined purchase on the ground for too long, which releases the pressure on the opposition relinquishing any advantage you may have had.

5. Your front row is being popped up either individually, or as a block of two or three players together.

First and foremost, adopt a lower position when crouching before engagement and stay low during the scrum. Front rowers must push their chest downward and forward. Law 20.3 (c) and (d) states that props must not exert downward pressure. May I add that exerting upward pressure doesn't help your team either; on the contrary, it negates and stops any forward movement you may have generated previously.

This creates a difficult situation for player and referee. My opponent is allowed to apply upward pressure but I'm not allowed to exert downward pressure. The reality is that most loose head props (No. 1s) will try to push up the opposite tight head prop, and if the No. 3 doesn't prevent that then that player is in trouble. The natural reaction is to respond with an equal and compensatory force that neutralises the upward pressure and, at the same time, stabilises the scrum.

This is why we see the outside arm of the props being used to exert downward pressure onto the opposition's shoulders; they do not do it to collapse the scrum. I think it would be a harsh referee who would penalise an action that makes the scrum safer, but this is another example of a law that is too prescriptive. It should say: "Props must not exert pressure that takes an opponent down."

When I played tight head I always started with my right arm well locked in a medium position (elbow pointing out and not down) denying the loose head any chance to push on my ribs or sternum or get right under me.

6. The opposition's force is shifting your whole pack, which is unable to establish a stable footing.

If your legs were locked in your initial position, you have no way to counter the force you've been subjected to. Your body position is probably too high, so everyone must bend their knees and the front row must aim to get underneath the opposite front row.

I always insisted during my coaching clinic sessions that locking or holding the scrum is a very defensive attitude in that you are preparing your body to receive rather than give. Worse than that though, you are mentally giving in to the opposition's initiative. An extra effort is required by the second row to be tighter and to provide more weight. Equally, the back row must also provide more weight, as well as ensuring that they pack down early enough to make their weight count on the engagement hit.

Too often the back five conserve themselves for starry work around the paddock. The second rowers and the flankers should all regard themselves as being part of the second row unit, and the four of them should go in together as a tightly bound pushing team. To enhance this contribution the number eight must seriously lock together the two second rowers.

7. Your loose head prop No. 1 is being pulled down and dominated by the opposition No. 3 who is also boring onto your hooker.

The first step is to improve the grip between hooker and loose head prop. Make it as tight as you can so that both operate as one unit. The same thing must happen with the tight head prop, regardless of comfort or discomfort.

The second step is to improve the grip of the loose head prop's left arm. This must be early and decisive and, depending on the physical ability of your prop, could be a short, medium or long grip. As the loose head prop is in a tighter position now, this player should be well positioned to use the head to exert upward pressure onto the sternum of the opposition's No. 3. To complete this operation the inside shoulder of the loose head prop should be applying a compensatory downward pressure on the neck of the opposite prop, not to take them down, but to create a destabilising force to counter the other side's initiative.

8.   Your tight head prop is being popped or dominated by the opposite prop.
The first question to be asked is whether the problem is due to their being underpowered. This could happen as a consequence of being too loose or lacking weight from the second row.

The hips may be moving wide and angling too much onto the opposition's hooker which is called boring. The right shoulder must lock the scrum up, exerting a downward pressure onto the loose head prop's neck as that player will be trying to drive you up. This right shoulder must be very strong and the grip should be short to keep that side of the scrum very low.

9.   The opposition's scrum is taking the initiative after the engagement.
It is crucial not only to have a good solid hit on engagement, but to chase the weight and maintain the pressure. The scrum should be edging forward as much as possible even before the put-in, whilst taking care not to be penalised for it. This edging prior to engagement is about getting the feet in the ideal position to effect a favourable connecting line.

10. The opposition is anticipating your put-in and is snap shoving your pack.
In my experience, if you use too many calls during preparation, you provide the opposition with an easy target for attack. It is best to have only two calls, one for preparation and the second for execution, or to disguise it whichever way you wish.

11. Your front row is having an off-day. Or is the opposition playing a blinder?
Everything that happens in the scrum, whether good or bad, is the responsibility of the whole eight. Neither the front row nor the tight five can take the credit for the results; these are the products of teamwork. However, a front row that has very good communication and problem-solving ability will always provide better opportunities for their team than lesser counterparts would.

12. Your scrum has no authority; it is being dominated by a lesser pack.
A good hooker, leader, or organiser has a better chance at having a dominant scrum than others that are more passive or less organised. Being in the heart of the scrum, the hooker can feel what is happening or what is missing, whether from the front or from behind.

Moreover, hookers will anticipate what is going to occur, so are able to correct or redirect forces as they come. Their communication with the scrum half must be impeccable, as hookers are able to tell when the pack is ready for the put-in and when it's not. This may surprise some readers, but I am talking from personal experience, having played not only both sides of the front row, but also as a hooker for several years with the Tala Rugby Club in Cordoba.

13. In wet weather, how low is too low?

Taking into account the anatomy of the players, the scrum could be set at a minimum height dictated by the length of the props' thighs (perpendicular to the ground) plus 5 cm (5 to 10 cm), which is the distance of the knees to the ground. The second row and back row must also aim for the mandatory 5 cm off the ground.

The lower the centre of gravity, the stronger the pushing position, with the added bonus that the lower the front row, the easier it will be to get underneath the opposition's front row. This is universally agreed to be the best position to be in any scrum. At this juncture it is important to remember that this low body height applies to a dry and firm ground. This position allows you to utilise just the front half of your soles to gain a stable footing. Conversely, in wet weather conditions, you are forced to change your body position substantially, adapting your angles to the softness of the ground.

We saw in the 2010 European series how the Wallabies suffered ingloriously on soft, rainy grounds. In these conditions we must utilise the entire sole of the feet (using all studs) to maintain grip and balance. As a result your body will be higher than normal, allowing for a firmer footing.

This is not just an automatic response of the body to the weather; it must be trained time and time again until the pack acquires the ability and skill to adjust to the different conditions.

14. Your hooker is unable to hook.

Maybe your pack is in a very low pushing position, or the opposition has forced you to adopt this position. Even though your pack may look strong in this position, your hooker is unable to strike for the ball. A greater effect will be needed from both props to engage the scrum at a higher position and maintain it.

It is very difficult to lift the opposition's front row when you are already in difficulties. Your hooker should learn to chase all the weight and shift it to the left leg, leaving the right leg free for hooking.

Solving this problem and others makes you realize the importance of very good communication and understanding within and between the front rowers and the back five.

15. The opposition baulks and gets you in an over-extended leg position.
We must not be deceived by this feint which involves a lull in pushing before their big shove. The over-extended leg position happens because we haven't chased the weight. From the moment we engage we must shuffle our feet forward adjusting our pushing position, always having legs bent and ready to move forward. As soon as we do that we must move into edging mode by adjusting our feet to chase after the weight. This means that when they baulk, we are ready to give them a double or triple shove.

16. How much recovery time is needed after a scrummaging session?
According to the principle of recovery for strength work, your sessions must be carefully spaced. No heavy scrum sessions should be carried out less than 48 hours before the match. This 48-hour gap should also apply between sessions.

If your team is playing on a Saturday, any heavy scrummaging should be done on Tuesday or Wednesday. Recovery time is essential. I am fully aware that probably 80% of teams in Australia face this predicament, and that the most important scrummaging session takes place on Thursday night. However, I repeat that this session should not be too heavy, since the players will be performing in less than 48 hours.

17. Am I responsible for the players' performance?
Shouldn't they know what they are doing? Many players won't always do what is best for them. I feel it is appropriate to emphasise that coaches are not only responsible for organising the work that takes place on the field, but also for the recovery and recuperation of the players. Allied to these two imperatives are nutrition and rest which are intimately related to human performance or under-performance.

Of course we don't have to be experts in this field, but nobody and nothing can stop us from exercising common sense. We do have to keep an eye on lifestyle and the habits that may affect their performance.

18. Do I have to limit myself to what happens on the field during matches and training only?

The answer in short is no! A lot of young players have boundless energy, and literally burn themselves out with too much excitement, or suffer from a lack of organisation, structure and discipline. Here is where we can make a difference, teaching them how to establish energy regeneration systems for themselves. This means that by the time they become seasoned adults, they will be fully prepared to confront the demands of rugby and life in general. After all, it is the job of a mentor to help them, educate them and prepare them for life, improving them as individuals and as future members of our communities. This is the real function of sport and should be part of the coaching mission.

It seems to me that the professional era has neglected the primordial function of sport which is preparing young men and women for the future vicissitudes of life (good, bad and otherwise). Players in the professional era seem to be too pampered, protected and excessively looked after by agents, managers, sponsors and, at times, even the coaches. There may be a few exceptions, but it appears to me they are few and far between.

There is nothing wrong with being paid for the time dedicated to preparation, for playing and for taking and accepting the risks associated with the sport.

I feel administrators, coaches and players are all responsible for the well-being of rugby, so that it serves not only the players, but also the supporters, the spectators and the community in general. Not enough of those at the top are willing to support or share with the infrastructure that gave them their privileged position. We are all told that the national players are the rain makers, but they should from time to time remember whence they came.

A friendly warning for players, coaches, teachers and parents

Anything that goes inside your body is, or should be, your concern. I am specifically referring to illegal substances, performance enhancement drugs or treatments, recreational habits, etc. You may choose to ignore it for privacy or for other reasons, but be aware that everything adds up and counts toward performance on the day and you are likely to suffer the consequences sooner or later. An aspiring athlete will appreciate guidance from the voice of experienced coaches, mentors and real friends. If you think I'm excessively cautious or strict on this area let me remind you that rugby post-1995, became professional attracting all sorts of evil, whether from inside or outside the sport. Many people do not care about long-term consequences; all they care for is the short-term results no matter what. Rugby 2015 is very different to what it was pre-1995. Being forewarned is being forearmed. First and foremost weigh up your own objectives vs risks and be true to yourself. You don't need to be part of somebody else's band wagon or circus either!

CHAPTER
8

Scrum practices and physical conditioning

SCRUM PRACTICES AND PHYSICAL CONDITIONING

Scrum training

The way to acquire sound technique is through practice and repetition with the aim of consistently performing to the best of your ability. The repetition will not reap the dividends it should unless the key factors are right, so the scrum coach must look after the necessary corrections during the routines. Scrummaging requires you to attend to quality and quantity. The natural or normal consequence will be a gradual growth in confidence. There is no quick-fix in this area. Many hours of good hard work will produce great results, but remember that everything must be solid, progressive, consistent and with follow-through. Therefore, it is not only the technique but the physique and the will that get trained at scrummaging practices. The discipline and attitude developed during scrummaging sessions can easily be transferred later to the other phases of the game, such as line-out, ruck, maul and restarts as indicated by Ray Williams OBE in his assertions on the scrummaging subject.

A brief five year review of world scrummaging

Rome was not built in a day, nor was the Italian scrum competitive after just a couple of scrummaging sessions. The Italians beat France in the 6 Nations tournament in March 2011; they owe at least 70% of that victory to their very solid scrum ('la mischia').

The world order with the scrum has changed in some countries. For the last 10 years, New Zealand has developed a national scrummaging program with Mike Cron in charge. Cron has done a great job in ensuring more consistent performances and performers. In my opinion, New Zealand has the best depth of quality in almost every position.

The Argentine Pumas are back to their powerful best. They have gone back to the basics and fundamentals of old times and are now reaping the rewards of concerted hard work and intelligent planning.

France on some days are absolutely awesome and a handful, while on other days it plays like a completely different team. Their scrum academy led by Didier Retiere keeps producing first-class props, along with solid second rowers and back rowers (e.g., Thierry Dusautoir).

England, at times, are up there with the best; they know how to single-mindedly do it but occasionally get distracted or demotivated by irrelevant or insignificant issues, or inferior opposition and they pay a heavy price. They have a tendency to over-promise and under-deliver, the price they pay for being the favourites. They also have the biggest depth of players and forwards in the world.

Georgia seem to have entered the conversation of International scrummaging. They have troubled many fancied countries and certainly are carving themselves a nice reputation as giant killers.

South Africa have long demonstrated a great tradition and success in this field. They were the quickest to adapt to the 2013 pre-bind sequence of engagement. I was in touch with Pieter de Villiers dissecting the laws, techniques and tactics necessary to succeed in it. Nonetheless, they somehow dropped off the race in 2014 when the Springboks were unmercifully done by Argentina. I have no doubt that their overall pride will bring them back in no time.

Other countries I have not mentioned here could generally be rated or classified at best as competent but most of the time as inconsistent and even substandard. For the last 30 years, Australia has been jumping from picks down to troughs where the ups have been very sporadic and the downs long and slow.

In any sport, techniques are not a permanent commodity, acquired and kept forever! The ability to execute a certain skill is fully dependent of the state of mind and fitness levels. These abilities are fickle, flexible and adaptable to circumstances (sometimes for the better and other times for the worst).

There is, however, a flip side because unlike with some of rugby's more innate skills, you will see an early improvement once you start practicing properly, with the emphasis on *properly*. Poor practice will only engrain poor techniques and bad habits, but the mere act of doing a lot of scrummaging at practice will improve strength and confidence.

The reduction in the number of scrums per game is not a reason at all to do less scrummaging, particularly with the amount of resets we have had to endure in recent times. There may be fewer scrums but they are no less important for that; on the contrary, when a pack is literally crushed, this has terrible psychological consequences in the whole team for the rest of the game.

Let's all bear in mind that one piece of possession from the scrum or the lineout could assist in generating up to 20 phase plays. A scrum win can put your team in the best position to dominate possession and position and, therefore, gain control of play for long periods of time which should lead to points.

Moving away from the technical and tactical aspects, let me touch briefly on some subjective elements that may not be fully apparent to some coaches. These are linked to the mental and emotional dimensions of the player. I am referring to the authority, the superiority and the domination developed whilst training and acquiring the skill of scrummaging. The desire to dominate and be on top of the opposition and the will to be in control of positions during the game are extremely important and must be coached too.

This mental superiority comes from having confidence in knowing that the work has been done beforehand. The Welsh coaching legend Ray Williams used to say, "Success comes before work in one place only—the dictionary!"

There you have it! In my opinion the five pillars and factors of scrummaging are:

» Sound technique
» Superior fitness
» Respect for the opposition
» Pride in our team and what we do
» Respect for and cooperation with the referee

These factors, along with the total dedication of the individuals, are the tools that will generate the confidence to build the mental toughness and the will to win. It can't be artificially manufactured without the practice.

Another quality of the pack that must be trained is the 'collective mental urgency' or anticipation needed for the thinking and execution of every movement. Once again all of the above are the responsibility of the eight players, and they must execute them together as one unit. We, the coaches, are merely the teachers and facilitators.

As you will have appreciated by now, my constant theme on scrummaging is the whole before the parts. The scrum is an ensemble which works better when the individuals are in harmony. Obviously the ensemble can be better with better individual contributions, but if the harmony is not there then there will be no prizes at the Rock Eisteddfod.

We must remember that the human brain is fickle. It is easily attracted by distraction; has a concentration that fluctuates without knowing it; and a selfishness that creeps in like a lizard to a puddle. So synchronization and timing need to be mastered—all together now!

As a coach I have, for many years, utilised this simple yet effective actions checklist to remind myself and players of all the nuts and bolts required in fine tuning a scrum, never forgetting the combination and the knowledge that the sum of the parts is what makes the whole so powerful.

All these have been mentioned in the various sections on the scrum structure, but it's not going to happen in a game unless it is rehearsed at practice. So here they are again.

NUTS AND BOLTS ACTIONS CHECKLIST:

1. Sprint to the referee's mark as soon as you hear the whistle.

2. Have a mental and physical urgency in everything you do.

3. Give your full attention to scrum tactics and calls with a common direction for all. Information must be stored in your brain before preparing for the engagement.

4. Check and ensure correct feet positioning.

5. Check and ensure correct binding and grips.

6. Check and ensure correct head position.

7. Check and ensure back and body position.

8. Check and ensure leg positions and angles of flexion.

9. Engagement with the opposition pack requires controlled aggression and authority within the law.

10. Follow the referee's instruction.

11. Maintain forward pressure after the hit.

12. Ensure mental concentration on the coming call.

13. Explode forward on the call all together and with exact timing.

14. Advance with short steps.

15. Adjust your feet positions after the initial shove and keep your legs flexed.

16. Sustain forward pressure, mounting pressure on and on and on.

17. Always be prepared to reset the scrum again with no fuss, if needed. Enjoy the opportunity to pack another scrum against your opposition.

18. The whole scrum must drive forward, not up or down.

19. Eight for one and one for eight!

20. Perform like an orchestra. That means eight different players and instruments, the same script and one conductor all playing in unison.

Practice reminders

» You may have to share the ball and the put-in in the scrum! However, you may challenge for possession at every scrum.

» You may not win every ball, but you must try to win every scrum.

Scrum superiority is achieved by:

(a) Doing the whole work set beforehand

(b) Acquiring and applying yourselves with very sound techniques

(c) Achieving superior fitness: strength, power, stamina, aerobic and anaerobic fitness

(d) Having respect for the opposition, the referee and the laws at all times

(e) Having pride in your team and what you do!

A proposed new scrum proficiency assessment centre

As not every club has knowledgeable and qualified personnel (e.g., forward or scrum coach), I believe there is a way to overcome this deficiency and to up skill and develop aptitude in front rowers, in particular. Clubs might have to contract offsite consultants and services to conduct a theoretical and practical competency-based evaluation.

This is tantamount to an individual scrummaging skills audit, if you like. This initiative will never replace the collective work necessary, but it may go a long way towards up skilling and increasing safety for all forwards. It could also have the added benefit of forming part of a well organised and monitored national scrum risk management program.

Scrum machines

Some coaches may argue that machines do not provide a realistic situation. My answer is that if you are not ready to manage live scrum sessions firmly and with discipline, you are wasting time and energy, and even risking injuries.

I would suggest that this knowledge base, skill and attitude certification be carried out every year (or two years, as required) on a mandatory basis. It could also be used as a protection strategy for all personnel involved and a very handy tool for insurance purposes. I leave this plan open for consideration and implementation by all administrations.

I am often asked, "When do you do live scrums?" My standard answer is, "When both packs have a sound technique and are fit for the tussle, but more importantly when the person in charge is really in charge and the players have sufficient maturity and discipline."

When using mechanical aids it is highly advisable to double check that machines and equipment are fully operational well before starting each training session, as accidents can easily occur through lack of maintenance or insufficient supervision. Catastrophic injuries have occurred at practice on a scrum machine, so all-round safety principles are just as important here.

I am also asked what the characteristics of a good scrum machine are and what one should look for. A good machine must have the standard qualities; it must be strong, sturdy, simple, moveable and durable. If you use the machine as you should, it will eventually break down, so I'm inclined to say that the less sophisticated or complicated the better. It's a mechanical machine and some parts will break one day.

Whatever the machine, I like to see how much weight or resistance there is and gauge the reaction of the pack to it. So, if one night the pack is off for some reason, I will not punish them with more weight; on the contrary, I will ease off to keep the motivation factor alive. When they respond with good work, then I will increase the load. This means that observation, review, adjustment and situational management are all part of the discerning eye required for scrum machine work.

Make sure you have after-sales service and the budget for it. In this day and age of tight financial resources, it's more than likely that the machine will be used by at least 10 teams in a club, so it's got to be accessible and moveable, and its weights have to be removable or easily adjustable.

In late 2010 French rugby produced a state-of-the-art high-tech hydraulic and computerised scrum machine. If you think of scrummaging as an art you would describe it as the Stradivarius of the genre, but if you think of scrummaging as an engineering exercise you would describe it as the Rolls Royce of the range. Either way it comes at an estimated cost of 200,000 euros and the privileged driver of it is French scrum coach Didier Retière.

The well-known English Rhino and Powerhouse scrum machines offer a great variety of models and proven service.

A good session should go for no more than 30 minutes and no less than 25 minutes (approximately 60 scrums), and a big session no more than 45 minutes (approximately 90 scrums), but in both cases it's the quality that counts. If the pack has no energy or is demotivated for some reason, then I'll make 30 scrums and we'll compensate for the shortfall with something else.

That's why instant visual monitoring and recognition is very important to me, and I guess it is for the players too. It's true that they like to see for themselves how much they are doing or are not doing. Machines will provide you with a static situation where the forces can be controlled while checking the positions and techniques. From here we can progress to moving and shifting the machine. This is good for strength training and observing the technique in a dynamic situation.

What is not advisable is to push against any machine or piece of equipment that is fixed, bolted to the ground or packed against a stand or a tree, etc. PLEASE DO NOT DO THIS EVER.

As a motivational factor in training, it is important that every energy output has a desired positive outcome. Furthermore, the potential for spinal cord injury at the neck and lower back levels diminishes considerably when you are displacing or moving an object that provides resistance.

The sort of segments you might work on with the machine are:

» Warm-up
» Grips drill
» Body height variation
» Tightness
» Intensity and incremental pressures
» Reaction, speed off after pushing
» Engagement, disengagement and resetting the scrum
» Shove, double shove and shoves combined with wheels
» Left and right wheels combined with shoves
» Work with varying numbers of players
» Sustained pressure drill

If you have people watching, keep them at a reasonable distance so their presence or conversation doesn't interfere with or distract the players running around the machine or in the vicinity. This also silences those would-be coaches eager to demonstrate how much they know at somebody else's session! Players must hear only one voice at scrummaging sessions.

Live scrum practices

Live scrums are excellent as a means of fine tuning and testing out your players, and for complementing training with machines. This is because they provide an almost 90% simulation of the match situation. Additionally, you can train and counter the tactics corresponding to the front row, as well as the whole scrum. Unlike an opposition pack, if you have a machine it is always available, but it is limited in the range of dynamics and forces that confront you in the match scrum. Machine and live practices are complementary and both necessary.

As valuable as live scrum practice can be, the coach needs to be aware of a few points:

» It has to be done in a very controlled and organized manner.
» It requires discipline and cooperation not only from both front rows in particular, but also from all 16 players. If the session goes for too long, it will become an

energy-sapping exercise with the potential to degenerate into untidy scrummaging that benefits no one. Such sessions can also develop into ego-driven battle royales, where some individuals will look for short-term personal satisfaction with regard to a selection-related pecking order within the club.

When these events happen, both teams can suffer unfortunate consequences with injuries that might disrupt the teams for quite long periods.

To build control and confidence, the sort of routine that can be used is to pack the scrum and then direct the scrum to do the following: walk forward, walk back, move it sideways, then back, wheel it one way and then the other. After you have done this at the natural level, do it all again at a lower level and so on and so forth.

A strong and close supervising eye at live sessions will be very beneficial, but I'd like to stress to coaches that the players' energy consumption is far greater than on a machine. It is important to take into account the psychological energy, the physical contest and the adrenaline flow generated by the competitive instinct during such sessions, and consequently I recommend that they be done at least 48 hours before the match to allow sufficient recovery time.

Attire, uniform and gear

PLAYING JUMPERS AND JERSEYS

The evolution of synthetic fabrics in the last 30 to 40 years has certainly been a boon for the merchandising world, and it has infiltrated many sports, including rugby. The marketing of the latest playing jumpers claims several new features and benefits:

» Improving aesthetics
» Reducing dehydration
» Making the ball easier to catch when holding it against your body
» Making the ball carrier is more difficult to tackle.

All this may or may not be true. Certainly true is that:
» More often than not the price tag is higher, which produces extra revenue for those involved in the trade.

» Previous jumpers become redundant and obsolete, forcing the prices of new jumpers up.

Well, all these features may be true, but nobody has yet asked a prop or a second rower about the grips being easier or harder with these new fabrics. I don't need to ask the question because I don't sell rugby jumpers to supporters. And, besides, I know the answer already; it is very difficult to grab hold of those flimsy jumpers. I think the old cotton or wool or even a 20% polyester/80% cotton jumper should be reinstated for all forwards!

Training sessions

We should always try to replicate playing conditions as much as possible. This should mean a strong pair of shorts, strong quality jumper and proper boots with studs or cleats. Unfortunately, to replicate a match in some competitions this means using jerseys which are unsuitable for scrummaging, but for safety's sake I would use practice clothing that does allow firm grips.

A foot or toe injury could take a long time to heal and it will keep you off the field and out of the team until it heals. If head gear, shin-guards or any other prosthetic supplement is used, keep using it because your body is used to it; do not change that. Psychologically, our minds detect the smallest variations in habits and we don't know what the likely reaction will be!

JUST REMEMBER THE THREE PILLARS OF PREVENTION!
1. Safety first.
2. If in doubt, DON'T.
3. Prevention is better than cure!

Scrum conditioning

My comments apply to scrummaging in particular, but also to rugby in general. There are nine points to work on to achieve adequate scrummaging preparation!

1. Prepare for contact in its various forms with all the required techniques, such as where to place the head, how to use the opposition's momentum to do some of the

work, the foot and leg positions needed to achieve balance and stability, the use of the body's assets and avoidance of dangerous positions, such as a combination of a hyperflexion, hyperextension and twisting of the neck.

I have spoken of the need for front rowers to take the initiative in gaining a strong position. This not only gives the players an advantage over their opponents, but also limits the options of the other front row. It is for this reason I recommend that rugby players get some basic training in wrestling. In a one-on-one situation the speed and technique of a good wrestler can make an untrained rugby prop look weak and clumsy. Between 1984 and 1987 I played several times against a champion All Black prop named Gary 'Axle' Knight, who also won a Commonwealth wrestling bronze medal, and the skills he brought to his position made me realise how much it pays to be smart in contact for balance, stability and, more importantly, safety. Cross-training can be of real assistance here.

2. Practice appropriate drills and technique correction during them. Too often players are allowed to continue making mistakes that then become ingrained instead of being eliminated.

3. Proper stretching before and after practice and matches is necessary. This prevents injuries, pulled muscles and also helps the athlete to become stronger, as well as aiding quicker recovery.

4. Cool down post-training and post-match with attention being paid to any injuries that might have occurred during same. Injured players and over-eager coaches tend to rush the rehabilitation period, but it is better to give nature as much time as it needs for natural healing. Remember too that it doesn't take much to reduce a good player to an ordinary player where an injury is being carried. A golden rule is for the coach to protect and put the injured player before the team's needs and any personal ambitions.

5. Maintain a positive mental attitude by following the laws and understanding the principles of the game. You need to foster a respect for the referee's decisions, a respect for the opposition and a respect for officials involved with the administration of the game. Needless to say, of course, you have to have respect for your own teammates. In a not-so-disciplined team, tempers occasionally flare, and this is the most damaging thing for the team and an encouraging factor for the opposition. So there is no room to lose your cool!

Some players are prepared to put their bodies on the line to a point where it shows a lack of interest in their own welfare. We all admire courage, but if your game is all crash and bash then a body not built for abuse will respond accordingly. Having some respect for your body will not diminish the respect that others have for you.

6. Follow the guidelines and rules of thumb for adequate position selection according to age, size, shape, ability and strength. Some body configurations are unsuitable for some positions. You would never put a string bean with a long neck in the front row.

7. Utilise training aid equipment, such as tackling bags and scrum machines that lead to improved technique and fitness. Coaches are responsible for double-checking and for ensuring that equipment is fully operational and safe before the training session!

8. Pay attention to the use of protective and safety gear: strapping, shoulder pads, head gear, shin guards, etc. This can extend to the testing of running styles which can lead to the design of footwear which relieves strain during the constant exercise of running.

9. A very effective and uncomplicated safety for coaches to follow is:
    Fitness + Nutrition + Rest + Recovery = Top Performance and Risk Minimisation

The two parts of the body most at risk are the neck and the spinal cord. The joints, such as knees, ankles, shoulders, are much more exposed to risk in contact sport, but never with extreme consequences. However, we know very well that the outcomes of accidents or injuries to the neck and spinal cord can be elevated to the catastrophic category.

The protection of these areas must be uppermost in our minds when preparing a conditioning and development program for our players. When it comes to basic strength training I could supply a separate dissertation, but in this more general discourse I shall outline some principles and explain the basic exercises that can be carried out in a weight room.

I will now attempt to explain or provide a definition of some activities, disciplines and qualities that are closely associated with the fitness preparation for rugby. There may be some myths or misunderstandings among ordinary folk, but I'm sure that a specialised professional trainer would know the differences and the intricacies of each subject. It must always be done within the sporting needs and within a corresponding specific framework. There is no point in squatting 400 kg if we cannot apply it within the specific context of the particular sport. For example, after engagement a scrum may last for 5 to 15 seconds, but immediately after that we need to run and make a decision or two on the go: whether to tackle; pick the ball up; support a ball carrier; catch the ball on the full or envisage where the next phase will occur and be ready for it. Rugby is a power game and *power* by definition is a combination of strength and speed, so in developing strength one must be careful not to sacrifice too much speed.

Strength training

For the uninitiated, strength training is one of the forms of training which uses resistance against muscular contraction. This builds muscle strength, anaerobic endurance and the size of the skeletal muscle. Most common is the use of gravity (e.g., weights or body weight), hydraulic or elastic resistance. Strength is one of the most important fitness components for rugby, not only for performances on the field, but also a must for durability and injury prevention.

Body building

Body building is a discipline and sport that uses intensive muscle hypertrophy with weights aiming at body modification. One of its main objectives is the aesthetics and public exhibition of the body in competitions. This sport requires very strict diets which are conducive to muscle definition with a very low body fat percentage. It is essential that rugby players go to the gymnasium to develop power and not beauty. Also be aware that a percentage of body fat is very important for the immune system to function efficiently, particularly in fighting infections and assisting in injury recovery.

Sports conditioning

Sports conditioning is the sports-specific preparation for a particular activity. This may combine a number of disciplines like strength training, interval training, aerobic training, swimming, running and other specific activities conducive to promoting skills and fitness. Athletes and rugby players may benefit from individualised programs, but we mustn't forget that they also need to train with the specific sub-groups (e.g., forwards and backs) and also the whole team together as often as possible.

How to avoid losing mobility

One of the principles of weight conditioning and flexibility is that the more flexible you are, the stronger you could become and vice versa. You may or may not have heard of agonist and antagonist muscles which happen to be involved in the same movement, yet are opposite in action. For example, when we do a biceps curl, we are contracting the biceps (agonist) and simultaneously stretching the triceps (antagonist). So in the same movement both muscles operate differently. This means that more flexibility equals more strength. In conclusion, we must train the flexibility to maintain mobility, but also to get stronger. The same principle applies to all other muscles of a moving part. The quadriceps and hamstring work in unison, so if you strengthen one without strengthening the other something has to give, and so it is with many other sets of muscles.

Strength conditioning

Strengthening the neck, back and abdominal muscles

Beginner, Intermediate and Advanced Players

The three programs are discussed in the next chapter, but specifically I'll outline some simple neck exercises. It is important to make a differentiation between the three levels of intensity:

(a) Grab a round weight, a brick, a book or even a bag of sugar (1 or 2 kg to start with)

(b) Lie prone (face down) on a bench or a table leaving the head free to move horizontally

(c) Place the weight on the back of the head, extending and flexing the full range of motion (15-30 repetitions).

(d) Turn to the supine position (face up) with the weight on your forehead and repeat the same motion (15-30 repetitions).

(e) Lie on your side, shoulder off the bench, and weight on your ear, and repeat the same motion (15-30 repetitions).

(f) Repeat on the other side (15-30 repetitions).

This is the same exercise I used to do three times a week in my heyday when I would handle up to 15 kgs for 160 repetitions. Mind you, it took me at least ten years to get to that level. My neck grew to 50 cm in diameter and it became my safety belt. As my neck developed I found that I had to buy bigger shirts with more and more having to be cut off the sleeves.

Seriously though, you must start with 1 or 2 kgs and gradually increase the weight as you feel you can control it throughout at least 120 repetitions. This is my preferred system because you can gauge progress at all times.

Advanced

The forehead bridge involves arching your body off the ground with all your weight supported by your toes and your forehead. Your hands are usually clasped behind your back.

By carefully rocking back and forth and also sideways with most of your weight supported by your neck, you can give the important neck muscles a pretty good workout. Even skinny necks can be thickened up by 5 or 6 cm by this exercise, along with the work done in real scrums.

The back-of-the-head bridge is similar, except your navel is pointed skyward instead of at the turf, and the weight is supported by the soles of your feet and the back of your head.

Another really simple neck exercise involves pushing on your forehead with the heels of your hands and using your neck muscles to resist the pressure (isometric contractions). The drawback is not being able to gauge the resistance which is one of the reasons isotonic contractions are better, along with being able to achieve full range of motion.

CHAPTER 9

Player safety and scrum safety

PLAYER SAFETY AND SCRUM SAFETY

Spinal injury prevention and successful scrum management

Scrum safety became such a passion of mine that the only adjective that I can use for the knowledge and importance attached to it is *vital*.

Dealing with collapsed or collapsing scrums

The law states that front rows must not do anything that is likely to collapse the scrum, and then goes on to say that the referee must penalise strictly any intentional collapsing of the scrum. It would be much better to say that the referee should penalise dangerous intentional collapsing of the scrum and let the referee decide because there are times when an intentional collapsing is called for as a safety measure. When a front rower's head is exposed to the combination of neck hyperextension, hyperflexion and twisting, there exists a real danger of spinal injury.

In order to protect our neck and spinal cord, muscular tone and flexibility are paramount. Thus, the importance of a proactive weight training program can never be overstated.

This chapter will cover three truly vital physical areas:
» Neck muscles
» Back muscles
» Abdominal muscles

These three main muscle groups will protect players' spines and minimise the risk of spinal and neck injuries. This needs to be done through serious and consistent conditioning in order to promote three fundamental qualities: strength, flexibility and endurance. Information on types of programs, and the principles and components of an injury prevention program are addressed shortly. Only after we've taken care of those three muscle groups should we work on the legs, shoulders, arms, etc.

Dealing with collapsing scrums requires a preset proactive strategy that is simple, effective and well-known to all players involved, as well as to referees and coaches. Every collapsed scrum has some risk implications but the following protocol applies to those collapses in which an immediate threat has been detected:

» The person who first realises that the scrum is collapsing must call "May-day" or "Down." My preference is for the latter because it is one simple, clear and direct instruction for the tight five and back row to execute.

» The first symptom occurs when one or two of the six front rowers start going down on the head or shoulders.

» When the weight and force of the whole scrum goes down to the ground it is almost impossible to stop it! Dead weight can't be countered.

» the chosen call must be immediately and firmly ordered; it's not a request but an order.

» The three back rowers are to disengage immediately by stepping back and leave other players to come out in their own time, thus de-powering the scrum straight away.

» When the front rowers of either side, the hooker or both touch the ground the immediate reaction should be to straighten their bodies by kicking their legs back, and lying on their chest and forehead, with their head preferably face down ('eating dirt' is the safest position for the spine).

» The same technique applies to the second rowers, who should kick their legs back.

» Once both tight fives are flat on the ground, the entire weight and force has been taken care of by gravity.

» Second-rowers may start disengaging slowly.

» Then, if everything is OK, the loose head prop comes up first.

» Then, if everything is OK, the hooker is next.

» Then, if if everything is OK, the tight head prop is last to come up.

When the call is voiced it means the tight five in unison drop to their knees or chest and straighten their legs. At the same time the back row will detach from the scrum.

There is a perception that the dangerous combination of neck hyperextension and twisting occurs only on the ground, but this is not so. The front rowers' necks are exposed and at risk all the time.

Principles of a sound injury prevention program

Full attention must be given to the following components when preparing athletes for competition. These are fundamental principles that will provide for a solid preparation for any sport:

» Correct techniques (as previously described)

» Neck muscles (strength and flexibility, full range of motion)

» Abdominal muscle control (abdominal stability)

» Back muscles (lower and upper back, strength and flexibility, full range)

» Scapula and shoulder stability (strength and flexibility, full range)

» Fitness and conditioning (aerobic, anaerobic capacity, endurance, power and general flexibility)

Remember that, no amount of enthusiasm or assistance displayed after an accident will ever make up for the prevalent apathy which allowed it to happen prior to the accident.

It is up to us, the coaches, teachers and professionals, to work in conjunction to reverse this trend, and to provide safer conditions and guidelines for the practice of contact sports. Finally, I'd like to emphasise that positive mental application, combined with adequate fitness and sound techniques not only provide the basis for good play, but are also the best insurance against injury that we have.

Upon this realisation we take action to prevent or minimise the consequences of the implicit risks and so it is with coaching rugby. If we take the time to properly prepare the athletes, then accidents become acts of God as opposed to avoidable misfortunes. Unfortunately, we tend to be reactive and change through events and necessity only. Suffice to say that in this area the stakes are too high not to be proactive in implementing all the precautions. My mantra has always been "Preparation, preparation, preparation; and never compromise on safety."

Summary and conclusions

Much of this calls for some change in our thinking, and overcoming our resistance to change. The majority of human beings are by nature very often disinclined to make changes because we prefer to stay within our comfort zones. That is not to say it can't be done swiftly or easily which we automatically do when we see that our family, our properties or our relatives are under threat or at risk of anything.

CHAPTER 10

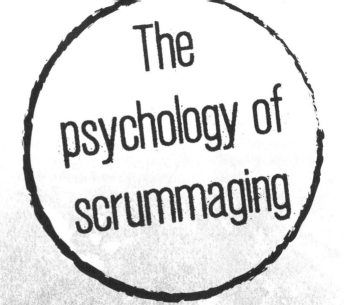

The psychology of scrummaging

THE PSYCHOLOGY OF SCRUMMAGING

"The psychology of competition"

'From the jungle to Twickenham 2015 RWC Final'

By Michael N. Fox - Performance Psychologist

Our inherent competitiveness was born in the jungle. For it is there that our brains evolved. It is there that aggression and fear became wired in to our being to enable us to survive. Most of our brain is not designed for cognitive function (thinking). The majority of our brain is quite primitive. Its function, primarily, is for survival.

The present structure of our brain is the result of a subtle continuous improvement program. The basic apparatus has changed little in the last several million years. The majority of our brain and its basic structure and function is shared by most vertebrates. What differentiates us from the animals is essentially a thin layer of cortex—thinking brain—that covers this essentially primitive apparatus.

Because of the similar structure, we share many behaviours and emotions with other species. This is the realm of ethologists who study species-specific behaviours. Indeed, noted ethologist, Konrad Lorenz, won the Nobel Prize in biology by looking at aggression, competitiveness, territoriality, jealousy and other instinctual behaviours that we have in common with many other kindred species. We are designed for a primitive environment.

We are designed to deal with dangers—real physical dangers. We developed in a world in which fight or flight had real value—actual physical survival. This development occurred over millions of years. Those of our ancestors that were most aggressive, most competitive survived. It is these aggressive survivors who pass on their genes to us. And while our brains have changed little from our time in the jungle, it has only been several thousand years since we moved into the city. Our time in civilisation has been a veritable drop in the bucket.

Our primitive brains and our proclivity for violence and aggression had to be quelled in order for us to survive in this new environment. Our instincts and violent tendencies had to be controlled. Sets of rules, laws and police became part of our new world to force us to function peacefully in society. Religions and codes of conduct such as the Ten Commandments were provided and internalized to shape behaviour. Without this, aggression and competitiveness would cause pandemonium.

'The need for aggression to be expressed'

However, there seems to be a need to be able to express either actively, or vicariously, what is prohibited by the laws and religions which serve to control primitive behaviours.

The Romans developed the circus to provide an outlet for experiencing (visually) mortal combat, rape and other behaviours not tolerated within their society. On Saturdays, Romans would go to the Coliseum, get their fill of watching gore and then go back to the toga factory where they worked during the week as peaceful citizens. The need to express or experience the most base and instinctual behaviours not accepted within our society persists. If you want to write a book or produce a movie that will be successful to the masses, it has to transgress things that we cannot do based on the Ten Commandments.

Animals living in groups, actively seek to raise their status in the group—that is to move up a defined hierarchy. Those that have higher status often have better ability to acquire sexual partners, food and territory. There is a payoff for being competitive. The fittest survive and provide their genes for the evolving species. However, these intra-species competitions have also evolved into a sort of game or ritual in which the competitors do not kill one another.

This, too, is beneficial for the species' survival. Ethologists call this ritualised aggression. Stags lock antlers, birds strut, monkeys howl and dominance is demonstrated without bloodshed and death within the group. Some behaviours seem brutal and others choreographed.

But the phenomenon generally serves to prevent interspecies killing while fostering competitiveness. With humans, sport serves the same function. It fulfills our in-built need to compete. It becomes a socially acceptable venue for displaying aggression. It defines hierarchies.

Team sports also sate another need that encompasses the in-built aspects of a pack mentality that is also part of us. In the jungle, like other social animals, humans hunted together as a family and later fought other humans as tribes evolved. Rugby is almost the rawest expression of acceptable human pack competitiveness in our present environment. Animal packs that hunt and fight together produce relationships that mirror those developed with sporting teams.

When competing against another group, intergroup rivalries cease and individuals bond together like a team. This occurs with both animal and human groups. When there is real danger, such as for soldiers in war, the bonding becomes intensified. The same thing happens in sport when competition is important and team members have battled together.

The bonding can last forever. There are friendships, but the bonding that occurs amongst teammates can often be at another level. I have witnessed this with platoon members during the Vietnam conflict. I have witnessed this with ex-Wallabies, such as Topo and some of his 1984 Grand Slam and 1986 Bledisloe Cup team mates, who battled through those test matches to end up victors. I have witnessed it with others, such as police who have worked and battled together through adversity. In each of these, success and survival depended upon teammates. Each of these produced unique understandings and feelings that outsiders cannot really appreciate. The bonding is part of the richness that a sport such as rugby and particularly the scrum provides.

'The psychology of scrummaging'

By Dr Steve D. Mellalieu and Prof. Peter C. Terry (Psychology)

"Every scrum I ever went into, I set the agenda. I had to make sure the rest of them were as focused as me, especially the back-row forwards. I mean, somebody had to make sure that the importance of the scrum was fully understood. As props, our heads were on the block. Nobody blames the back row if the scrum goes back. It's a war, right?"

Gerry McLoughlin, former Shannon, Ireland, British Lions and Munster tight head

Of all the elements of the beautiful game played with the oval ball, without doubt the one that currently produces the most debate, controversy and outright frustration for player, coach, spectator and official alike is that of the rugby scrum. The aim of this chapter is to draw upon our combined experiences of playing (from both the inside—second row—and outside the scrum—scrum half), coaching and sport psychology consulting in rugby union to give an insight into the psychology of the scrum.

Specifically, we give our take on what constitutes the scrum from a psychological perspective and focus on the various techniques that can be employed by coaches to complement and enhance the tactical, technical and physical elements of scrum practice, preparation and performance for the individual player and forward pack alike.

This chapter comprises three sections. First, to orientate the reader toward the mental side of the functioning of teams, we present a psychological model of scrum performance. We then talk about the notion of team—specifically scrum—psychology and the various factors that contribute to the collective scrum function. Finally, we provide some advice on coaching players within the forward unit and how their personal preparation and performance can be maximised or enhanced at scrum time.

A model of scrum performance

If we think about the performance of a rugby union scrum in basic terms of outcomes, we can use the following simple equation:

$$\text{ACTUAL SCRUM PERFORMANCE} = \left(\text{POTENTIAL SCRUM PERFORMANCE} - \text{PROCESSES LOSSES [Coordination and Motivation]} \right)$$

Potential scrum performance is what your pack of eight forwards can achieve if they all produce a maximum force at the precise time, in the correct technical way, with the correct tactics for that particular scrum. As coaches we strive for perfection and that flawless scrum from our eight every time. In reality this rarely happens, and so achieving consistency in terms of scrum outcomes becomes a more realistic aim. So what actually goes wrong? Why doesn't your team's scrum achieve its purpose every time? In simple terms, the scrum is susceptible to what psychologists call process losses. Process losses are the factors that conspire to prevent that perfect set, engagement and subsequent drive. We can separate process losses into two categories: coordination losses and motivational losses.

Coordination losses are just that, the inability of your forward eight to coordinate their individual efforts to achieve the desired collective scrum outcome. For example, think about scrum practice when coaching junior age grade forwards—immediately visions come to mind of second rows pushing their socks off at different angles, but with no unity or coordination, resulting in a dysfunctional, unsuccessful output.

Motivational losses refer to the psychological factors that influence your forwards' ability to maximize their individual and collective efforts when they pack down. Ever had a new eight to work with who are not performing because they are not used to how each other sets up or packs down? Ever coached an eight whose scrum has deteriorated over a run of matches and now resembles a shadow of its former self in terms of confidence and performance?

These issues, and many others you might think of, are examples of psychological, specifically motivational, losses that can contribute to a pack of forwards being nowhere near its potential come game day.

In the following sections we present a range of strategies that can be deployed at the unit or individual level in order to minimise these coordination and motivation losses respectively and, therefore, produce a more robust and consistent performance for your forward pack at scrum time.

All together now—Part 1

Scrum coordination

Effective coordination of technique in a rugby scrum is a combination of task-work and teamwork. Task-work refers to the execution of the relevant skills by each individual player (e.g., physical force generated with correct technique), which combine into a collective forward effort that determines the success of the scrum.

Subsequently, teamwork is essentially the coordination of all those individual efforts to produce the desired outcome (e.g., the coordination of the engagement, chasing the hit and the subsequent drive from the eight collectively).

From the scientific research into high-performing teams we know that getting everyone on the same page is vital. This is referred to in psychology as a shared mental model—essentially the collective understanding or knowledge of what your pack is trying to achieve, or what needs to be done at any scrum during a game. Shared mental models in high-performance teams are based on a common understanding of team members regarding the task, one another, task goals and strategies. All the best scrum and set-piece teams from history attest to experiencing this shared mental model as a factor contributing to their success—a kind of sixth sense if you like. To enhance shared mental models and the subsequent coordination of scrum performance, we can adopt an off- and on-field approach, or preparation and practical work respectively. From an off-field perspective we can draw on what is now routine for most successful sports teams and organisations—that is, to engage in preparatory, discussion-based scrum sessions that seek to develop a vision or focus for what your team's scrum wants to achieve, underpinned by clear expectations, goals and strategies to advance that vision.

Commonly, teams will develop a mission statement for their overall modus operandi as to how they wish to play, train and behave for a season or tournament. Applying this

psychological efforts of your pack. Of the numerous psychological factors in high performance sport, we focus on two of the most pertinent to the scrum: cohesion and confidence.

Building a cohesive scrum

Cohesion refers to the ability of a group to remain united in pursuit of its goals and resist disruption from outside threats. Often referred to as the level of chemistry or team glue, the annals of rugby union history are littered with accounts of team chemistry being attributed as a major factor underlying successful championship or cup winning teams and their respective playing combinations (Charlie Faulkner, Bobby Windsor, and Graham Price; Gareth Edwards and Phil Bennett; Nick Farr-Jones and Michael Lynagh; Tim Horan and Jason Little; Wayne Shelford, Michael Jones, Gary and Alan and Whetton). We can think of the cohesiveness of our eight in two ways.

Firstly, there is the social cohesion of the pack or, the degree to which members of your team like each other and enjoy each other's company. Although this has anecdotally been perceived as important by coaches and players (e.g., team bonding and social activities), there is actually little scientific evidence to support social chemistry as a predictor of team performance. Task cohesion, or how well the team or unit works together on the pitch or practice ground in pursuit of its collective goals, is much more important for performance. Scientific research tells us that task cohesion increases performance in interaction sports, such as rugby union. Moreover, the more task cohesion, the greater the influence on its individual members in terms of their ability to conform to the team's norms or performance expectations. Teams which have a higher task cohesion can better resist disruption or external threats from the opposition or from outside sources than teams with a lower cohesion. Teams that stay together longer tend to be more cohesive, which leads to improvements in performance. So the thinking goes that if you seek to build task cohesion on the pitch, your pack will collectively be enhancing its motivational efforts.

There are two elements to task cohesion. The first element is the individual player's attraction to the group. Some players sign or move to a club because they like the way the forward pack plays or operates, or the attitude it displays (this goes back to our scrum philosophy and culture that we talked about nurturing in the previous section). Others, particularly in less cohesive packs in the professional game do their individual jobs, but just don't seem to be going the extra mile to give their all for the cause of their fellow pack members, perhaps because their attraction to the group is not that great. The second element to task cohesion is the level of team integration, that is how well the forward pack actually believes they are a collective, united force. The stronger the pack's belief and collective unity, the greater the cohesion.

There are four main sources or factors that predict cohesion, and in this respect they represent areas that we as coaches can seek to enhance, develop or manipulate in relation to the scrum. They include environmental, personal, leadership, and team factors. Environmental influences relate to factors, such as the size of the team. Research tells us that as the size of the group increases so cohesion reduces, largely due to the difficulty of effective communication and coordination of scrummaging activities.

Bigger in this respect may not always be better. Take the 2005 Lions tour to New Zealand, which was one of the best resourced to leave UK shores, and comprised one of the largest touring parties of players. Although this was intentional in order to ensure sufficient cover in playing positions, adequate player rest and recovery, and quality of practice, performances on the field were disappointing.

In this respect, we know that for every task or group activity there does appear to be an optimal team number or size to maximize cohesion through effective communication and player efforts and actions. Too large a group size and the motivation and coordination losses will become more and more prevalent leading to reduced performance. In terms of leadership, research tells us of the style that the leader, captain or coach, the relationships they establish, and the behaviours they exhibit, all contribute to team cohesion. We can all recall good captains, coaches or pack leaders who communicate in clear, consistent, unambiguous ways regarding team goals and objectives. These leaders command respect and lead to the creation of an effective eight. Team factors refer to the collective characteristics of the group; the norms or expectations in terms of work ethic, practice quality, etc.; the desire for the team's success; and lastly the level of team stability or turnover in the starting eight.

So how do we build cohesion? Firstly, if red flags appear in relation to any of these four factors, a coach can direct subsequent interventions specifically at these sources (e.g., poor leadership, high player turnover, lack of shared values or goals). We also present some key pointers to build task cohesion in the scrum. Of course, many can be applied to any unit or group operating in the game, or beyond.

Team environment

Togetherness can enhance cohesion. When members of a team are repeatedly put in close physical proximity, feelings of cohesion often increase. Exclusive forward only training, practice pitches, changing areas, weights rooms and training camps are all examples of engineered proximity. Introducing group distinctiveness is also a relatively simple way to contribute towards team cohesion. This can be achieved by having a forwards only kit or apparel that distinguishes the eight from the rest of the squad (e.g., the front row club), or by having collective and individual awards for scrum performance–strikes against the head, pushover tries, a medal or ring for 50 games, etc. Even just emphasising the history and tradition of the forwards who have represented the team, club, province or nation can be a good move towards reinforcing the scrum philosophy and culture at a team or club. Any Munster or Llanelli Scarlet's player, coach, supporter, past or present will be able to recall, or at least acknowledge their team's famous victories over the New Zealand All Blacks. Appropriately relevant events, and tales of prior bravery or achievement on the field, can all serve to build history and tradition and instill pride and cohesion in the current pack of forwards.

Team processes

As well as enhancing our scrum environment, as coaches we can also build cohesion by working on the actual process of the scrum. For example, sitting down with players to work on scrum philosophy by setting clear scrum unit goals and objectives is more strongly associated with team success than merely setting individual goals for players. Moreover, player involvement and participation in the goal-setting process helps to build cohesion. Encouraging team sacrifices among and for the pack (whether that is time, financial or personal) is also known to contribute to cohesion.

Research tells us that when high-status members of teams (e.g., captains, pack leaders, experienced old heads, internationals) make sacrifices for the group, cohesion is enhanced. In similar ways, the promotion of cooperative behaviour develops cohesion (e.g., encouraging rival hookers to work on throwing practice together for the good of the cause; second choice pack members rehearsing an opposition team scrummage to create a more realistic live scrum practice session for the starting eight).

196

Conformity to team norms

Developing a scrum philosophy, vision and culture will help to produce a conformity in the pack's expectations and standards, both on and off the field. Evidence from scientific literature tells us that greater conformity to both task (on field) and social (off field) norms contributes to enhanced team chemistry. A more cohesive pack of forwards will stick together on and off the field, and be more likely to buy into team codes of conduct, formal or informal, and take regulation or policing of those rules more seriously.

In summary, team chemistry is a much sought after component that hard work alone will not necessarily produce; it has to be nurtured and developed with much careful consideration from all the key people involved at scrum time.

Building a confident scrum

It's an age-old phenomenon that as a coach you have a player who has all the skills and physical talent and displays them on the practice ground, but lacks the confidence to deliver in the heat of the moment in the big match. Apply that principle to a unit context and you may have a collective lack of belief or confidence from your eight in their set piece work. So how do you build scrum confidence? In simple terms, confidence in one's ability to successfully execute a task, at the team or individual level, is situation specific. We all have elements of our game, coaching or officiating, that we are more confident in than others. In the first author's own rugby career in the second row, making big tackles on his right shoulder was a walk in the park, but making effective tackles on the left shoulder was a struggle!

So just as players have varying levels of confidence in different elements of their game, so do the back and forward units. Evidence of this is the use of the collective from players in post-match reviews and interviews following poor performances. Rhetoric such as 'we scrummed badly' or 'our scrum fell apart today', all give an indication of a low level of collective belief in the pack. Essentially, there are a number of ways that coaches can seek to build scrum-specific confidence in our eight. These focus around several proposed sources of team confidence that include: performance accomplishment, modelling, verbal persuasion, physiological activation and motivational climate.

Performance Accomplishments

Performance accomplishment is about making sure your scrum has gained recent positive performance or experience of mastery, either in practice or in matches. Essentially, if your eight experience success in a facet of their scrum performance (e.g., holding the opposition's drive, disrupting the opposition ball with a wheel), they will have an expectation that they will perform equally well in future situations of a similar nature. If we think of Gerry McLoughlin's quote at the start of the chapter, he was confident in himself and his fellow front row members' ability to hold their own, because they had been there and done it before. This phenomenon can essentially explain why an eight's confidence in its scrum gets stronger the more success they gain, and equally less confident the more failures they experience!

Modelling

Modelling can also be a means to enhance an eight's collective beliefs. It sounds a scientific term, but it's basically a way to describe that seeing oneself, one's pack or another side doing the business can build confidence. Watching video reviews of your eight performing successfully is a simple way to achieve this, or if you are up against a particularly tough scrummaging pack in an upcoming game, then you can show footage of other sides' packs doing the business successfully against them, and this will help to enhance both individual and collective feelings of confidence in your pack.

Verbal Persuasion

Verbal persuasion is the coach, pack leader or old head inspiring the players to achieve a successful scrum performance. This is essentially the power of the spoken word and its effect upon a pack's collective beliefs. Pre-match or halftime team talks are common examples of verbal persuasion strategies. Quite often the most effective ones are those that take place between the pack leader and their forwards during a break in the game or behind the posts after conceding a score. The more the players can believe in the person doing the persuading, the better effect it will have.

Physiological Activation

Research tells us that individual and collective beliefs in a player or their team's physiological state can enhance confidence. This goes back to the old adage that if you feel warmed up, strong and sharp you are more likely to feel confident. So if your pack hits the machine before a match, or better still has some live hits, eight on eight, then this will further contribute to enhancing team confidence. Pre-match warm-ups are not just about preparing the body, but about bringing together a pack of forwards to the collective belief in their physical and psychological readiness for the challenge ahead. This in itself will build better performance accomplishment experiences, better team confidence, and so on.

Motivational Climate

Motivational climate is the training and playing atmosphere that is created by coaches, leaders and players in practice and in matches. In performance-focused climates the emphasis is on outcomes, results, social comparison and individual ability. A mastery-oriented coaching climate promotes effort, hard work, improvement and teamwork leading a team or group to have better ability to reflect and analyse their performance. Clearly, there are times when a mastery or task climate is warranted, such as during preseason, or when the emphasis is on developing the technical components of the scrum. At other times a performance focus is warranted, such as in pre-match briefings on scrum tactics against a particular opponent when the focus is on achieving specific outcomes.

Motivation, focus and confidence

The principles used to ensure your pack of forwards is collectively motivated, focused and confident can also be applied to the individual player at scrum time. For example, in terms of maximising individual motivation it is important to work with players to encourage them to develop the ability to set themselves clear targets in practice and around games. This ensures players are being stretched and worked to their full potential. In addition to unit or team goals set by players and coaches at scrum time, individual goals should be encouraged that focus on the process or quality of an individual player's role. For example, rather than just seeking to hit ten live scrums at practice, players can seek to make ten quality engagements, ten effective strikes, etc.

At game time it also helps to provide a specific focus for players to direct attention and concentration to the important roles or jobs required of players during games. All players will have outcome goals for the match (i.e., to win) and to an extent personal performance goals (e.g., percentage of successful tackles carried, line out completions), but a focus on the processes (e.g., shape of back, foot position prior to engagement) gives the player an immediate focus that is within their control, which, if executed successfully, will lead to attainment of subsequent performance goals, and hopefully the desired outcomes.

A further way to enhance individual motivation and focus is to develop a sense of role clarity regarding a players' job at scrum time. It is advantageous for coaches and captains to work with players to ensure that they know, understand, and accept their respective roles at scrum time.

Skill practice

Practice Like You Play

Simulating match conditions physically, tactically, technically and mentally will allow a player (and a forward pack) to practice coping with the various demands of scrummaging. The closer the match simulation conditions are to the real thing, the better the potential learning experience. However, because of the contact nature of rugby union, simulating match-like conditions often becomes difficult, impractical or downright dangerous. So how do you seek to maximize skill, development or practice time? In addition to physical practice of a skill, one of the most common psychological strategies used to enhance technical and tactical development and match day preparation is mental practice.

Research into mental practice shows that a combination of mental and physical practice results in greater performance gains than either mental or physical practice of a skill alone. In certain skills in the game, such as place kicking and throwing, players can physically practice to their hearts' content without any fatigue issues, until the skill becomes grooved. In skills where physical practice is limited or constrained, such as at scrum time, then mental practice can provide a nice top-up. The beauty of mental practice is that the possibilities are endless; the only limit on what a player can imagine, rehearse or simulate is their imagination itself!

The technique of mental practice can be used in a number of different ways. For example, when it comes to skill development, mental practice may aid a loose head prop working on a particular engagement at the scrum; the bind and drive of a second row; or the back row move run by an eight. It can also be used to build confidence and reduce nerves in the lead up to a match by imagining a successful strike against the head, a pick and drive against a physical back row, or a clean crisp 8-9 to put the scrum half over close to the line. During games, mental rehearsal can also be used as part of a pre-scrum routine to help focus a player's efforts as they are binding up preparing for engagement. Following games, mental reviews of scrums by individuals can also be used to augment standard post-match video analysis procedures (e.g., What did that last drive feel like where the scrum wheeled?, What was going on when we were penalised for collapsing?)

Skill execution

Developing Pre-Scrum Routines

Success at the elite level in any domain of life requires an individual or team to prepare thoroughly and execute performance under the demands of a variety of stresses and strains. Rugby union produces a huge challenge in that players are constantly required to respond to a changing environment and the options in front of them. Then, following an infringement, enforced breaks in play occur, and players have to refocus their efforts and attention once more towards the tasks at hand. Often the ability to refocus can be hampered by fatigue, pressure, distraction or a combination thereof.

One way in which performers in all sports manage such distractions is through the use of pre-performance routines, such as pre-shot, pre-kick, pre-throw, or pre-match. Performance routines allow a performer to consistently go through a systematic cognitive, emotional and behavioural process to prepare the body to do the business. The most obvious manifestation of pre-performance routines in rugby union is the place kicker preparing to take a pressure shot at goal.

Research confirms that pre-kick routines are consistent in terms of actions and timing down to the split second, and we can apply the same principles to individual players come scrum time. For example, every member of a pack will have specific skills to execute at scrum time, so they should ensure that they focus on each step of their pre-scrum routine.

A routine is, very often, idiosyncratic to the individual. However, despite this variety, a routine will generally comprise some element of thinking, feeling and doing. For example, a loose head prop picking themselves up from the bottom of a ruck ready for a scrum, after a high number of phases, may first engage in some behavioural activity or doing (e.g., increased deep breathing to regulate heart rate and calm themselves down), which may be followed by some thinking (e.g., where the location of the scrum is occurring on the pitch, potential tactical consequences, scrum calls). Once they get to the binding point with their hooker they may then go through a prescribed set of activities: physically binding and twisting, setting feet, checking they are calm, thinking about the outcome of the scrum, and then focusing on a specific point of contact or approach with their opponent.

Throughout this process, triggers or keywords can be helpful to ensure the pre-scrum routine is consistent and that all the correct technical coaching points are being adhered to. Indeed, the use of triggers and keywords is helpful in all facets of skill development in individuals. Pre-scrum routines can also be used in training to enhance the quality of scrum practice by ensuring the player is as motivated or warmed up for the scrum session as possible. Players then can be encouraged to adopt these strategies during game practice or simulated scrums, and finally into live matches.

Scrum management

Pre-, In-, and Post-Game Review

Given the direct confrontational nature of the scrum, a key challenge is countering and getting the better of the opposition, whether at the collective or individual level. Research shows that experts in all domains of life have learnt how to problem solve and make decisions more effectively than their less successful counterparts. Largely, this is due to the quantity and quality of their experiences—through practice and game time—and how they reflect upon and learn from these experiences. If we go by the ten-year rule of deliberate practice regarding expertise, our forwards, especially the front rowers, would need to have played over 300 games and hit 6000+ scrums to be experts. In most cases in professional sport we do not have the luxury of this amount of time to allow expertise to develop naturally, so any way to improve the quality of experiences to develop expertise, particularly reflection and learning, is important.

As coaches we spend a lot of time in discussion with players, undertaking analysis to work out the opposition in advance of matches, and even more time post-match when it doesn't go to plan! While these forms of activities all contribute to enhancing reflection and learning, often a problem occurs with players who are unable to react successfully to novel situations on the pitch when it matters. This is often termed game sense or game management.

Working out your opposite number, or opposition scrum—the ability to successfully reflect in game upon what is working and what is not—is the hallmark of an expert. The first step in encouraging this development of scrum management is by developing players' pre-match opposition analysis and post-match reviews to help build critical thinking and reflection skills. This can be assisted by encouraging players to consider specific, structured reflection questions (Who? What? Where? How? and Why?) in group and individual preparation and review sessions. The skill is to effectively build the ability to reflect into live simulation scrum sessions at practice—via directed questions during breaks in play—and then seek to encourage players to engage in reflection, individually or collectively, at appropriate times during matches (e.g., stoppages for injury, half-time).

Use of 'What if?' scenarios during live practice as discussed earlier in the chapter (e.g., seven-man scrums due to a sin bin, certain officials penalising technically the way your front row usually scrummage) can further help players to think on their feet and problem solve in situ.

Referee management

How many matches in the professional game and at test level are won and lost on the blow of a whistle and the direction in which the official's arm is raised, often due to a collapsed scrum or an incomplete engagement?

How players and coaches alike work with and manage officials (and how officials reciprocate!) is now becoming a big part of the game. Impression management is where individuals seek to manage others' views of them and their actions. A key to successful impression management lies in the interpersonal skills of the individual; ultimately how effective they are at communicating, verbally, and non-verbally, with others.

We often see poor examples of players dissenting to officials, or captains overbearing themselves to reverse or minimise the damage of an infringement, only to result in further irritation of officials, and potential further punishment consequences in the game.

Sounds obvious but the trick therefore is to work with, rather than against the officials— know your enemy! Do the key protagonists involved in scrum time (e.g., No.9, loose forwards, front row) understand how the scrum is refereed and more importantly how to communicate effectively with officials regarding this process?

At the professional level referees are themselves now being trained in communication skills (verbal and non-verbal) so player body language and interaction is even more vital. Knowing when to lean in and politely argue your case or point out the alleged error in an official's decision, or when to shut up and retreat ten metres, is a skill in itself.

Similarly, off the field, at whatever level you are involved, there will invariably be a few local referees who will regularly officiate. Get to know them better, and get them to know you better. Inviting them along to coaching sessions, discussing the nuances of the scrum and their views—away from the pressure on the field—will help to enhance shared understanding and shared mental models at scrum time, in practice, and games.

Conclusion

The information presented in this chapter represents some of our thoughts and views, together with a light brush of the science regarding the psychology of the scrum and the ways in which some of the factors that contribute to an effective unit can be harnessed and developed. We hope that there is something in it for everyone—whatever level of playing, coaching, managing or support. If nothing else, we hope we have thrown some ideas into the mix to stimulate the grey matter to help enhance your own rugby-related practice, whatever that may be.

CHAPTER 11

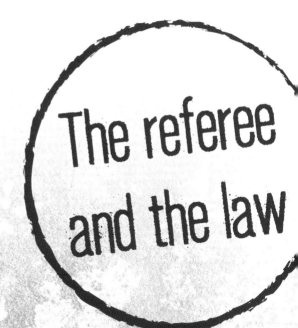

The referee
and the law

THE REFEREE AND THE LAW

Some may say referees are a necessary evil but I prefer to call them essential on the basis that without a referee we cannot play the game! Despite having played for 22 years at top level, I never had the courage to grab a whistle, and instead have given the referee my outmost respect.

The ideal best referee's review is when people say they have been invisible or unnoticed during the match and nobody talks about them afterwards. These days touch judges' collaboration and technology such as the TMOs, the ear pieces and the microphones make it impossible for the referee not to be noticed by the spectators. The result is too much interruption, too many breakages and the breakdown of one of the sacrosanct principles of rugby: CONTINUITY.

Referees are todays' law administrators, the enablers of the game and the spectacle, the facilitators on the ground, the judges of the Supreme Court, the whistle blowers. As much as we can elevate them, we also want them to let the game flow more for continuity and entertainment's sake.

I propose that referees should be incentivized to achieve a higher percentage of continuity without stoppages.

Spare a thought for the people that carry out the thankless job of allowing a match to take place when they know most of the time they cannot please both teams; this is a real handicap and an intrinsic restriction for the job ahead. When we undertake to do a particular job with such conditions, we may well say we will be severely challenged. Therefore referees deserve a lot of respect, sympathy and a bit of empathy.

They are condemned to a role, either by choice or by nature, because they cannot play anymore or because they choose to continue their involvement as referees. In this post-playing role their kicks come from completely different stimuli than those of the players, whether they be physical, emotional or psychological.

We must be grateful to referees for their dedication, unselfish giving and for being humans (with all the errors that mere mortals may commit).

In the last 20 years since the advent of professionalism the game has gotten faster, and players are faster, stronger and fitter.

Referees have been given more responsibilities and more demands have been imposed upon them. Their job is very complex.

The constant probing of the media has exposed every little detail that referees cannot see when refereeing 30 players (e.g., J. Kaplan allowing Wales to use a fresh ball in a match against Ireland and scoring a try).

I believe the referees were left behind in this race and are now disadvantaged; the likelihood is that these contributing factors will shorten their careers.

Professional referees are under pressure to keep or enhance their careers, and to do that they have to please those that have a large input into controlling their livelihoods. They must also be very conscious of peer opinions, image and the power that they wield in relation to match outcomes.

Those with extroverted tendencies who think they have star qualities are attracted to the theatre to which the professional game lends itself through television and its worldwide coverage.

I have mentioned before the GSB factor (game-show-business) and referees are not immune to the vagaries that exist inside the mass entertainment bubble.

There is subliminal pressure from administrators for referees to consider some situations commercially; there is spin from coaches pressuring them to watch the opposition on certain aspects of their play; there is pressure to get the media off their backs if they are being labelled in a negative way; they are pressured by home town crowd reactions; and they put pressure on themselves by being aware that unpredictable results are likely to attract extra scrutiny.

They are given a very complex and detailed law book that contains inconsistencies, and are then told which parts of it they should ignore and on which parts they must follow to the letter.

I don't like the refereeing system and I despair that there is too much of a refereeing influence in the international governance of our game. Why does the game have to bear the expense of neutral referees being flown around the world when all referees are supposed to be neutral? The concept of neutrality under this system is illogical anyway, because coming from a third country doesn't in any way guarantee impartiality. In a World Cup how would the best referees feel about refereeing games at the business end of the tournament knowing that they can't preside over the final if a team from their own country is in it? The same implications, temptations and opportunities are there for anyone who is unscrupulous. Country of origin has nothing to do with refereeing integrity.

Referees: the enablers

Why can't the touch judges be amateur locals? I venture to say that the top amateurs are probably better referees who are just not prepared to give up their professions to go full time. I say this as an Australian who sees the game bleeding at the grassroots level, while so much unnecessary expense is happening at the sharp end. My real point is that under the current system and with all the pressures I have mentioned, how can the professional referee focus entirely on what he should (i.e., facilitating the playing of a game that is played fairly and within the spirit of the laws and with no thought for the ramifications of how he does it)?

What we want is for the referee to be a player, to play the game, to enjoy the game, to be for the player and not against the player, and to teach and encourage players to play the laws instead of being the policeman who says, "Caught you!" As corny as it might seem we need to get back to the idea of the referee being the 31st player!

As it is commonly applied in CBT (Cognitive Behaviour Therapy), the correct expression of ideas, feelings and emotions leads to behavioural change. Therefore the terminology utilized breeds attitude and there needs to be some attitudinal shift with rugby refereeing. Wouldn't we all like to see the usual terms used in officiating parlance being replaced with the following alternatives in both word and deed? Referees can play their part in the transformation of the product but the change is equally dependent on players and coaches having a positive approach.

» in charge = enabler
» authoritarian = facilitator
» arcane = transparent
» autocratic = consultative (particularly with touch judges and television match officials)
» boss = one of the stakeholders
» supreme = fallible, but just and consistent
» in charge = yes, but collaborating
» players and coaches = proactive collaborators or stakeholders

The key is having 31 people playing in the knowledge that only one has the authority to pull things up if the others depart from what has been laid down in the law book for a fair contest. It brings to mind an analogy that this is not different to a big theatre production play where many people play their specific roles and when everybody does so (under the leadership of the director), everything comes together and all participants as well as the audience enjoy themselves by all being part of the one spectacle.

Some time ago I had the pleasure of discussing a number of innovative ideas with several internationally experienced referees, and I'd like to share with you some of the outcomes and comments:

» Love the idea of simplifying the whole process
» Love getting rid of four steps
» Unanimously want to stay with crouch and pack calls
» Think that pack is a good, positive call
» Change of mentality is understood and accepted
» Sharing responsibility amongst the stakeholders is also a good initiative
» Very impressed with our list of collaborators
» Very happy that something is being done
» Everybody agrees that at the moment scrummaging is degenerating and is a cause of major concern for all and sundry.

References and citations

» Australian Rugby Union Safety Kit. (1996).

» Buenos Aires Rugby Union. (1997). *Guide for coaches.* Argentina: Buenos Aires Rugby Union.

» Gallaher, D. & Stead, J.W. *The complete rugby footballer.*

» Hopkins, J. & Cotton, F. (1979). *Rugby.*

» Howell, M., Xie, L., & Wilkes, B. (2000). *The Wallabies: A definitive history of Australian test rugby.*

» Marks, D. & Burkett, T. (1998). *Forward play: National Rugby Union coaching plan.*

» McGregor, L. "Touch, pause, engage." Retrieved from http://jonathanball.book.co.za/blog/2011/06/20.

» McGregor, L. "Why Trevor Manuel turned his back on the Boks and how to keep a scrum tight." Retrieved from liz-mcgregor-why-trevor-manuel-turned-his-back-on-the-boks-and-how-to-keep-a-scrum-tight/.

» Milburn, P.D. (1990). *The biomechanics of rugby: Scrummaging.*

» Quinn, K. (1991).*The encyclopaedia of World Rugby.*

» Rodriguez, E. (2012). *The art of scrummaging: A rugby scrum thesis.* Sydney: Rugby Friends of Sydney.

» Ross, B. *Scrummaging, Myoquip.* Retrieved from http://www.myoquip.com.au.

» The Rugby Football Union. *Why the whistle went.*

» Rutherford, D. (1983). *International rugby.*

» San Isidro Club. *The decade of SIC: 1970-1979.* Buenos Aires, Argentina.

» Tala Rugby Club. (1981). *Rugby in black and white.* Cordoba, Argentina.

» Villepreux, P. & Brochard, F. (2002). *Modern rugby.*

» Wakefield, Lord W.W. *Rugger.*

» Wales Rugby Union. *Rugby pathway*. Retrieved from http://www.wru.co.uk/downloads/pdfs/WRU-Rugby-Pathway2008.pdf.

CHAPTER 12

Our expert collaborators

OUR EXPERT COLLABORATORS

Information about all factors that involve *Rugby—The ART of SCRUMMAGING* can be of assistance to a number of stakeholders, not the least of which are coaches, players, referees, lawmakers and rugby journalists. The opinions of any one person with the normal qualifications of experience and study have some value, but a compendium of opinions from similarly qualified people has more, particularly when the issues are being shared as they are here.

I am very grateful for the contribution of the expert collaborators whose letters and comments follow. All are concerned about the welfare of the scrum in the sense that it remains a very important identity in the game of rugby. We all want to see scrums take less time and result in much fewer collapses and penalties.

To achieve this we need better technique, better attitude and better coaching, as well as better laws that will take a lot of the guesswork and disregard for the law out of refereeing.

I feel equally indebted to all the contributors and for the most part I am putting their comments in alphabetical order. There are, however, three venerable elder statesmen with whom I would like to lead. The most revered front rower in World Rugby, in my opinion at least and many others would agree with me undoubtedly, is Sir Wilson Whineray with whom I shall start. Sadly two months after my book was published Sir Wilson passed away in Auckland, New Zealand, on 22nd October 2012. He is remembered as one of the most respected All Blacks of all times.

At this point I need to remind you that these are the exact comments I received from my Expert Collaborators before publishing The ART of SCRUMAGING in August 2012 and they were made when the old sequence of Crouch-Touch-Pause-Engage was still part of the scrum law.

Introducing our expert collaborators

Sir Wilson Whineray, KNZM, OBE

Sir Brian Lochore, ONZ, KNZM, OBE

Sir Nicholas Shehadie, AC, OBE

Kevin J. Crowe, OAM

Alistair Baxter

Dick Byers

Mike Cron

Colin Deans

Gaven Head

Andrew Hopper

Peter Horton

Jake Howard

Philip Keith-Roach

Malcolm Lewis

Andy McIntyre

Ray McLoughlin

Philip Orr

Emilio Cesar Perasso

Heinrich Rodgers

Peter Sloane

Pieter de Villiers

Cobus Visagie

Jon White

Sir Wilson James Whineray, KNZM, OBE

Ex-Patron of NZRU, 32 New Zealand Caps (1957-1965), 30 as Captain

I would like to commend Topo for the energy and thought he has put into this project. There is a general view that scrum laws should be examined when the laws are looked at again after RWC. The four-step process to set the scrum seems a little too much, but the touch call to bring the scrums closer together is very valuable, especially applying to younger or less mature players. I have not seen the final report but know that many experienced people have contributed.

Sir Nicholas Shehadie, AC, OBE

30 Austrtalian Caps, Captain, Former President ARU, 1987 Rugby World Cup organising team

Thank you for sending me a copy of *Rugby—The ART of SCRUMMAGING*. It was in the early 1980s, as president of the ARU, that I became concerned with the neck injuries that we were experiencing in the front row.

With the assistance of a very dear friend, John Yeo, AO, we got to consulting with many old props and forwards and then devised a method for school and junior teams to pack with their feet closer to the centre of the scrum, thus packing higher. This was adopted and to my knowledge no further neck injuries have occurred in GPS schools which, at that time, were considering banning rugby. Today in senior rugby the crouch-touch-pause-engage method is ridiculous and does nothing to help the game, the scrum or the spectators. In scrum law 20.5, how can a referee tell how the ball is put into the scrum when he stands on the opposite side of the scrum half? It makes me think they are not interested in controlling the put-in.

Topo, I see nothing wrong with your comment where you say: "The aim is to get more safety at less cost." In my time the referee would never touch any member of a scrum during a game. Furthermore, I feel the referees today think the spectators have come to watch them. I very much look forward to seeing the completed book.

Sir Brian James Lochore, ONZ, KNZM, OBE

25 New Zealand Caps 1964-1970 (recalled from retirement for 1 test in 1971), Captain 1966-1970.

I will make my points in chronological order, not in terms of importance.

1. It takes far too long to put the scrum down once the ref calls for a scrum. Players think it's time for a spell. Any delaying tactics should result in a short-arm penalty immediately.

2. Refs instructions should be crouch-engage. No touch or pause calls. You don't say ready-steady-go in a 100m race, because you would always have a break. Same with the scrum; every referee has a different rhythm. Also the prop is aiming at

the place to grab his opposite and, by having to touch, it becomes difficult to be accurate.

3. The scrum should not be able to be moved around by more than 90 degrees. This would encourage scrums to push instead of wheeling. We would have many more clean scrums. I feel very strongly about the points I have made.

Thanks for getting people's thoughts together.

Al Baxter

69 Wallaby Caps, 130 NSW Waratah Caps, 121 Super Rugby games, 2003 RWC (runners up), 2007 RWC (quarter finalist)

Topo, many thanks for including me in your expert collaborators team. I have read your document with interest. I'm in agreement with a large part of the document and also have a few comments to add as follows.

Summary:

In my opinion, one of the key elements that sets rugby union apart from rugby league and American football (and to a lesser extent, soccer) is the highly physical and tactical contest at each stoppage of the game. Constant competition for possession of the ball makes this game a greater challenge both mentally and physically for the players that play it, and hopefully more exciting and mentally rewarding to those who watch it.

The rugby scrum is fundamental to this and it deeply concerns me when people talk about fixing it by removing aspects of the physical contest of the scrum. However, in saying that, I think it can definitely be improved for the players and spectators while keeping, and allowing for, robust competition in this part of the game.

Rugby—The ART of SCRUMMAGING is an excellent document to start this process and to help improve the modern scrum. Essentially I am in general and wholehearted agreement with the majority of the technical and organizational points, as well as those concerning attitude and mentality.

The points where my opinion differs to those discussed in the document are:

» Feet positioning on setup suggested by you for the No. 1.
» The singular importance of bind and grips above balance and tension.
» The non-neutral head position of the front row immediately prior to engagement.

Of the points of law, I think the ability for a referee to act by strategic principles of law, as opposed to an exhaustive checklist of possible infringements, would be of great value. Additionally, the amendment that I think would most quickly and easily assist with the improvement of the scrum is simply the shortening of the referee's engagement sequence.

Technical points

Feet Position for the No. 1:
I feel that the prop's feet should be as close to perpendicular as possible to the intended direction of force, so that knees, hips and shoulders are all aligned to go in that same direction (whether it is inward, outward or straight). Just as with squatting and power cleans, the most force is produced most efficiently when the hips and shoulders are perpendicular to the line drawn between the toes. Also, as a prop it has been my experience that when one foot is further behind or in front of the other while keeping hips and shoulders forward, then either the back leg becomes over-extended and above the optimal knee/hip angle of 100° to 120°, or conversely the front knee and hip become too bent and under the optimal pushing angle.

The singular importance of bind and grips above balance and tension:
I feel that binding and grips are just one component of three for the entire scrum to be tight, together, balanced, steady and safe. The two other important components are balanced, even weight between the feet and as a scrum, and core and shoulder stability of the individual—that is, balance and tension.

Head position of the front row immediately prior to engagement:
Having the head position fully up in the front row before engagement means that the front row will have to quickly duck their heads into the neutral position so as not to have the top of their forehead be the first point of contact with the opposition's shoulder! As well as being a safety issue if somebody is too slow to get their head into a neutral

position, it is also a stability issue. If the front row has to quickly duck their heads on engagement, then there is a risk that their shoulders may follow (even briefly), placing them in a position of having shoulders below hips and increasing the risk of collapse. Having heads in a neutral position (or very slightly above neutral), with still eyes looking forward at the opposition, removes the need to duck on engagement but still allows the opposition to be watched (albeit over the eyebrows).

Points of Law:

In refereeing of the scrum I entirely agree with Topo, Ewan McKenzie and Dick Marks' comments relating to a less-is-more approach to scrum refereeing. I think that more discretion (and ultimately responsibility) should be given to the referees, particularly at the professional level. The referee should be allowed to judge on simple, strong scrum principles, as opposed to a highly prescriptive checklist.

The Engagement Sequence:

As with most others I think this should be reduced in length. At the very least I think that the pause call should be removed. Referees are already leaving long pauses between each call, so there appears to be no added benefit of pausing then saying, 'Pause', then pausing again before proceeding to the engage call. Ultimately, though, I would like to see the call at the senior level being simply 'Crouch-Engage'. The referee could call 'Crouch' when the two packs are ready and formed at an appropriate distance apart then, once the packs are in a still, stable and balanced crouched position, the call of 'Engage' could be given for the two packs to engage.

I hope this helps in the general discussion which is currently badly needed in order to improve this sovery important aspect of rugby.

Dick Byres

Referee, 14 international matches, inaugural IRB Referee Selector Panel 2007, recipient of IRB Referee Award for Distinguished Service.

My first point is that, although you refer to the IRB Medical Advisory Committee recommending this change to the law, in the background (as I understood it at the time), there had been a number of serious cervical injuries in the UK and the insurance companies were applying pressure to the IRB. Thus, although your treatise goes down very technically detailed lines, there may be some background political issue that needs to be addressed to satisfy an invisible stakeholder.

On my second point, I have asked around and generally get the answer that, with the even cadence, packs were anticipating the referee's call to get the early hit.

All I was wondering was whether this was the real cause of the uneven cadence requirement for 2011. Was there a technical paper presented to Super 15 coaches and referees? For players at the community level rugby your points are particularly applicable. As good and as safe as it sounds, this precautionary principle doesn't take into account the ability and inability of the players, varying fitness components, skill levels, anthropometry, cultural levels or different psychological aptitudes.

Two important points I would like to stress:

1. The top rugby practitioners of recent years all suggest that the present method of engagement is contributing to the slowness of packing a scrum and to the frequency of collapsing in modern scrums. Their views must be listened to.

2. Whilst I leave the actual engagement process to the more learned members of the front row, I refer to the other point that former front rowers and hookers lament, that being the fact that crooked feeds are a blight on the game. Could I suggest that the current method of having the putting-in half back come from the referee's left means that crooked feeds will abound? Feed it from the left and immediately collect it at the back of the scrum is the result. I suggest, therefore, that the half back be made to come from the referee's right-hand side. The half must, therefore, step around the referee and square up to get the ball in the tunnel. This must give a better chance of getting a credible feed. In fact they will often ask the referee, in his pre-match chat, to make it an even cadence which is not too drawn out.

Mike Cron

NZ Rugby Union scrum coach (2004-2011), All Black scrum coach, 2011 Rugby World Champions, Wales scrum coach 2002-2003 (RWC 2003)

Topo, you have outlined very well the finer points of scrummaging in the draft document you sent me some time ago. I thought I would look at the things that allow a player to scrummage correctly, and some tips for coaching scrummaging. There are three main areas relating to scrummaging that a player needs to nail to be able to achieve his greatest influence at scrum time.

1. Balance

This is huge. All players need to be able to crouch and hold in a balanced position without being held back too much by a fellow player. If props are held back too much by their locks and loose forwards, they end up in the perfect pushing position at the preengagement stage (too early), but once the referee calls 'Engage,' the props engage and are not only over-extended on the hit, but also are generally angling downward. On the hit they are very weak through the legs and core region. This leads to instability on the engagement causing a collapse, or at the very least inconsistency on the engagement. Using a dart board as an analogy, the prop engages angling toward double three on the dart board, whereas he should be aiming at the bullseye.

I work a lot individually on players' set-up. I use a mirror in the gym for a player to see himself after he has completed a set-up. He can then change his finished position if he has to readjust. A study carried out in Australia a few years ago revealed that a prop's technique changes slightly every time you add another denominator. For example, a prop doing a set-up by himself will change slightly once he binds onto a hooker. This will change slightly when you add a lock and so on.

The main area to address is the hips. When a player bends either into the ¾ set or full set-up position his first movement must be at the hips. He has to cock his hips like a duck's arse. This allows him to get into a strong set up position. Scrummaging is like completing a squat in the gym, except you are doing it horizontally instead of vertically.

I noted with interest a study carried out in England relating to props getting into a good set-up position. The study showed that a lot of young props found it difficult to be fully balanced in a good set-up position due to a restriction in their dorsi-flexion (ankle). This meant that they ended up setting up on their toes with very few sprigs in the ground. The study found that an older, mature prop had far better range through his dorsi-flexion and could have a much flatter foot on set up, and therefore more sprigs in the ground and better balance. Interesting!

2. Engagement

It is important for front rowers to have their chest in front of their knees when they go into the crouched position. If their knees are in line with their shoulders, they will need a large gap to be able to engage to end up in a strong position. This gap will not be given either by his opponent or the referee, so he must learn to engage off a shorter hit by having perfect technique on the setup.

When you go into the set-up position your knees should be in line with your chest. When you engage, your knees move towards the target. If the knees do not move, a front rower will not be able to meet his opponent in the middle of the tunnel and will, therefore, be beaten on the hit.

Speed comes about by all players being in a balanced set-up or crouched position. The weight is on the balls of their feet. When the referee calls 'Engage,' the players with a split stance, normally hooker, locks and No. 8, release their leg, and all 16 feet of the eight players are on the ground and roughly square when the front rows engage against their opponents. Each coach will have his own idea about where the feet position should end up. But the principle is the same.

On the engagement you want all your players to have a flat back, head in the neutral position, hips/thigh angle at roughly 120 degrees, knee angle roughly 120 degrees and tension through their body. You want the power from the ground to go through each player's feet, up through the body and into the opponent. The halfway range of a joint is 120 degrees which is considered the strongest position. But every prop is an individual. For example Owen Franks engages with his knees at 90 degrees on the hit on a regular basis and still scrummages strongly.

3. Staying strong with movement

Each forward has to have the ability to stay strong with movement. This is the difference between scrum-machine training and live scrummaging.

I do a lot of drills from one on one, one on two, etc., and build it up to finally have eight on eight. The drills include straight-line pushing, as well as lateral movement drills which get the player to individually feel his body and adjust his transfer of power accordingly.

4. Key points to scrum coaching

I do one third of coaching on a scrum machine and two thirds off the machine.

I never use a scrum machine that does not have spring-loaded pads, and the pads have to have the ability to be adjusted to allow for different sized front rowers. This ensures that the front rowers engage with their spine in line and not angling in on an angle, which encourages poor technique and also has an injury risk.

I always use primer (warm-up) drills prior to putting a full pack into either a scrum machine or live. In every scrum session I include neck exercises which is an area overlooked at times. Flexibility is a very important area to continually work on, particularly for front rowers. They need to have the ability to adjust to various forces.

I use video feedback at every scrum session. Where possible this is done out on the field at the time. If not practical, then the session is certainly videoed so the coach and players can view it later that day. There is no substitute for repeating correct technique regularly.

Kevin J. Crowe, OAM

Representative player; International referee and touch-judge; coaching director; delegate to the ASRR (Australian Society of Rugby Referees); member of the Australian Rugby Union Laws Committee; president of the QRRA (Queensland Rugby Referees Association); appointed by the International Rugby Board through the ARU as technical advisor to the 9th South Pacific Games.

I am an octogenarian and some would consider my views to be irrelevant and outdated. They do involve old values, but they are not irrelevant to the modern professional game. The professional game is different and has required significant adaptation, but that is not an excuse to discard principles or to change traditional and time honoured relationships.

It was interesting and refreshing to read TOPO's insight into the present dilemma regarding the scrum engagement in today's rugby. His passionate plea for a review of the scrum engagement law for the safety of the players, particularly the front row, is long overdue. *Rugby—The ART of SCRUMMAGING* is a very well presented publication. In order to address this safety issue, one has to assess the situation presently against what was offered in the past in over a century of international rugby. The scrum is not only a means of restarting the game after an infringement, but it is the focal point of the game. It attracts players of all shapes and sizes and executed efficiently, it can gain a decisive advantage for the team.

The past

For most of the game's history there did not appear to be a problem on scrum engagement as we breezed into the twentieth century. The game progressed and prospered between the two world wars using the same formula in the scrum, and the game reached greater heights from 1946 to the Rugby World Cup in 1991. Over this entire period the scrum was the vehicle that guided the team to fame or dismal failure. The front office of the scrum was the front row. This tight-knit club comprised players with rare courage earned over years of exposure. I have had the pleasure of refereeing international and test rugby over twenty-two years, and during this period Australia hosted test and international matches involving all the International Rugby Board countries. With this broad sample I have had a bird's-eye view of some of the best scrum engagements in rugby history, including some that

I played in. Let me give you a sample of some of the older front row identities that I have either known or studied at close quarters:

All Blacks: Ron Hemi, Kevin Skinner, Ian Clarke, Wilson Whineray (Capt.), Ken Gray, Dennis Young, Brian Millar, Bruce McLeod and Tony Kreft: British Isles and Ireland: Karl Mullins (Capt.), John Robins, Tom Clifford, Ronnie Dawson (Capt.), Syd Millar and Hugh McLeod.

Springboks: Jan Lotz, Fanie Louw, Phil Nel (Capt.), Piston Van Wyk, Chris Koch, Jaap Bekker, Abie Malan, Andy McDonald, Hambly Parker and Hannes Marais (Capt.).

Wallabies: Neville Cottrell (Capt.), Eddie Bonis, Bill Cerutti, VinceBirmingham, Ken

Kearney, Nick Shehadie, Doug Keller, Bob McMasters, Eric Tweedale, Eric Davis, Jon White, Peter Johnson, Tony "Slaggy" Miller, Roy Prosser, Jake Howard, Stan Pilecki, David Dunworth, Chris Carberry, Tom Lawton, Enrique Rodriguez, and Andy McIntyre.

My total experience covers some sixty-five years. Over that period I did not see a scrum reset, except for early sorting out in the front row which soon settled down even in slippery or dangerous conditions, so it says a great deal for player responsibility and their own management. I realise that through emotional circumstances brought about by pressures from the outside, the scrum engagement in schoolboy rugby had to be de-powered. The reason could have been peer pressure in the front row. I worked on the committee engaged to find a solution, and after days of discussion and video watching the committee findings were to de-power the scrum in schoolboy and junior rugby by a sequence of instructions, namely: crouch, touch, engage.

This was sent to the International Rugby Board for a decision which called for a season's trial which was successful. It was returned for adoption, but to our surprise it went through with provisos; the changes to the scrum law were to be adopted across the board with the addition of the word pause. The scrum sequence now read crouch, touch, pause, engage. This meant that what was successful for over a century in senior rugby was now out of the hands of the players and under the commands of referees.

Solution

My experience with the IRB subcommittees is that they are very reluctant to admit mistakes and are much more inclined to compromise than to retract. With that in mind, and with safety issues being the flashing beacon in *Rugby—The ART of SCRUMMAGING*, I think it brings serious considerations to the negotiating table. Therefore, my personal approach would be three options, those being:

(1) Delete entirely the sequence crouch, touch, pause, engage, from Law 20 1(g);
OR

(2) Remove the word pause from the sequence, so that the call is crouch, touch, engage;
OR

(3) Compromise by moving the word pause directly after crouch so the sequence is crouch, pause, touch, engage.

My theory on moving the pause forward is to put it into a comfort zone. When the front rowers go into the crouch position, their body profile changes which may require slight foot adjustments and grip focus, and the pause would allow this to take place.

Referees' role

Rugby—The ART of SCRUMMAGING raises some pertinent refereeing questions, namely:

1. What should be the relationship between the referee and the referee assessors?

2. What should be the relationship between the referee and the law book?

3. What should be the relationship between the referee and the players (in terms of coaching them, telling them when to pack in stages, telling them when they have to deliver the ball from a ruck or maul, etc.)? The relationship between the referees (doers) and the assessors (tickers) should be meet and greet.

(1) The doers receive their representative appointments at the beginning of the season where they have the time and opportunity to review each appointment weeks before the match by video or consultation with his peers, or perhaps they have refereed the teams at some time the previous season. With this input and preparation they go into each match fully organised and aware of any problem players or flash-points (e.g., restarts, breakdowns, etc.).

On the other hand the tickers come into a prime stadium seat armed with a clipboard and various pro forma sheets attached to record all facets of the referee's performance. I don't mind their gathering information for a whole range of statistics that would be of some use when making next season's appointments.

However, the ticker has no right to burst into the referees' dressing room armed with a sheet of ticks and comments, when all he has been doing is using a pencil and warming his arse. There is no relationship at all.

(2) The relationship between the referee and the law book must be intimate and sacrosanct. The law book is the very fabric of the referees' being. The referee must be able to in an instant quote the law and its reference to an incident. I used to sit in the sun the morning of the match, whether it were a schoolboy game or an international, and run through the laws, and on the long lonely training runs during the week leading up to the match I would test myself on the laws.

It helps of course if the laws are clear and if the referee is given some discretion in applying common sense rather than being hamstrung with minutiae.

The law book should be the bible and the referee's master, not the administrators or appointment boards. They can make the laws but after that there should be a separation of powers, and it annoys me that appointment boards are made up of too many former referees.

(3) What is the relationship between the referee and the player? I consider the referee the 31st player, unobtrusively melting into the game; I am a great believer that it is the players' game and I think this may stem from my being a former player extending to representative level.

The referee must allow the players to set the tempo and, as the game unfolds, the referee can sense their attitude. A referee can establish authority through his own human management skills. Legislating authority and control to the referee has gone too far and I think this has been a factor in our present predicament. The referee is not only instructing players but also in some cases coaching, as in the scrum engagement. The attitude adopted by some referees has slowed the game down remarkably and in most cases the referee has lost the respect of the players. Good luck, TOPO.

Colin Deans, OAM

Hooker; Hawick RFC; 52 Caps for Scotland, 1978- 1987 year.

When TOPO asked me to write some comments for his book *Rugby—The ART of SCRUMMAGING* immediately came to mind a Scrummaging Technique booklet I wrote back in 1999, which I revisited. First up I realised I didn't have any mentions about the very unpopular and controversial engagement sequence C-T-P-E. This engagement management system (disliked by just about 90% of rugby people) was adopted around eight or nine years ago in the name of safety. This may well be true and, if that's the case, I applaud and support that.

Nonetheless, I'd like to ask three questions about these current practices, because these days I see a lot of time lost with resets and collapses, something I never liked because I know this is dangerous for everyone involved:

(a) Is the scrum the solid structure that used to be and needs to be?

By the looks of resets and collapses it doesn't appear so.

(b) Is the ball being put in straight?

No, it is actually very predictably rolled onto the second row eliminating any possibilities of challenging for possession (tight head).

(c) Have the hooking skills improved?

In fact, on the contrary, they have almost disappeared because referees allow the ball to go onto the second row instead of into the middle of the channel. Therefore, this occurrence in my view has transformed scrums into a pushing contest only.

From a personal point of view it really disappoints me that the old art of hooking is being lost to the modern day scrummaging game where size and power prevail.

I suppose we could easily blame the Argentines in the 1970s and the French in the 1980s for this when they started to play three props in the front row, but you must never forget Tommy Lawton (1984); what a size he was! Daniel Dubroca was a great club player but played at prop; he could not get into the French team in that specific position so to accommodate him they selected him at hooker. This was great for the way the French played the game, but when lineouts came along Berbezier the scrum half had to throw the ball into the lineout as Dubroca couldn't!

What also disappoints me with the modern game is how very few hookers strike the ball now, the use of channel 1/2/3 ball which was developed in the 1980s and 1990s is sadly totally lost now. I would say that this is due to the pressure that is exerted in the power scrum.

But I still do believe that teams who would use the channel ball would benefit greatly from its use, especially when the rules dictate that the opposition backline is five metres behind their own No. 8's feet. A quick channel 1 ball coupled with a quick scrum half would test any defensive line.

If a scrum is under pressure there is no better way to convert the negative situation into an opportunity to take the feed in channel 1 ball. And if the opposition push your scrum back, the ball has gone and they are all in front of the ball carrier and have to work very hard to get back into a defensive position.

This does work and very well as I played in numerous games with a small pack who often would struggle to hold our own in the scrum, but channel 1 ball laid this to rest.

A couple of reasons for the disappearance of the striking against the head may be:

1. Non-coaching of this art

I do not see any reason why a hooker should not strike against the head and steal a few balls, as balls won against the head are great possessions to use to your own advantage. I am of the opinion that maybe we should change the name of the hooker position to thrower as there seems to be more emphasis on the accuracy of the throw in at the lineout, rather than the channel of the ball in the scrums.

2. The crooked feed being allowed

This is a very important point that does not help in the scrums and the art of hooking. The manner in which referees allow the scrum half to feed the ball into the second row again confirms that very few hookers have to hook the ball as it is rolled into their second row. The hookerf the ball in tn in this position is to push and not to strike. You can have the scrum half doing this with no penalty given, but if a prop's foot slips and the scrum is dropped you can be assured that the referee will automatically penalise one of the props and probably the wrong one!

My own personal view is that the modern day coaches have been too much in favour of the bigger scrum always wins scenario, when in actual fact they should be looking at coaching striking of the ball, as well as coaching the use of the lost art of channel ball, to its full advantage as Scotland had to do for years.

Andrew T. (Andy) Hopper

1990-2012 coaching and refereeing in the UK.

I have been an avid student of the scrum since my school days. Hooker was my position, which meant that I had full responsibility for the setting up of the scrum and its outcomes. Like many others, I've witnessed, with some dismay, the transformations that have taken place in the last 30 years and more particularly in the last 15 years with the advent of professionalism.

I strongly believe that to correct the problems we currently have with our scrum, the whole approach to scrummaging, the mindset of players, coaches, referees and administrators at all levels needs to change. The scrum must return to being a proper contest for the ball again and be respected for it.

» The root cause of scrum problems is crooked feeding.
Crooked feeding has resulted in the deskilling of the hooking role. Today, some hookers are just paddlers assisting the crookedly fed ball on its way through channel 2. Others are spectators who watch as the ball is rolled through the loose head's legs. This is an embarrassing nonsense—and a fundamental law breach ignored by referees.

Due to scrums being uncontested in terms of possession of the ball, coaches and players see the purpose of scrums as an opportunity to force the opposition into conceding a penalty—or hoodwink the referee into awarding one. Referees expect to whistle for penalties and are looking to do so. All too often, there's a shrill blast for something obscure—then the most blatantly embarrassing crooked feeding goes unpunished! It's absolutely ridiculous.

Despite the clear and obvious flouting of the fundamental law for the ball to be put in straight, the IRB remains inexplicably incapable of taking corrective action.

Making the scrum a real contest for the ball again would turn the emphasis away from a penalty fest. The focus of teams would return to ensuring that they won their own scrum ball, the technical hooker would re-emerge and a faster ball would be produced.

» The problem of the command sequence.
The C-T-P-E commands take many referees 6–9 seconds to get through. Keeping loaded packs on the pause command for several seconds is ill-considered and flawed. It simply increases the risk of collapse—it's screamingly obvious. The problems resulting from the variations in time taken by different referees to voice C-T-P-E, result in more deeply tedious and unnecessary whistling for early engage. The negative and debilitating consequential effects of C-T-P-E cause much alienation and frustration for players and spectators alike (and, may I add, for the majority of referees too).

The engage command sequence must be changed, and there are two possible options:

1. **Retain crouch and touch, but delete the superfluous pause command.** The referee gives the engage command as soon as the props are seen to touch and then the final command is bind! Takes 2 to 3 seconds when crouch and touch are given together.

2. **Replace the commands completely with two simple ones: set and engage. Takes 2 seconds.**

The view that the scrum is just a way of restarting the game is a dangerous folly and one step away from the unedifying ridicule of totally uncontested scrums. Rugby league made the mistake of allowing its scrum to become a way of restarting the game and now it is a sad, inconsequential debacle and a pointless waste of everyone's time.

Our scrum is and should be sacrosanct, a massive part of rugby's very identity which defines the game. It must be a proper contest for the ball, not the foregone conclusion and penalty fest it has degenerated into.

The IRB owes it to real rugby enthusiasts to show vibrant initiative, authority and leadership in reestablishing our scrum to its proper function and identity. After all, by doing so, they will facilitate their own job and responsibilities for the administration, marketing and caretaking of our game.

Gaven Head

Level 3 Coach, ARU 1993-present; director of rugby, Sunnybank 2006-present; community rugby manager, Queensland Rugby Union 1994- 2005; consultant, ARU 2006; 20 years of coaching at national age, state, premier and 1st XV level.

The inevitability of law

One thing that I have learnt to accept as a rugby coach is that the current law and the associated application by referees are two variables which you are unlikely to change or influence in the context of a match or a season. I always approach my coaching with the following taxonomy.

1. **Law**

What is the current law and what is the range of action that it permits you to do?

2. **Environment**

What are the factors specific to your team, game or venue that make the situation unique?

3. **Tactic**

Based on 1 and 2 what is the most appropriate tactic?

4. **Technique**

What skills or techniques are required to execute the selected tactic?

5. **Coaching**

You then need to devise methods of teaching and training the skills.

6. **Application**

The players will apply both the techniques and the tactics in a game.

7. **Refereeing**

Referees will interpret your performance with respect to the law.

8. **Review**

The performance of your players and the interpretation of the referee will provide the feedback for your next coaching cycle.

The scrum law is one of the most prescriptive in the game which defines what you MUST do more so than the bounds within you must perform. It also claims to be based on safety. While this may be debatable as to whether it prescribes ultimate best practice with respect to potential injury, it is obvious that mutual compliance is a safer option than looser forms of management moving towards anarchy.

As such I have found that it is best to accept the inevitability of current law and its interpretation within the micro confines of a game or a season.

Law

With respect to the law there were two areas which the paper focuses heavily on:

» The engagement sequence
» The feed

The engagement sequence

With the recent increased interpretative policing of this area of the game by the referees, I have found it easier to adopt a strategy of compliance rather than look for a loophole. In doing this I took the concept to an extreme and was aided by the experience of my daughter in another sport.

At the time the interpretation for the engagement sequence in all levels of rugby was adopted, my daughter emerged a gifted freestyle swimming sprinter. Not knowing much about swimming I become a spectator at many meets, sometime paying significant money to travel to championships in remote venues for what might be a performance that would last less than 30 seconds.

At one of the first meets I watched a young swimmer break at the start. As the swimmer climbed from the pool they were met by the referee and removed from the event. There were tears and anguish and my immediate thought was of the time and money that had been spent, and the swimmer was effectively sent off for not complying with the officials' voice prompts.

At the same time I was coaching Brisbane State High School 1st XV. This team contained a number of players who would play Australian Schoolboys in the front row and forwards. I used the analogy of the swim start with these players to reduce our infringement turnovers at scrum time, and ensure that we maintained our competitive advantage by ensuring the scrum was set.

While the technique will vary, the base physical concept of the loaded swim dive is not too different to that of a front rower. The athlete should be in a balanced, stable position with their muscles mechanically and physically loaded.

As power relates heavily to speed, both athletes need a fast response as soon as they are commanded to do so by the relevant official. Front row players who try and engage early tend to not do so with speed and, therefore, power as it telegraphs their infringement. Any advantage of an early engagement is therefore minimised. I would prefer slower reaction speed but a faster, more powerful action that produces a more dominant response.

The lethargy I faced in rugby is that the players knew that their punishment for an early engagement was not as severe as that of the swimmer, so I altered this by focusing on it as a key performance indicator, and introducing intense training environments where they had to exhibit ultimate compliance to my engagement sequence calls (e.g., running penalties for noncompliance). Not only did this improve our engagement sequence, but it created a heightened awareness at engagement time that actually improved other elements of our scrum.

By introducing a zero tolerance environment we took the referee out of the game. It is interesting that I have coached some of these players at club level now after they have returned from super rugby and ARU U20 teams, and the lack of focus has seen them revert to a far less focused mindset at engagement time.

The feed

I witnessed one of the most amazing things with respect to the feed at the SANZAR forum in Perth that preceded the 2000 Super 12 season. The IRB referee training manager had explained that the referees would be policing the put-in to the scrum. The culture at the time was that rugby was becoming entertainment more than a game and the coaches had introduced a concept that was plotted in a quadrant map. The argument was that we should be penalising negative play rather than Illegal play. The coaches argued that crooked scrum feeds were positive illegal, and their acceptance allowed them to concentrate on more important areas of the game as straight feeds would encourage more scrum contests and, therefore, more time would need to be spent on scrummaging.

Positive Legal	Positive Illegal
Negative Legal	Negative Illegal

The referees were accepting of this and it was only the late arrival of the IRB referee assessors who altered their opinion when they informed them that while they might be appointed to super 12 fixtures they would not be considered for test matches if they did not police the scrum feed.

Another issue on the scrum feed is that in my experience in hooking, a straight feed provided me with a consistent environment in which I could strike for the ball. I found it very frustrating when a scrum half fed the ball crooked, thinking he was helping me, and I missed my heel. The ball might lie still in the scrum rather than be effectively channelled, and this would result in me as the hooker or one of the locks having to lift their foot and compromise their body shape to move the ball.

This would compromise the rigidity of our scrum making us vulnerable to be pushed or wheeled. While loss of possession is an option, it was the effect on the quality of possession that was most noted.

Tactic

The concept of tactic in the scrum is something that it is very hard to teach or communicate. I agree with the comments of Ewen McKenzie that if you have never been in the front row your opinion really lacks authority. I think that referees are currently looking for random markers to penalise the scrum, rather than really understanding what has happened. I also agree with the comments that it is not a preferred option to collapse a scrum. It is an escape or a release from pressure and, ultimately, someone is responsible for a poor or illegal tactic or technique.

One of the great things about scrums is that it is a Paper-Scissors-Rock environment. No one tactic or technique is all dominating. While the mass of the packs has always been critical, it has become more important now that the scrum engagement is so heavily policed and there is less leeway in the alignment of weight across the front row. As someone who was not a large player, I am not sure this is a good thing and it is one of the reasons why uncontested scrums have become a key tactic for coaches in lower grade and junior rugby.

Scrum engineering

The comments on the structure of the scrum are interesting and require contextual clarification. The scrum is a combined eight; however, there is a tendency for people to hide within that eight.

I have a belief that if the scrum is to be square, stable, strong and synchronised, it requires all players to be performing as an individual as part of a unit. By breaking the scrum down in a training environment it focuses on the individual performance of each player. One of the key areas is stability. I find that many players lean on other players in the scrum and, as such, they are neither stable nor strong. They also require other players to push back to hold their weight which reduces their efficiencies in loading to elicit a powerful engaging force.

One of the critical areas for this is the locks and is covered in the book.

» Should a lock's primary binding relationship be with their prop or the other lock?
» Should we use a hip or a crotch bind?

You can achieve using either strategy as long as the player is square, stable, strong and synchronised.

Front row binding on the opposition

After body shape and foot positioning are set up, the bind on the opposition's prop is one of the most important requirements.

If you were to fight someone you would use your grip to fix or shift their body position to give you an advantage. As such, getting your grip first and getting a dominant grip are critical to ensure you can apply a force and that they cannot escape.

Too many props think that these grips are merely a compliance with law for the neatness of the scrum and place little strategy or focus on this. The bind is the only weapon a smaller prop has to defeat a larger prop within the sanitized law environment we currently have.

This is another reason why I do split my scrum for training. It creates a competitive environment for players of equal ability where my loose head and tight head can practice their engagement and bind in a competitive environment. It is easy to get a bind on a scrum machine or on the second team prop, but the combative and competitive nature of the front row is perfectly suited to matching your own tight head and loose head for mutual gain at training.

Clustering

The scrum is an eight, but I actually believe that if everyone is performing optimally as a unit it can have the strength of 12. I only break or cluster the scrum at training to ensure each element can perform at its ultimate level.

Outside foot

I like the comments on the outside foot and I think that there needs to be more work done on the footwork related to how a scrum moves.

Like with like

I think that this is extremely important. Again I could offer more from personal playing and coaching experience, however, there is no debating that there is little correlation between the culture and dynamics of a scrum at the highest levels of the game and that which exists even at Premier club level, not to mention school or junior rugby.

This opens a large range of issues and arguments as to how we develop scrummaging players and how we maintain the scrum as a core identity within the game at all levels. I am not sure how we achieve this but I am pretty sure we are not doing it credit at the moment.

Peter Horton

19 Wallaby Caps 1974-79; senior lecturer at James Cook University and Fellow of the Cairns Institute.

If you can achieve any sanity in this matter we will all benefit. I have some initial bilious comments to make before I actually get to read the tome which, strangely, is not dissimilar to documents that such people as Phil Keith-Roach wrote a century ago.

Apart from the biomechanical analysis, which is in many ways a basis for all coaches to gain some cynical advantage or other and will always cause unstable and at times negative approaches to our wonderful art, I have one or two issues that do not concern the players, but the referees and the laws.

Firstly, I am sick and tired of referees trying to instruct players as to their craft; they should have no role in coaching, instructing or warning. I think that they talk and discuss too much in all aspects of play. You never hear NFL refs calling players to get back on side, telling players the ball is out, or to get onside or to roll away. And certainly why should they say when the ball is out of scrums, lineouts or rucks and mauls, let alone have a discussion which is invariably conducted with either churlishness or, which is even more annoying, a sense of authority! And what about all this all good pals tone? It's nauseating.

As an aside, we did an experiment decades ago to prove to refs that they have not a clue as to who is at fault in a collapsing or popping scrum. I think it was about 80% of their calls that were incorrect! Also I think their increased engagement has turned the players' brains off, leading to self-restraint and control being taken out of the players' hands and minds!

Why should the refs warn a player he is infringing or tell a player not to continue to do something, such as detaching his shoulder from a scrum?

All the ref has to do is see it and penalise it.

I am not sure what you mean by protocols if you are talking about general administrative lines of communication with the IRB. If it is the protocol of the scrum assembly it is that protocol that is at base of all the nightmares!

The four calls, which are inevitable, are utterly different not only from ref to ref (which is very apparent), but from game to game and at times scrum to scrum, which is a major problem. Simplify the whole entry process, and make it consistent!

I have been thinking about the possibility of standing the scrum closer, hands to be placed on the opponent's shoulder, crouching (not as low, perhaps 60 degrees, with head high) and packing, maintaining the hand on the opponent's shoulder on contact. The calls could simply be crouch and pack and entry would be closer—and higher—with a more stable position upon contact.

Pet scrum issues

1. An essential issue is that we should not repack won-scrums; the logic defeats me here, just clear the ball! Why should we pack another scrum in which the odds of an injury are increased? Obviously, if it is an absolute fight with no chance of the ball emerging, that is another issue, as is the excessive refereeing of wheeling scrums!

    As you suggest, a maximum of three attempts to pack a single scrum then a free-tap kick with no direct kicking within at least three passes would be an interesting notion.

2. Another absolute necessity is that we have an utter commitment to have all forwards actually packing before contact and no off-setting of the No. 8.

3. Defending half backs should stand behind their scrums and not be able to advance: the high levels of interference cause so much stuffed delivery at the No. 8. This idea did actually work in U19s or some junior age years ago. Why should they have such access?

4. The refs MUST police the scrum feed, which should go down the centre of the tunnel. That way the hookers actually have to strike! (I see Colin Deans agrees with me here.) A novel idea I know, but I really think this does add to the destabilisation of the scrum by adding to the loads. It might mean we see some contests!

5. Take the refs out of the scrum technology debates and stop with all their, at times, puerile and uninformed prattle. Also, have we actually ever seen a touch judge (assistant referee) get a scrum call right? I will not mention the abomination of the rolling maul that cannot be stopped by tackling the leading player.

You will have dealt with some of these no doubt but I think these things should be considered. I have not read your treatise, the use of this word will no doubt confront all the heavies. Such people tend to hate being shown their inadequacies! Remember anti-intellectualism rules!

However, looking at it with an editor's eye it looks very impressive—another reason it might be received negatively! Bravo, I will now look at it more deeply.

Jake Howard

Wallaby prop 1969-1973; Wallaby forward and scrum coach 1990-1993, 1996-1997; 1991 World Cup winners.

I thought of reiterating a few points on some key factors for your thesis. You have already covered everything and more.

GENERAL PRINCIPLES
» Hooker and props have to work with referee
» Hooker should be in control of scrum
» Front row has to work as one unit

» No passive scrums
» Middle four are the engine of scrum, flankers and locks
» Most powerful flanker and lock on the tight head side
» Shoulders must be on for the engagement
» Have to put each prop in a strong safe position
» The loose head shouldn't put too much weight on the inside foot as this will force him to rebalance later on

Other points
» Everyone must understand their job and role in scrum.
» Don't respond to disruptive opponents.
» Avoid resets as penalties can occur.
» Don't be tentative, engage on call from referee.
» Chase your feet as you go forward.
» Always be mindful of the scrum role within the framework of attack and defence of the entire team.

Philip Keith-Roach
Scrum coach to the winning England 2003 Rugby World Cup side.

Topo has done an amazing job on his scrummaging thesis; he's also brought together such a remarkable bunch of people who all want to see the scrum playing its full and constructive role in the game and at the same time protecting the interests of the players—a great contest but a safe one as far as possible.

At the moment the scrum is often a blight on the game and dangerous as well. What are euphemistically referred to as repeated resets are often the result of repeated collapses. Collapsing scrums hold untold, unquantifiable danger. Collapse has become almost accepted as if it's unavoidable—an extraordinary state of affairs. The IRB must act. The scrum has morphed into something it was never meant to be and it's so straightforward to fix. The IRB's continued inaction and lack of logic make them look incompetent.

The law book already holds most of the clues to the way forward. We need to marry up the best of the old with the best of the new. Coaches and players have to do whatever it takes to adapt to current practices.

The amount of collective force top scrums now deliver is absolutely staggering, as is their efficiency, technique and training. So when two well-trained outfits collide the forces are absolutely extraordinary. However, it is the IRB that has the responsibility to set out what those practices should be.

The scrum is meant to be a two-part process. The ref makes a mark. The scrum is engaged and the front rows come together and bind up on the mark. Once the ref has ensured that the scrum is stationary on the mark square to the touchline, and the front rows are correctly bound to the opposition, only then should he allow or instruct the No. 9 to put the ball in and the pushing contest plus hooking contest to begin.

Currently there are two laws which seem to cause confusion. One says the scrum must be square and stationary before the ball can be put in. Unfortunately the other says that the put-in must occur immediately once the front rows come together. It's that law that's causing the chaos and means both teams load up for maximum power on engagement. This leads to massive forces as scrums smash into each other to win the hit, win the scrum.

The result is instability; the scrum moving off the mark; collapse, etc. So much is focused on the hit—too much! What to do? Cross out the law which says to put in immediately when the front rows come together.

If the IRB takes away that part of the law, they instantly take away the incentive to focus on the hit. If the forwards know there will be no put-in until the scrum is square, stationary and on the mark, and the law book already states that "neither team can push the scrum away from the mark until ball is put in," then there is no longer an incentive to smash into the hit.

In fact, there's now a real disincentive to do so. The referee makes a mark; the scrums bind up as two packs of eight on either side of the mark; referee gives the command, "Crouch and hold" and once both front rows are fully crouched, the referee says, "Engage."

The front rows come together over the mark. The referee checks that the scrum is stationary, correctly bound, etc.; then, and only then, does he instruct the No. 9 to put the ball in. The contest starts with the put-in and with the scrum set square and stationary. The referee can now judge the put-in so much more easily. The result is that collapse on engagement will fall to zero.

A great pushing contest just started when the scrum is correctly set and as the ball is put in, hooking will come back into focus. What's not to like about that? Even parents and medics will have their worst fears allayed, and it's so much easier for the referee. He or she has time and process on his side.

Malcolm Lewis

January 2010, Cardiff Society of Welsh Rugby Union Referees; worked for the Welsh Rugby Union for nearly 18 years, first with Ray Williams and then with John Dawes.

Statement

For some time the scrum has been an unsatisfactory part of the game and the recent changes to law 20.1(g) with the formation of the scrum have made things worse.

Law 20.1(g)

The referee will call crouch then touch. The front rows crouch and, using their outside arm, each prop touches the point of the opposing prop's outside shoulder. The props then withdraw their arms. The referee will then call pause. Following a pause the referee will then call engage. The front rows may then engage. The engage call is not a command but an indication that the front rows may come together when ready.

Sanction

Free Kick

Reasons

Management of the scrum is generally poor and inconsistent. This is mainly due to the inconsistency of referees within games and between referees, making it extremely difficult for players and coaches. There is inconsistency in the management of each scrum which then has had an overall effect on scrums throughout the game. Players are confused and hesitant in their actions as to how the referee is going to approach each scrum. This inevitably leads to resets, illegalities and time wasting.

The recent changes to law 20.1(g) have added considerably to the time it takes for a scrum to take place. This, in turn, adds to ineffectual play when the ball in the scrum is technically still in play but no one is playing with it; adding frustration to spectators, players and coaches.

Referees are inconsistent in applying the new instructions. The major disparity is with the pause instruction and the decision then as to whether the engagement is early or correct. Players try then to guess when to hit (make contact) with the opposition. The hit has become important because the front rows, in making contact first, have a significant advantage in deciding where to put their head and shoulders and how and where to bind. Referees in allowing this give a major advantage to one side. However, as stated above referees are inconsistent in giving the relevant instruction causing unnecessary free kicks or penalties.

A major reason for this inconsistency is lack of knowledge in the technique of scrummaging or an attitude to ignore current laws. It does seem as if they are limited in the tactics of scrummaging and so just let things go.

The throwing-in at the scrum has become a nonentity. Very rarely is the ball thrown in straight and very rarely is it penalised. Very often the ball is thrown straight to the second row's feet giving a huge advantage to the throwing-in side. No longer do we have a contest between hookers. The defending side, in order to compete, has to resort to mainly illegalities.

This has been a problem for many years but, despite repeated attempts by the IRB directing referees to be stricter and rectify this, nothing has changed.

Overall I believe the increase in the amount of time taken up with scrums, together with the many unnecessary resets, has had a damaging effect on the game as a spectacle.

Suggested solutions

1. Two instructions:

(a) Crouch. When the referee is satisfied all players are in the correct position and ready he then gives the instruction.

(b) Engage. The engage instruction will only be given when the referee is ready, and that will depend on when he is satisfied both packs are ready. It will do away with any pattern of timing referees seem to have adopted particularly with touch-pause-engage. This will dramatically lessen the time taken up with scrums and do away with the sham of touch (players very rarely touch where they are supposed to—on the tip of the shoulder). Then there's a pause before the instruction to pause is given, making two pauses before engage which is totally unnecessary.

2. Referees, touch judges and assessors are to receive specialized instruction on scrummaging which is updated each year. They will go a long way to understanding the scrum if they know that front rows rely heavily on where they put their head and shoulders and how and where they bind. Much of the technique required for scrummaging has deteriorated. Due mainly to the changes in law and the fact that front rows very rarely if ever compete for the ball at the throw-in, front rows have not had to concentrate so much on the expertise of front row play.

This will ensure that there is a fair competition to win the ball and, the length of time taken for scrummaging is decreased dramatically.

3. Assessors are much stricter in their after-match briefing to referees. As this problem has been ongoing for such a long time assessors must share some of the blame. I have resisted the temptation to give technical answers to the problems because Topo has covered this area extremely efficiently in his treatise.

Although I could query some tactical appreciation of the scrum, it would appear nitpicking and would only be a personal view on tactics and technique.

Andy McIntyre

Prop, 38 Australian Caps; Australian Universities.

You are appealing to three different animals:

1. the front rower (and perhaps coach) who wants to get better
2. the administrators
3. the referees

I'm sure you appreciate that with a large proportion of the second two groups you need to make your message to them short and direct.

With respect to the finer details of the art of front row play I think you have done a great job. My comments include:

1. Introduce some flexibility into the techniques. As you know not all the rules apply to all players because of different shapes and combinations of players, and you can't be hard and fast on what is going to work. Players need to know that if one thing is not working then you try something else. Some things just don't work on all oppositions.

2. I used to change my position of grips on players according to my hooker and the opposition. There is no one size fits all.

3. Having the inside foot up in a shove did not always work for me at tight head. It really depended on my hooker and who I was playing against. If I had to change my grip or angle I quite often had to change my foot position to suit—a kind of priority of techniques was put in place and my foot position depended on the first two.

4. Don't assume these guys know stuff. A lot of information and knowledge has been lost over the last few years. Very basic stuff like the combination between the hooker and half is not a high priority. Many hookers have no signals anymore.

5. They need some explanation of why you use different channels, etc. That stuff is a mystery to them. Even back row moves are rare these days. They would rather just throw the ball to a guy standing off the edge of the ruck these days—painfully boring stuff that loses the crowds and slows the game down.

6. A discussion of what scrum you use and where you use it could be added. The basic Aussie or even Kiwi player has no idea about how the tactic, and the subtle way of screwing the scrum left or right at any particular part of the field, may give your backs an advantage or stuff up the opposition.

TOPO, all the very best in your pursuits and keep persevering because your chosen road is not an easy one.

Ray McLoughlin

40 Ireland Caps 1962-1975; 3 British Lions/Ireland Caps 1966-1971.

TOPO, I am responding to your email of 30 July 2011. It is good to connect with you. I have been an Australia enthusiast since I first visited there in 1966 and a keen follower of Australian rugby since I visited a coaching week in Sydney in 1977, at the invitation of Peter Crittle and Dick Marks.

As we both know, Dick spent close to 25 years overseeing the transformation of Australian rugby from an also-ran to a super power and, of course, a team of which you were a member won the Grand Slam in 1984 which was the first move into super power status. Dick has been telling me about *Rugby—The ART of SCRUMMAGING* and I have read the draft which Dick had available to him. It is indeed a formidable document, most impressive in its scope and detail and so much of it evokes so many memories of my playing days, now so long ago!

Rugby—The ART of SCRUMMAGING will make an excellent scrummaging manual for coaches, players and rugby aficionados. Once again, it was good to hear from you. And let me add congratulations on your invitation to the 2011 Oscar du Rugby!

Philip Orr

58 Ireland Caps, 1976- 1987; 1 British Lions/Ireland Cap.

Congratulations on putting together a first-class manual on the scrum, and also the excellent contributions from Dick Marks and Peter Fenton. So many of your comments echo my own views, it's uncanny. For example the text regarding the front row transmitting the shove and the back five generating the shove is what we have been preaching for years.

I cannot find fault with anything I read in *Rugby—The ART of SCRUMMAGING*. I have two additional comments which may already be mentioned but I'm not sure:

1. I fully endorse your comment that, when dealing with the front row assembly, props should maintain head up at all times. In addition, I have found when instructing young props that they are inclined to look in toward their hookers during assembly,

and even during the scrum. I always suggest to them that they should not look into the scrum but should concentrate on looking out, which has the effect of keeping their backside in and keeping their body straight to enable better transmission of the shove from the back five forwards.

2. I generally insist on having the team scrum half put the ball in at any scrummaging training session, and he is told to put the ball in so that it lands on the same spot in every scrum. Hookers must know exactly where the ball is going to land so that they can adjust their stroke, sweep, or strike accordingly and send the ball down channel 1, 2 or even 3.

However, this comment is totally irrelevant unless the law on the put-in is refereed as it is written (i.e., Law 20.6 (d): "The scrum half must throw the ball in straight along the middle line, so that it first touches the ground immediately beyond the width of the nearer prop's shoulders.").

Emilio Cesar Perasso

1956-70, played for Monte Grande RC, Pucara RC and San Isidro Club; 1966-present coach, manager, selector, administrator and educator; 2005 and 2006, president of the Argentine Rugby Union (UAR).

We all agree that in rugby, a scrum disputed cleanly, rigorously and openly, with due respect for the laws and the spirit of the game, is a necessary ingredient in contesting the possession of the ball which is the essence of the game and the scrum contest must not be devalued or dispensed with.

Rugby in 2011 lacks open spaces and the scrum is the only device which groups together 60% of the players in a reduced area, thereby proportionately producing spaces from which attacks can be launched. The way in which the scrum is currently being played is something that justifiably is worrying everybody and is the result of what has been happening for some years now.

The problem is based on consistently not respecting and not applying the laws. Whether some of them need modifying in either word or interpretation can be debated but, above everything else, the current situation reveals a lack of understanding, teaching and implementation of what the scrum represents in terms of both its philosophy and its technique. Over the last 40 years, I have personally participated in many workshops, lectures and talks where this problem has been analysed and, generally speaking, opinions have been universally shared but these initiatives have not gone beyond the rhetoric.

On rugby pitches and generally during practice and coaching sessions (which are then reflected in the games), I have not seen that accepted opinion being incorporated into the game. What we constantly see is players with enormous physiques, a lot of strength, very little technique, no disciplinary control and even little regard for fair play!

The scrum, in most cases, has ceased to be a contest between two packs and has turned into something like a street fight which generates scrum collapses, resets, repetitions and multiple law infringements.

In Argentina, we have an expression which says: "Como muestra solo hace falta un botón," which when translated means something like: "The proof is in the eating of the pudding." In this case, I think the proof is in sincerely answering a basic question: Is law 20.6 (which refers to how the scrum half should put the ball into the scrum) being applied? The answer is definitely no!

Now then, if we cannot implement this law (which perhaps is the easiest to carry out and to judge), how can we apply and judge all the other complex scrum laws. Many of these are not easy to understand and require a specialised knowledge not often available to referees who haven't participated in a scrum.

To finish up, in reply to the kind invitation to join Topo's excellent initiative, I would like to say that we are faced with a problem that, in some ways, is threatening the future of the game. With the IRB at the top of the list, everyone should give a quick and forceful response in order to rectify what might still be rectifiable.

Heinrich Rodgers

Former Blue Bull (120 Matches) and Springbok Prop (5 Tests Matches) 1984-1994.

I will refer to law changes which primarily have two very important functions:

» To improve the spectator value of rugby.
» To improve safety for players.

Have the new law changes succeeded in doing that?
The best way to determine the outcome of the law changes is to study IRB statistics since these changes took effect. Having played prop from the age of 7 up to international level retiring at age 32 allows me the arrogance of ignoring statistics. My opinion is based purely on experience and on observation.

Scrummaging perfection is attained by practising body position and timing for hours on end. The variation in the length of the engagement calls by different referees disrupts this perfection. A well-timed engagement by both packs could not possibly create injuries. One can understand that the lawmakers needed the two packs to engage in a controlled manner. Shortening the call to engage in order to get referees more or less to synchronise their timing might produce a better result.

One of the advantages of rugby as a team sport is that it accommodates different body types to participate on an equal footing.

The law that punishes the loose head prop whose elbow touches the ground first, does not consider the prop with superior upper body strength and who makes use of the short-arm technique when binding on the opposition. It is difficult for seasoned props to determine which of the two opposing props was at fault when a scrum collapses, let alone the tiny former back turned referee. To simply punish the loose head touching the ground first when a scrum collapses because of his short-arm binding technique is similar to punishing a taller player for a high tackle against a shorter player simply because of a difference in anatomy.

The direction the art of scrummaging is taking in South Africa. I do not have sufficient insight on the direction junior rugby is heading in other countries as far as the development of props is concerned, but I can give you my concerns regarding such development in my home country of South Africa.

South Africa enjoys the luxury of senior boys' schools rugby being played at a high standard. It is mainly from our top 20 schools where we see our future Springbok props emerge. These schools are all coached by highly qualified and skilled coaches. Amongst the rest of the schools, skilful coaches are scarce. This could possibly be attributed to fewer men of quality entering the teaching profession. In my definition of coaching skills, I also include interpersonal skills. It is expected of a good coach to build a man with character, instead of someone capable of playing rugby only.

The result of this scarcity of quality coaches is that the unskilled coach transforms the 18-year-old lock that has stopped growing (in height) into a prop, or the loose forward that has stopped growing at an earlier age into a hooker. The former loose forward normally has good ball skills.

His skills outside of the front row make him stand out and the unskilled coach deems himself a specialist in terms of talent identification.

The fact that the technique to survive in the front row is a skill which is honed over many years in the front row eludes the coach who is not aware of the specialised skills required to become a prop.

A mediocre prop, in terms of technique, is able to disguise himself in a good pack of forwards nine times out of ten. All he needs is a powerful lock and loose forward behind him and a good hooker and prop next to him. Good timing practised as a pack will improve the poor prop's abilities. He will be exposed though the moment he comes up against the prop who has honed his skills since early childhood, and who was allowed time to gain experience and to determine which techniques best match his specific body type.

Playing in this position from early childhood develops the core muscles needed to prop up a scrum, negating the need for law changes. Those changes more than likely were intended to cover the weaknesses in props because they were not given the correct coaching and training methods from an early age, or were moved from a different position too late in their careers. Heaven forbid the day comes when props are selected on their ball-handling skills or because they do 12 seconds on 100 metres dash without taking into consideration or ignoring their primary function, namely scrummaging and lineout support.

So, what will happen to the overweight 7-year-old to which rugby provides a supportive team appreciating what he brings to the sport (a solid scrumming platform)? We as former international props need to preserve what is important to us otherwise our trade is going to become extinct.

Peter Sloane

Front rower, North Auckland 1972-1983, All Blacks 1973-1979; coach for Super 12 Crusaders 1997-1998, All Blacks 1998-99, Highlanders 2000-01, NZ U21s World Champions 2000, Auckland Blues 2002-05, Northampton Saints UK 2006-07, Kintetsu Liners Japan 2008-11.

Keep it simple and safe

Rugby's biggest fan base sits in their home or bar lounges hoping their favourite team wins, and the more the ball is in play the more they enjoy the product like all stakeholders.

Coaches will tell you that scrum ball is the same as prime attacking ball, where 16 of the 30 players are in an area around 5m x 3m which means space for the backs to organise and utilise their skills.

Simplicity

1.   Pre-match

Referee reinforces to both front rows their responsibilities (e.g., ownership) and his (e.g., facilitator).

2.   Scrum

Referee marks spot and steps back.

3.   The call: crouch

Referee checks hips and shoulders and loose forwards all attached to scrum.

4.   Contact and pack

Let the contest be competitive and fair. Ball must go in straight.

When we listen to stakeholders around the world the game's Achilles' heel at present is the scrum. The work you and your support staff are doing on the scrum will help grow our game.

TOPO, good to see you have not lost your sense of humour.

Pieter De Villiers

Tight head prop, 69 Caps for France (1999- 2007); two Rugby World Cups.

I want to refer to the two paragraphs below that I copied out of your treatise, and give my opinion.

My experience is that the engage call has now became a command call as all players have realized that the quicker they get the hit, the more of a chance they stand to set their scrum. If the scrum is not set they do not have much chance of working together as a unit after that. It is exactly this reason that, therefore, makes your observation regarding the sprinter so true.

The scrum that gets to the hit zone first has a better chance to set. It is because of the small distance between two scrums in modern rugby that the speed out of the blocks has become such an important factor. I agree that after the hit the very important three dimensional work starts, but without a fast hit platform it will be in vain. The referee will call crouch then touch. The front rows crouch and, using their outside arm, each prop touches the point of the opposing prop's outside shoulder.

The props then withdraw their arms. The referee will then call pause. Following a pause the referee will then call engage. The front rows may then engage. The engage call is not a command but an indication that the front rows may come together when ready.

Nevertheless, I have seen in the last four years (since 2007) that this long, drawn out process creates a crescendo of anxiety in both packs that puts such a focus on the engagement that, when finally untethered, they crash in with nothing in mind other than the hit. It's not unlike the tension that bedevils sprinters as they wait to explode out of the blocks at the sound of the gun. All of the best.

Cobus Visagie

29 Springbok Caps; 1999 Player of the Year.

I tried to write most comments before reading the document to keep my view independent, but we are close in our assessment. Please see my following comments:

1. Most ignored rule

Until the ball leaves the scrum half's hands, the scrum must be stationary and the middle line must be parallel to the goal lines (or perpendicular to the touch lines). A team must not shove the scrum away from the mark before the ball is thrown in. The big hit-and-go scrums will be avoided if the referee always ensures that the scrum is stable and straight before put-in:

» No team can achieve an advantage on the hit.
» The contest starts only when the ball is put in.
» The process should be executed as quickly as possible.

2. What does the word prop mean?

I am sure it means they should prop it up. There is a tendency in the modern game for loose heads to put their left leg too far back to push, and they ignore their responsibility to keep the scrum up. I believe the law should require loose heads to keep their left foot forward to ensure they prop up the scrum.

Because the tight head will not be allowed to hit you out of position on the engage, the loose head's body position will not be compromised at the start. Loose heads are below the tight head and should always bear the biggest responsibility to keep up the scrum. The only exception is when a tight head throws his feet back to enable a collapse.

I played three years professionally until 2009. I did not change my technique by putting both legs back like all props do now, and my technique and scrum ability remained superior. I always believed that the only player to rival my scrum ability in the modern game was Carl Hayman; he had the perfect (modern) technique. However, every time (about six games) we played, we managed to dominate him. There were a number of reasons, but the essence was that I scrummaged in an old school front row that could still lift a tight head to the level needed to best handle him.

In the modern game the manipulation of height is completely ignored and the players know only how to scrum one dimensionally. All they know is to go hard and lower and that is why they struggle to make adjustments. If I had my right foot forward I could control the changing distance better. Because my weight was on the outside foot that was forward, I could change the position of my scrum leg that was back. As a single action I believe this is the best way to improve the scrum. Even in the 1995 World Cup you will see that the loose head props do not have their left feet very far back.

3. Angle of attack

The most basic rule of the scrum is to keep your shoulders above your hips, but this is never refereed. Michael Foley's only plan against me in his playing and coaching career was coaching his front row to hit me down until the referee forced everyone to scrum higher and limit the game to 50/50 penalties going both ways. I blame the Aussies for this mess when their scrum was weak in the 2000s.

4. Another aussie technique

This technique (which was shown to them by naughty Argies) is folding props in underneath the hooker. Although I agree that this is good technique to be tight, I believe it is against the spirit of the game and causes uncomfortable angles for players to scrum at. Everyone should be square and their shoulders out.

5. Put more pressure on the loose heads to bind first

If the loose head binds firmly and quickly and is not allowed to ever put his arm down, this will ensure that he works the scrum into the best possible position for not losing his bind or not having to put his hand on the ground.

6. Position of the referee

The refs should stand at the opposite side of the scrum from where the ball is put in, because:

(a) the real battle is on this side between the tight head (of the team in possession) and the opposite loose head;

(b) he needs to be there to ensure the scrum is stable after engagement and before the put-in;

(c) he should then insist that he sees the ball come in through the middle of the scrum; if not it's a free kick for a deliberate skew put-in.

7. Not refereeing the put in

This is one of the main reasons why scrums are collapsing at the rate they are. No one is trying to hook anymore and it is too low to do so. If the ball is put in only when the scrum is stable and if the ball is put into the middle, everyone would scrum higher and the scrum would be safer. Once the scrum is stable over the mark it should be a pushing contest and a striking contest and this ridiculous refereeing outside the law needs to be addressed.

(a) When a scrum is dominant and they keep the ball in, they are scrumming legally and straight. I now often see that referees tell the No. 8 to play the ball. Why? There is no such law; it is really pathetic and a technique used mostly by the southern hemisphere to de-power the scrum.

(b) Teams are an arm's length apart and the referees pull the teams even closer, thinking it will make it safer, issues which are covered in the treatise. The standing and crouching issue is a big one and, after testing this, I have determined that two teams can reach more than 2.5 meters if both teams crouch and lean and touch each other's shoulders.

(c) Referees don't know what the really important things are in the scrum, like a tight head folding a loose head in by binding on his arm. This is also a big issue as, with shoulders below, it is difficult for the loose head to get stability. The practice should be penalised. The loose head not binding and putting a hand on the ground gives him a major advantage and this practice should be penalised out of the game.

A major issue that is not being addressed is the alignment of front rows and what we call crabbing (i.e., when the tight head or hooker wants to be aligned more right to gain an advantage or vice versa). Referees don't know what the reason is and they tend not to stop the pack from moving. At the current short hit distance these issues become acute when one team gets away with them. I hope these comments help but I am sure I could do a lot more at a live session. I have great passion for the scrum which I believe is a vital part of today's rugby; on the other hand I'm saddened by the ignorance of so many people that are stuffing it up for different reasons.

TOPO, the work you are doing is fantastic, because it will initiate discussion to bring full attention to the simple remedies needed for the current ailments.

Jon White

24 Caps for Australia; Walk of Honour at the Sydney Cricket Ground; Wallaby Hall of Fame; Greatest Waratahs 125 years; Wallaby Team of the Century.

Thanks for including me in your expert collaborators' team. I have read the abridged edition of your scrum document which I found very interesting, and it's great to see ex-players making a practical contribution to help the future of the game and its law-making process. I'd like to mention a few points close to my heart, some of which you have already covered but not all. I totally agree with your seven law-making principles.

Problems

1. Both packs being so close together makes it next to impossible to get sufficient time and space to extend body and back (hence properly straightening), and adopt a safe and strong position. I daresay in many cases this is dangerous.

Proposed solution

(a) The referee orders a scrum;

(b) announces whose ball it is;

(c) marks the spot for scrum;

(d) then with no crouch–touch–pause-engage, the timing is left to the players.

2. These days the prop deemed unable to hold up the scrum gets penalised (the law clearly states no downward pressure). The question for lawmakers and law enforcers should be why is it so? Through the universal principle of action and reaction we can arrive at the conclusion; it is pretty obvious to me that the stronger man is doing the pulling down.

Proposed solution

Apply a short-arm penalty for most scrum-perceived infringements. Games should not be won or lost on scrum collapse as this encourages the stronger scrum to milk penalties.

3. You have already identified the problems of not putting in the ball fairly, and it's about time that referees policed and implemented the law with the same rigour as they do with the lineout.

4. I watched the 2011 Rugby World Cup in New Zealand with a lot of my friends, but invariably the whistle fest, as we call it, spoilt the spectacle. The common gripe is the abundance of scrum penalties to either team and for highly questionable reasons, which are usually wrong. I have spoken with many referees in my life, generally after games, and I feel that the referee who has not played in the front row has restricted knowledge of it and, in my opinion, is not qualified to adjudicate. The short-arm solution would go a long way to diminish collateral damage and it would assist by lessening the number of match results that are decided by referees' mistakes, whether these be a product of personal incompetence or of poor instructions.

I appreciate that your document is about scrummaging, but I wish one of your colleagues would carry out the same scrutiny of the breakdown where rucking has been downgraded almost to extinction. This has turned the contest for the tackle ball into a shambles. At the moment the scrum is the only vehicle by which backs can line up in even numbers with some sort of a blindside. This gives them real scope for attack, but they are no longer getting it from a ruck.

This not only forces the forwards to congregate, but it also has the capacity to give them a quick ball. The game needs the quick, clean recycling that the ruck provided. I suspect the ruck has been virtually eliminated because it was looking dangerous, but this could have been cleaned up with severe penalties for stomping or kicking. The scrum can also be restored to a quick safe part of the game, and I trust that your effort will prevent it from suffering the same fate as the ruck.

It may sound like I'm advocating for a return to the old days, not so! Any move that will cure today's grey and confusing areas of the law will be a big step in the right direction. The present day law book is far too long and cumbersome and, in my opinion, it should be reviewed, simplified and reduced as much as possible.

CHAPTER
13

The engagement sequence

THE ENGAGEMENT SEQUENCE

So why are there still collapses? Right from the first pages of this book I have said that the basis of the safety factor lies in the theme of togetherness and tightness, and that the lack of this compression leaves members of the scrum unit vulnerable. Many other contributing factors have been mentioned in previous chapters and even more by the expert collaborators at the end.

These include:

» Not throwing in the ball straight or soon enough

» The C-T-P-E being a poorly constructed sequence and the Crouch-Bind-Set (C-B-S) have their problems too.

» Front rows too close

» Too much emphasis on the power of the engagement

» Lacking togetherness and common purpose

» Poor grips between both front rows

» Poor grips in second rows and back rows

» Poor technique

» Skin-tight jumpers impeding early and secure grips for the whole pack

Crouch-touch-pause-engage is what I call a sequence of steps. Others choose to call it cadence and there are efforts worldwide to make the timing of this consistent and slow. This is to make the scrum entry more controlled, compact and safe. What is interesting is that in some games there are many collapses, and in some games there are none.

The question about why there are so many collapses in one game and so few in the next is more difficult to answer. Obviously the difference in the two packs would have to be a factor, but the referee also has something to do with it. A good manager will always get a better result than a computerized robot. Players respect and cooperate with 'the enabler'. I sympathise with referees because in some respects they are asked to get very involved in a part of play in which they have no experience. The laws also encourage them to make impossible judgements about things like intention and cause.

I cast my mind back 30 to 35 years ago and even looked at some video footage. Some teams actually used to morph the scrums together. The front rows joined even before the second rows had arrived.

The scrum was effectively built or constructed and the only job the referee had was to wait for it to be steady and instruct the ball to be fed; the engagement was much gentler and the push came after the ball was introduced in the middle. I don't reckon we are far off a revolution on this topic and we could do worse than just turn the clock back a bit and see if a better solution might lie in the past.

I am betting the players and referees would like it to be a bit simpler and self-regulated. I always say that less is more.

I should begin by saying that I can understand why the current law had to exist until the completion of the Rugby World Cup. In saying that, I also welcome the news that subsequent to that event, a review is in progress and I hope the many views expressed in this publication will assist in the reassessment. Now that the Crouch-Bind-Set (C-B-S) formula has had a fair trial we need to be proactively looking for better alternatives.

From what I can gather the change to the current crouch-touch-pause-engage law was driven by insurance assessors. It is a pity that more consultation with experienced scrummagers did not take place at the time because they would have forecast the eventual outcome of the law creating more problems than it solved, including safety ones. There may have been a small reduction in injuries since the C-B-S, but more particularly by the stopping of the charge/hit in August 2013. However, since then other problems have developed in this area. In my view the jury is still out and more intelligent, common sense solutions are needed.

To use a building analogy I get the distinct impression that we are preserving the facade of the building (the cosmetics) while neglecting and compromising the integrity of the main structure.

In any case I would take more notice of Phil Vickery than the statistics which differ only marginally. The new engagement sequence was introduced on safety grounds, but the recently retired England prop Phil Vickery believes it has actually made things more dangerous.

I think that the players and the spectators have always enjoyed the physical aspect of the scrum where brawn and brain are more or less equally represented. Nonetheless, it doesn't have to be or become a Roman circus where the victor kills the conquered for the pleasure of the crowd. The rugby flock wants a contest but not the one we have that continually holds up the game.

We have in recent years been experiencing a gradual intrusion of the referees' role into the technical minutiae of engagement and other intricacies. These are areas which should remain in the coach and players' territory. The referees' domain should and must be the law and discipline enforcement while enabling the continuity of the game to progress.

Since the start of professional rugby they have been required to produce an Aide Memoire which is nothing more than a set of laws outside the laws. These have resulted in the condoning of a lot of illegal practices which, in the past, have included lineout lifting and crooked scrum feeds, hands in the ruck, the concept of a gate, and the NFL practice of being allowed to bash out players that don't have the ball.

The other problem with high-performance referees is that no one is allowed to criticise them. No wonder the refs feel bulletproof! They have immunity and impunity! As highly paid professionals shouldn't they be criticised when they do a poor job? Furthermore, they need to understand and accept that as one of the stakeholders they are responsible for the protection of the whole game and not just the laws!

In the modern game, responsibility has shifted and widened as the volume of influential stakeholders has increased. It used to be just players, referees, administrators and spectators. Coaches were added universally not much more than 40 years ago, and when the game went professional in 1995 all the commercial stakeholders—broadcasters, sponsors, consultants, suppliers, insurers and so on—needed their say.

The game is now required to put on a show as part of the mass entertainment industry and, with its huge increase in turnover, the game has now become a business. Some of the niceties of the amateur game have disappeared but all the stakeholders have to face up to realities and contribute to the new order involving the game, the show and the business.

A scrum shouldn't take more than 15 seconds or so to complete. It is interesting that opposite views exist on this question of timing. I am all for the packs taking a little time to form up, but once that is done the engagement and the put-in should proceed without the delay that causes so much of the shenanigans and the instability.

Delays cause a buildup of unhealthy pressure. To give you one of the best graphic examples of what we are dealing with, power lifting and Olympic weight lifting are two very risky disciplines that have been practised for hundreds of years and they have some valid relationship to rugby scrummaging. Almost everybody involved in rugby knows that the scrum has the potential for risk, and that is why I emphasise the importance of preparation, the right technique and a positive attitude.

I have yet to see an Olympic champion weightlifter that stays under the bar any longer than the time they need to claim the lift. In the rugby scrum we have become accustomed to spending three, four or five times more than is necessary to accomplish our outcomes. This is not right because we are overusing time and energies that we are supposed to spend doing something else on the field. This fact annoys everybody including players, referees, coaches, administrators, spectators, television, media and sponsors. Neither the game nor the show nor the business is flowing!

Recommended risk reduction and time-saving solution

Here is a simple, practical yet very effective solution to reduce the time taken by repeated resets or collapses which invariably result in the annoyance of just about everyone. This is also an excellent way to prevent many potential unwanted injuries.

I'd like to propose that the lawmakers consider the following initiative and modification to the scrum law.

I strongly believe that limiting unnecessary resets would go long way to solve this part of the problem. **There shouldn't be more than two attempts to pack down a scrum.**

If two attempts do not produce a reasonable quality scrum (to referee's standards) then the ball should be awarded to the team not responsible for the original scrum. This ball mustn't be allowed to be kicked to touch or for goal until it has been passed or touched by three players of one team. This restriction is to avoid an unfair advantage, whether by territory gain (kick to touch), or points scoring (kick to goal) from this post-scrum phase.

This practical technical innovation to the law would substantially reduce the risk of injuries and improve safety by limiting repetitive engagements. During prolonged or extended scrummaging passages, players will more than likely lose concentration, fitness and endurance. My proposal is based on the assumption that there are down moments during the game when one or both packs become temporarily unable or are not fully competent to complete a scrum properly and within the parameters of the law. Repeated resets do increase risks of injury. This law modification aims at looking after the players at risk, without being detrimental to the team which wasn't responsible for the original stoppage and without affecting subsequent scrummaging.

Four-step engagement sequence

Detrimental and negative factors

» Too time consuming
» Difficult to synchronise with referee
» Too much guessing
» Mentally and physically taxing on players
» More steps allows more margin for error
» Weakens the scrum structure

1. In this sequence, the players' weight is cocked like a gun and players must be very careful not to jump the gun as it can affect safety and performance.

2. Unnecessary prolonged isometric contractions occur quite often in this longer sequence because of the timing variations with different referees. These contractions are fuelled and sustained by the brain, and they may provoke early fatigue, muscular cramps and even loss of balance when resetting scrums.

3. Excessive self-control and unnecessary energy are spent on the four phases where players have to be on alert without knowing the exact timing of the referee.

4. A pack instinctively and by training wants action. There is an expectation of the eight players to push and compete for territory and for the ball. This will help to dispel the well-entrenched misconception that the scrum is just to restart the game.

For the player, it feels like a cocked gun. Common sense would dictate that those steps would be done gradually in crescendo, reversing the times expressed above (e.g., set-up = 3 seconds; crouch= 2 seconds; engage). The duration of the engagement should be standardised so everybody knows exactly what's coming.

Newly proposed two-step engagement sequence

STOP PRESS: A ONE STEP "Silver Bullet" sequence solution will also be explained in Chapter 19, please read on.

The best call is simple and only needs two orders: one for preparation and another for execution.

Crouch — Pack

(a) PLAYER –MANAGED STAGES

1. Players arrive to the mark and get set.

2. Players take their positions and get ready.

3. The whole pack steadies up (e.g., the second and back rows have one knee on the ground).

(b) REFEREE-MANAGED STAGES

    1.   When the referee deems both packs are ready, he or she calls crouch and checks both sides and may even jog around the scrum to check both sides of the scrum (e.g., all knees off the ground).

    2.   Then, when scrum readiness is achieved and all is steady, a monosyllabic action call follows:

» Both packs must be stable, straight, square and controlled.
» This will bring both packs together coming from a stationary position.
» Time between crouch and pack will be at the referee's discretion, but it is understood that it shouldn't be too long.
» The ball must be fed in straight through the tunnel.

REAL AND TANGIBLE HOLISTIC BENEFITS:

» Time-efficient and effective
» Easier to synchronise and referee
» Less strenuous on players and more definite
» Fewer steps results in less margin for error
» Responsible approach
» Safer
» No guess work
» Standardised
» Uniformed

This new two-step sequence reduces and alleviates players from prolonged isometric contractions which could easily lead to imbalance and earlier muscle exhaustion (i.e., cramps). Time between crouch and pack will be at the referee's discretion, but both packs must be stable, straight and controlled.

On engagement there will be a quick adjustment from both packs to achieve maximum balance, but in this day and age of power scrums, I have no doubt that the referee is in the best position to assess safety and scrum readiness of both packs and decide when the ball must go in.

Nonetheless, play must resume as quickly as possible and without delays. This last point is for the benefit of everyone involved, including the stakeholders.

My sixteen-step solution explained

1. Both packs arrive without delay at the mark. Both front rows set themselves at a distance of approximately 1 metre (100 cm) from each other (feet position distance).

2. Front rows assemble and remain tight in a standing position!

3. Second rowers must join together first, place outside knee on the ground and join the front row.

4. Back rows take their position without pushing.

5. All eight players must be tight and bound to the player(s) closest to him or her. Players are responsible for keeping both packs steady and ready.

6. Referee stays clear of the front rows' tunnel and observes the players getting in scrum readiness mode.

7. Referee will give an audio-visual signal when he or she considers all players to be ready. Both arms and hands out and followed by a decisive command calling, "Crouch." The audio-visual signal is extremely important because the second row more often than not is unable to hear the call.

8. Players maintain steady foot positions with bodies tight to each other. The front row has hands at shoulder height ready to bind properly on the opposition props' jumpers, heads up, eyes looking at the point of contact and where the head will fit, and all backs always parallel to the ground.

9. Referee takes the necessary time until totally satisfied that the 16 players are settled in scrum readiness mode.

10. The best indicators of scrum readiness mode for the referee will be:

    (a) Front row: Backs straight and parallel to the ground before engagement.

    (b) Back five: Connected to the front row and ready to set themselves with back parallel to the ground at the moment of engagement.

    (c) Second row: Outside knee on the ground, inside arm bound to each other, outside arm bound onto the front row (round the hips or through the crotch).

(d) Flankers parallel to touch line and tightly connected with shoulder to their prop's gluteus and body leaning onto their second row.

(e) No heads to pop up in the tight five or back row.

(f) No heads dropped towards the ground (a steady gaze frontwards is mandatory).

(g) The three back rowers are tucked in well with the second row.

(h) A positive attitude is evident in the scrum when all are disciplined, wanting to play on, and are ready together as they wait for the corresponding calls.

11. Both packs are responsible for remaining in a steady and ready position.

12. Referee, when satisfied with the scrum readiness, will again give an audio-visual signal this time lowering both arms (as in a racing start flag) and simultaneously calling "Pack" (an instruction to be executed immediately).

N.B. A short monosyllabic and positive command like pack is much better than engage and is a must here.

13. It is mandatory that both props bind on the back or flank of the opposite prop's jumper. The tight head must allow the loose head to do it first, and then the tight head completes the engagement by binding last.

14. Referee must check before the match that the jumpers of at least the tight five are made from an appropriate, substantial, non-slippery fabric (20/80% polycotton).

15. Both packs are to engage vigorously but without excessive charging or diving at the opposition. Referee will penalise any charging, overaggressive, dangerous or unsporting behaviour. Pushing will commence when the ball leaves the scrum half's hands and not before.

16. REFEREE gives a visual signal to the half back (no voice). The ball must be introduced straight in the middle of the channel at an even medium pace (i.e., not too slow, not too fast) to create an opportunity to contest the ball as fairly as possible for both sides. In any case, the put-in side will still have a slight physical advantage (20 to 25 cm closer to the ball).

(a) The referee should have the discretion to determine whether there is dangerous play or not and penalise accordingly.

(b) It's up to the coach to devise tactics and to prioritise energy expenditure over the various scrum stages (i.e., setting up, engaging, obtaining the ball or pushing after the put-in), but the current law puts some constraints on the options.

Law 20.1 outlaws pushing away from the mark before the ball is put in.

In (h) it says: "A crouched position is the extension of the normal stance by bending the knees sufficiently to move into the engagement without a charge"

In (j): "Charging: A front row must not form at a distance from its opponents and rush against them. This is dangerous play. Sanction: Penalty kick"

The problem with these laws is that they are about charging. This involves a forward rush which can't happen when the pack is restricted by having to form so close together (impossibly close as you will see elsewhere).

The reality is that you can generate enormous power launching from the crouched position. How do you think weightlifters can push 260 kgs above their heads? So a powerful hit isn't banned, only the action that moves the scrum away from the mark before the put-in is banned. With both sides uncoiling with forward acceleration this movement off the mark doesn't always happen but, in most scrums, the superior power of one hitter does move the scrum away from the mark, so the big hit definitely does cause illegalities.

If you want to eliminate the hit moving the scrum off the mark, then law 20 (g) has to say: "The front rows may then engage with a slow motion."

That sounds very quaint but I've learnt one thing: quaint laws and conventions often work very well.

One may well ask, "What is a slow motion?" It is the opposite of a fast motion which is similar to the term used in 20.6 (c): "The scrum half must throw in the ball at a quick speed..."

Specific mention of the slow motion would be sufficient for a referee to know when a front row is going beyond the hit (i.e., using excessive force). You can't get rid of the hit; you can only reduce the power in the clash.

It is easy to forget that there are psychological factors involved in the four-step sequence which, in my opinion, must generate player anxiety and frustration. This translates into a degree of negativity that may or may not be reflected when both front rows clash.

It is fair to conclude that excessive aggression may come from excessive frustration, thereby turning the hit into some form of release valve.

» I agree that the front rows' shirts should be conducive to easy binding and made from the recommended 80% cotton, 20% polyester fabric, or something similar. Swimming, with all the controversy surrounding the move, made changes to its costumes, and the change proposed for rugby is much smaller. As far as I'm concerned, this modification is non-negotiable and would be cheap and easy to implement.

» Binding on the arm is illegal per se, so I guess it's wise for the referee to vary his position on both sides of the scrum. The touch judge closest to the scrum could look at his side and the referee would take care of the inside. As an aside, props are required to remain bound until the scrum is finished, but a lot of them don't and are allowed to get away with it.

» Both tight head and loose head are subject to different and unique pressures. This is a technical aspect of the position, and the coaches are responsible for teaching sound and legal techniques which should fix the problem. The enabling role of the referee here is to enforce the law.

» One comment suggested that the lower scrummaging height might have something to do with the collapsing problem. It has always been the case that a counter to power scrummaging has always been to pack lower, but where power scrummaging didn't exist scrums tended to be 35 to 40 cms higher. That is not to say that the hooker didn't get very low, sometimes choosing to hook with the head, but the intense forces in the modern scrum have caused all high-performance scrums to get very low. This fundamentally changes the body position and forward thrust of the whole pack. Furthermore, sound technique becomes a very important factor in the low power scrums.

» There are many who lament the gradual disappearance of some skills from the game on the grounds that it reduces skill diversity and debars specialists in those areas.

From a purist's point of view, genuine and fair hooking contests are necessary if you believe that, in all contests, both teams should have a reasonable chance of victory. If there is a degree of uncertainty about possession, it will create more space and this would be a benefit to a game that is becoming more cramped due to competitiveness and the restrictive nature of the law. At the moment, both set plays in the lineout and scrum are far too predictable in terms of gaining possession.

I do understand that in many scrums both hookers may find it very difficult to get a foot off the ground due to the pressure and the low scrums. In the previous era there was less pressure, scrums packed higher, and a smaller and suppler type of hooker capable of striking like a snake was often selected. The crooked feed, nowadays allowed, does not encourage them to bother trying.

» It has been said to me that one way of taking some power out of the scrum is to allow back rowers to leave the scrum before the ball is out, which would have the added benefit of bringing back the creative moves we used to have.

I don't like the idea of having a third protected species in the team (i.e., backs, forwards and seagulls). The back row is loose enough already and we don't want to give those players more excuses not to push.

» It is my understanding that the IRB has commissioned a team comprised of Mike Cron (New Zealand), Ritchie Dixon (Scotland) and Brian O'Shea (Australia) for a two-year project at the University of Bath in England to study scrum forces and physics.

Funded by the International Rugby Board, the study will provide an in-depth analysis of the biomechanical forces among all positions in the scrum, using controlled live and scrum machine situations in order to identify better playing, coaching and refereeing techniques for this key facet of the game. Interestingly enough it doesn't mention lawmakers as a beneficiary of the research, but let's hope their inclusion is implied.

In the future it might be worthwhile undertaking neurological research to study the capabilities of referees and players in coping with the complexity of scrum law requirements imposed on both. It has to be recognised that some people have slow reflexes and if you disadvantage them too much, you are asking for trouble.

When comparing or considering rugby with other sports we must remember that rugby was always conceived as a participatory sport for a range of age groups, adding that players of all different shapes can and will be accommodated not only to play, but also to balance the team and the way the game is played. It has been evolving perhaps at a slower pace than other sports yet, since 1995 when it left the amateur ranks, rugby has had, and still has, a fair share of teething problems. It is still trying to find its own identity between the world of professionalism and the world of mass entertainment.

The fitness requirements for rugby players are quite complex, as every position has different demands. These include: speed, strength, flexibility, skill, supreme aerobic and anaerobic endurance, together with the mental powers of concentration and being able to deal with the unpredictability of the 80-minute game. Opposition, weather and referee are variables that the players need to adjust to as soon as possible as the game progresses.

Change doesn't always mean progress! The maligned engagement sequence of crouch-touch-pause-engage is the perfect example of what I'm talking about!

Nevertheless, sometimes significant progress can be achieved through small changes. When significant law changes are being contemplated it is imperative that they are trialled in a pilot program before implementation and full endorsement. I think that a number of alternatives should be trialled in the first year after the Rugby World Cup in a few carefully selected competitions, even if the IRB has to pay the unions involved to help with the experimentation. This is the only way to avoid the unintended consequences which sprang from the last set of scrum law changes.

I do not doubt the goodwill of all legislators because in this case their goal of increasing scrum safety is unquestionable. I have that same goal, but I think it is wise not to become too goal-oriented or we are in danger of missing the elephant in the room—the process. It is true that without a goal there is no process, but process-oriented people will strive and fight and move because they are looking to improve, even when a goal along the way has been reached. A partial goal has been attained in terms of achieving better injury statistics in scrums, but this comes at the cost of enjoyment and spectacle, so no one should rest on their laurels.

In August 2012 I've offered for consideration a 16-point plan, but this discussion about law has been a long and comprehensive one without arriving at any definitive conclusions. However, this was always the intention for this first step which has not gone beyond the counsel of my colleagues. As the responses roll in I believe we will see a clearer picture emerging for the future of the scrum.

Since 1996 when I started to write a very primitive scrum manual, now transformed with the help of some friends into *Rugby—The ART of SCRUMMAGING*, my aims have been to:

1. Ensure more safety for players by way of reducing the preventable risks.

2. Improve technique throughout the rugby world.

3. Acquire more scrummaging efficiency at less cost.

4. Dispel a number of common myths and hearsay that have been so common and create more awareness about the importance of this subject.

5. Assist coaches in becoming proficient in the art of scrummaging.

I feel have partially succeeded with the above objectives because a lot more people these days talk about it and have been talking about scrums and scrummaging.

Unfortunately and ironically an arcane law and official stubbornness have on the one hand helped me in that regard, yet on the other hand the lack of official support has made it all uphill and financially burdensome.

Let's now move into 2015 with some new nuances about scrummaging, more hope and more intensity. I promise some new ideas and a more liberal approach to expressing them.

With the help of MEYER & MEYER Sports, my new publisher, I really hope to reach many more countries, readers and rugby enthusiasts.

CHAPTER 14

TOPO's miscellaneous comments

TOPO'S MISCELLANEOUS COMMENTS

The degeneration of scrummaging since 2005

The engagement sequence of Crouch-Touch-Pause-Engage conceived by a group of referees in 2005 was, in my modest opinion, what started degenerating and affecting world scrummaging. The restrictive nature of this "staccato type" new ruling aimed at controlling the forces and restricting the competitiveness generated by 16 players down to the millimeter and millisecond. C-T-P-E was a convoluted sequence and a unilateral official decision that lacked several common sense principles. I firmly believe this approach became an over officious practice which had a detrimental effect in the scrum structure and its law. Even today we still endure some of those negative consequences.

In response, players and coaches developed other ways to channel their strength with additional tactics added to the legal moves. Hence the development of the hit, something that never existed in law books or scrummaging manuals. It was the over-compensation to being clamped down on by the referee who additionally had various interpretations; no referee would adopt the same timing of the engagement sequence which is absolutely ludicrous.

No sport in the world comes up with variations just 1 hour before the match, usually when the referee tells both captains and both forwards packs. Before the scrum law changes of August 2013 it was all about the brute force and intimidation of the bigger and more experienced packs.

With the new passive pre-bind engagement other over-compensation problems have appeared (e.g., now both front rows are in vulnerable and unsafe positions) and the gain is for the older, more experienced front rowers.

Hooking is an art on the brink of extinction, which doesn't bother me at all. In my view it is a contradiction in terms, because having 7 forwards pushing and 1 player on a different wavelength is not teamwork at all.

This new engagement sequence was strictly refereed for the first 12 months; the second 12 months, not so much. And now it's a dog's breakfast! Since 2012, I've been advocating for a two-step engagement with less complicated laws so to help the referees. Players also must take responsibility for the outcome and understand that when they muck up, they actually are increasing the risks of injuries which could be catastrophic.

Metaphorically speaking

Many times I've used a metaphor in trying to explain the function of the front row. The front row is like our parents: when we have them we don't notice it, but when they are not good or dead we feel very sorry indeed. The scrum is about all the players, not just the front row. Convincing the front rowers to push is the easiest job on earth. However, getting inside the minds of the back five is a full time job. Nonetheless, rugby is about the entire 80 minutes of rugby and not about the scrum only. Many people get pretty confused and misguided on this, particularly ex-front rowers. Coaches must allocate sufficient time to all main aspects of the game.

Rugby coaching is an artful job that requires a fine balance in combining men management and preparation time for ATTACK and DEFENSE. Also for TECHNIQUE, TACTICS, and STRATEGY. One of the keys to success resides in striking the ideal mix of time and energies invested throughout all the aspects of the game. And no less important in properly applying them during the match. Furthermore, there is no such thing as a "perfect game plan" so Captain and Coach need to be watchful and flexible in adapting to the variables (adversary, referee, and weather conditions).

Captains and their decision-making ability

The professional era (since 1995) has promoted large coaching and managing teams and as a consequence it has devalued and downplayed the important role of captains, vice captains and the team's decision-making powers.

I have no doubt that the people closest to the ball are the ones that are able see faster than anybody else the problems and the solutions developing during the match: first the players and the referees, second the coaches and third the officials.

Therefore, my ideal decision-making sequence would be as follows:

(a) See problems arising the earliest;

(b) Feel the opposition gathering momentum and ascendency in the match;

(c) Know whether players have had poor execution or have been nullified by the rival, or both;

(d) Make quick decisions; and

(e) Apply remedial action when and where needed whether tactical or strategic changes and adjustments

In conclusion, my view is that the coach's job is to equip and train players and captains on the up side and the down side of every single option and action. Once you know the likelihood of those different options occurring and the likelihood of consequences of those options and the benefits, then you can select what actions to take.

So, in a nutshell, coaching and parenting are very similar. The sooner our kids start making decisions by themselves, the better!

We certainly can and must provide them with the necessary intelligence, guidance and experience of years of practicing at life, which at times, like in rugby, can be a real minefield.

Yet, the selection and decision about what is to be applied and when resides purely and solely with the protagonists on the field. Of course pro coaches will climb down my throat for diminishing their jobs and responsibilities. In fact, I'm not diminishing it but enhancing it because results and outcomes are the ineluctable truth of performance.

TOPO

Scrums are hurting rugby

NZ Rugby Herald by Justin Marshall Followed by my comments (www.nzherald. co.nz) 21/03/2014

Here are five points made by Justin Marshall and followed by my comments following.

JM   1) Scrums are the big time wasters and the new interpretations of the laws have made it worse.

ETR: Clock stoppages in rugby are negligible. We tend to favour more continuity and currently, we don't have more than 5 minutes maximum of stoppages. The other irritating factor on this subject is the amount and extension of the TMO's referrals which are completely over-done.

One of my pet peeves and a source of distraction is when we see up to 10 people (e.g., ancillary staff, trainers carrying walkie-talkies, etc.) running around the players on the field while the play is on. This abnormality should be much more tightly controlled.

An average of 15 scrums per match at 1 minute per scrum would give you 15 minute of stoppages—of course I assume not every scrum will have to be reset but we need to start somewhere. I can take an educated guess that today TV appears to have more power than the IRB in regards to the length of the spectacle or show—an extra 15 minutes of satellite would be awfully expensive to justify.

I believe with the new physical and fitness demands on players at times they could be deemed unfit to sustain a full scrum. Therefore, I would suggest refs to reset it only once. If a scrum goes down a second time, then they should give a non-challengeable—tackles allowed after the 3rd pass—also to be a non-kickable tap ball—either to touch or posts—to the original put-in team. Thus, the ref limits a bad scrum to be set twice only.

JM 2) The defending scrum gets an advantage because it can manipulate the set piece wherever it wants.

ETR: This has always been the way, the only difference being that today everything has to be done almost at the turtle pace of the referee. The elimination of the initial hit, was a smart move by the IRB to stop the charge. What has followed around that directive has many flaws due to the lack of good understanding of the physics and biomechanics of the scrum, as well as players' attitude and competitive mentality. This has made the scrums ponderous, predictable and even more premeditated due to the slow forming process, here is where the defense has gained initiative!

There are two areas that have not been touched and need an urgent overhaul.

a) The scrum law needs to be brought into the 21st century, adapting to today's demands of a game-show-business format, referees and players (e.g., rugby is a much faster game than it was 30 years ago). This job needs to be done by professional lawmakers rather than referees or others.

b) The referees need to understand better their function as enablers of the game and not as managers, coaches, constable and referees; a clarification of their mind-set is needed. Refs are human and need less work or things to look for not more! More emphasis is needed to give priority to outcomes over process. Rugby is stuck in the minutiae of the 20th century.

JM 3) The manipulation of scrums by the opposition makes the ball stay in scrums for longer time,

ETR: With the new rules the non-put-in team, or defence, has some advantages due to the fact that the surprise factor has been eliminated from scrums. This is something those professional lawmakers need to have a good look at in order to maintain the team in position on the front foot.

JM 4) A good, dynamic No 8 used to be able to get off the back of the scrum and make a big impact.

ETR: The No 8 is used to getting in behind the opposition's back line and putting his team on the front foot. However, now that he doesn't have that stable launching pad, he can't have the same impact. More often than not he has to quickly feed it to the halfback or the No 9 scrambles away with it. This is one of the negative consequences of the new scrum laws. The No 8's game has been effectively nullified, making the defense in scrums so much easier.

Similar to points 2 and 3, the function of the No 8 has changed dramatically as things happen a lot slower and the demands to push in today's scrum are much greater. Thus he is no longer free to run. This also happens to the flankers. The consequence of all this is a slower ball and a slower game.

JM 5) As I've said, it's a clock-draining curse on the game. After all, it's a restart of play after an opposition error of some sort. If the new rules are working so well then why are we no longer seeing push-over tries? For me, it's simple - fix it or stop and restart the clock at scrums.

ETR: We all are suffering with this problem, and this is what encourages people to join other, more accommodating sports. I encourage you to continue voicing your opinion, those of your peers and those of regular Joe Blogs until something is done.

The new scrum laws have switched the concentration, attitude and strength from before the ball put-in (the previous hit) to after the ball goes in. This is what, by law, used to happen back in 2005 when the IRB asked referees to fix the problem. The new sequence, crouch-touch-pause-engage, was concocted and introduced, completely disrupting the engagement sequence that at the time was somewhat working.

The symptoms we see and have experienced in the past are none other than the reaction and frustration of super-fit players that are not allowed to channel their competitive spirit, physical prowess and winning attitude, all of which are the product of preparing to and playing rugby at their most competitive level possible. If you clamp down a player with laws, both the coach and the player will look for and find a way out or a way to explode to achieve advantage over the opposition.

These new scrum laws are on trial until August 2014 when they will be either ratified or rejected, so this is not fait accompli. Yet, knowing how the IRB operates, I'd say they will accept these changes because:

i) they have followed all the steps for law modifications by the self-imposed rules, and

ii) being bureaucrats as they are, they generally are disinclined to pay attention to other outcomes or public opinion.

Best regards,
ETR

Rugby referees' verbals: To be or not to be (08/02/2014)
Sport - NZ Herald News - **www.nzherald.co.nz**

Good initiative by the IRB in stopping referees' verbals and improving the scrum law! Now that authorities are mindful of these irritating interferences by the referees, they should continue eliminating all verbals during play.

Referees are flat-out ensuring and enabling the game to go on seamlessly! Thus, referees should not talk to the players because when they do, they are also letting the opposition know what is happening and what they see with their referees' eyes. Knowing about what the opposition is doing, whether legally or illegally, is an unfair advantage!

Refs must go back to the days of refereeing and enabling the game, not interfering or controlling with the tactics of the game. These days referees have got into managing the game and talking technique and tactics which should remain the domain of coaches and players. If something is not right, referees are the judges, and should therefore penalise the culprit and continue the game. No lectures, please! Rugby is a simple game, sometimes complicated by its laws and its officials. The removal of the yes, nine call to feed the scrum and its replacement with a silent signal between halfback and referee is getting approval, a step which shows promise.

ETR: I just go for no call from referees! Leave the player to work out when? When is a tactical decision foreign to referees!

Yes nine (9), put it in now scrum call to be axed by irb
07/01/2014
http://www.espnscrum.com/scrum/rugby/story/210459.html

The next thing to be seriously reviewed and scrapped is all the referees' verbal interference during play. Refs must not to talk to any of the players when the game is being played. On stoppages the referees may choose to address either or both captains by shirt number, "Captain" or "Sir."

Any other types of intervention are unacceptable and break down the discipline and figure of authority of the referees. Referees must not manage, coach or police. They are the rightfully chosen and educated enablers of the game and their attitude has got to change!

TOPO

"Richard Cockerill and premiership coaches are wrong, Irb's scrum moves are vital for the future of the game. By Brian Moore (04/09/2012)"
SCRUMS.....complex SCRUMS! - The Law - Problems and Solutions!

http://www.telegraph.co.uk/sport/rugbyunion/10284039/Richard-Cockerill-and-Premiership-coaches-are-wrong-IRBs-scrum-moves-are-vital-for-the-future-of-the-game.html#disqus_thread

The International Rugby Board has acted to address disaffection amongst the majority of rugby people with the elite-level scrum, a blight which has started to affect other levels of rugby and which, if left unaddressed will poison the entire game.

Hi Brian,

We have met once at the ex-players bar in Twickenham with our common good friend Jeff Probyn last November when Australia beat England (I'm not rubbing in anything, that was the fact). However you and I have played just about the same amount of international rugby so we both have contributed to up keeping the game into a good standard from our respective positions. We have a lot more in common than two people that meet for first time in a bar as we did.

A day before Easter 2013 the BBC Radio 5 Live put together a program about the scrum conducted by Eleanour Oldroyd, interviewing a large group of about 10 scrum experts. You were in studio with Phil Vickery, Phil Keith-Roach, John Jeffrey, Mike Cron, Nigel Owens, myself and others who were interviewed by phone about these changes that have now taken place. In the subtitle you mentioned: "DISAFFECTION AMONGST MAJORITY OF RUGBY PEOPLE WITH ELITE-LEVEL SCRUM."

I think it could be useful to ask ourselves why this is so.

(a) It has taken an inordinate amount of time for the IRB to fix this problem which started around 2003-2004. You may remember Ben Darwin suffering a spinal accident in the semi-final against NZ where Kees Meuws increased his estimation 1000 fold within the rugby community because he stopped the pushing without hesitation and protected Ben from further damage. I'm sure this incident has been in the back of the minds of many IRB personnel and delegates.

(b) For approximately the last 10 years, we have had 3 trials with lots of errors. The outcomes have not been positive. In fact these failed attempts have weakened the scrum structure because many people tried to fix it domestically and without regard for the other competitors.

(c) Although I support the intervention of the IRB, I also encourage them to be more expedient and precise—including consultation at all levels—because in this particular case, it has not been so. I'm well aware that a dozen elite coaches get to express their opinions and work at it.

(d) You as a lawyer would appreciate that law-making is not a job for coaches, referees or insurance assessors.

BM: What has the IRB done? It has altered the engagement sequence to effect a 25% reduction in the force of impact on engagement. This minimises the dangers that were clearly identified during a comprehensive three-year study, but that is all that is new.

ETR: It is pertinent to mention that the hit was a pernicious and dangerous practice that grew out of the players' frustration with the appearance of the maligned sequence,

C-T-P-E, and the referees varying the timing between steps (something that should have never occurred).

BM: More importantly, the IRB has instructed all referees to strictly apply the existing scrum laws, as clearly shown in its notes to elite referees.

ETR: I'm in full favour of applying the existing scrum laws: scrum square; scrum stationary; and ball put in straight in the middle of the tunnel.

BM: All players and coaches have to do is use the slightly amended sequence and comply with existing laws—ones that work.

ETR: In my opinion, the slightly amended engagement sequence doesn't go far enough to extirpate this cancer. Two steps is the safest and most efficient option: crouch and pack. Less is more.

BM: Last month I addressed the IRB and its top 21 world referees to reiterate the importance of the existing laws which mandate a straight feed and no early shove.

ETR: I won't suggest for a second that the above IRB meeting was a PR exercise, yet by the tone of your article it appears you have been converted!

BM: Though there seemed genuine intent to correct previous omissions there was also palpable angst about the flak this would attract. The referees must remember that the IRB makes laws and players and coaches comply, not the other way round.

ETR: As I said above, neither players nor coaches nor referees should be anywhere near a professional law-making session. The scrum drawing in your article No 2 is incorrect; it must be reversed. The backs parallel to the ground (90 °) is a reflection of the previous engagement with both packs formed at arm's length apart. Today, with the new sequence there is no launching so the legs are extended and backs are in an upright position (135°). This is a significant increase in risk.

BM: They have widespread support when they are firm and consistent, and it will not be their fault if they continually have to penalise players who refuse to play within long-standing laws.

ETR: This is the function of the referee especially with particularly stubborn coaches and players.

BM: The IRB and all true rugby fans have to back them and refute the gibberish already being spoken about this crucial issue. If they bottle it or gradually tolerate illegalities they will get—and deserve—no sympathy.

ETR: If the IRB gets their consultation processes right, including PR exercises and keeping the rugby people informed, reducing secrecy will garner a much better response from the rugby followers.

BM: Richard Cockerill, the Leicester director of rugby, castigated the IRB for making changes without consulting Aviva Premiership coaches. He added, splenetically: "It seems that if you are a [radio or TV] commentator and you whinge long enough about it, the law makers will do something about it." I do not know who he is talking about, but I do know the coaches were asked to comment collectively, and indeed their own players commented through David Barnes of the Rugby Players Association.

Moreover, since when has he needed an invitation to comment on anything and why are their views special, particularly when only two played in the front row? Even assuming Richard could have managed a meeting with the IRB in between disciplinary hearings, his contribution would have mirrored his further words. "I am not bothered about crooked feeds," he said. "You have a whole generation of hookers that have never hooked. It's a pushing contest, not a hooking contest."

ETR: Having read previous comments by Mr. Cockerill, it appears to me he needs to go to scrum school to straighten up a few facts and myths It is understood that a professional lawmaker would be equanimous, level tempered, objective and a professional devoted to detail.

On the other hand those coaches you have mentioned have only regard for themselves, their salary, their team and their club in that order. In other words, they lack objectivity!

BM: It would have been like asking an MP 10 years ago whether there was anything wrong with their expenses system. Rob Baxter, the head coach of Exeter, wrote a blog on this which is little more than a collection of non-sequiturs. He fears the de-powering of the scrum, claiming props such as Jason Leonard and Gareth Chilcott will disappear under the new laws, without appreciating that they played under the very laws he now criticises. Astonishingly, he avers: "These new engagement laws could just be the thin end of the wedge as we head towards a game where the scrum is simply a method for restarting play," before adding, "instead of depowering the scrum we should make it an even bigger contest."

ETR: Well, well, well, now I am very serious about the scrum school, and I'd like to be on the examination panel to see a few disjointed faces. Mr Baxter, what we should make bigger is the exit door! Let me just explain something very simple indeed: rugby 2013 is a combination of the game, the show and the business. You appear to know nothing about any of these ideas!

BM: The scrum is specifically defined as a means of restarting play; it is not meant to be the boring, dangerous penalty-fest it has become.

ETR: Not so! The law provides for what can and cannot be done, not how it is done. This is the tactical domain, decided by players and coaches. Not the law. Not the referee. Not the IRB. That tactical mix is a team's prerogative.

BM: When a team knock on or pass forward, the other side are supposed to have a good chance of getting the ball to play with, not face being penalised if they have a weaker scrum. Baxter, like Cockerill, accepts no responsibility for exploiting weak referees and coaching his players illegally to bind, shove, feed and not hook, when he writes: "For me this latest change to the engagement laws has almost been forced through by public demand, without commentators and supporters alike really appreciating the impact this could have on the game." They are joined by my old school colleague Jim Mallinder, the Northampton coach, in alleging that some sort of agenda is being pursued. Change has been forced because of the level of discontent, which they purposely refuse to recognise.

ETR: We need a bit of objectivity in this debate. This group of Premiership rugby coaches and the IRB have a big emotional issue in their hands. With objectivity we all need to look at the etiology of the problem. Many times conflicts and fights arise not so much because of what was said but because of the way in which it was said. The IRB has in recent times a poor record on law making.

BM: Personally I'm not against change and adaptation but we must remember that the unnecessary tinkering of the laws has lost faith and disenfranchised a lot of rugby followers. They had several attempts at re-skilling and we are still on trial and error? Recently you claimed in your column that this is the last chance we have to get the scrum right. I completely disagree because technically there are still a number of things that can be done to improve it. The fact that the IRB only listens to 12 or so coaches proves to me they have not exhausted the avenues. The agenda is simply to get the IRB to enforce its own laws; the likely impact is that the scrum is re-skilled, not de-powered. Those resisting change are already cynically playing the safety card; take note how this fraudulent line is pedalled in coming months.

ETR: From now on I will talk about scrum stigma because stigma is a euphemism for ignorance, hence the unfounded fears, scare mongering, etc.

BM: The Australian Rugby Club television show, Cockerill and Baxter, allege that enforcing the laws is dangerous because the striking hooker has to take his weight on his non-striking foot and is vulnerable when eight opposition players push against his seven colleagues. Yes. It is called hooking; the clue is in the name.

ETR: The TV comment was made by Phil Kearns, also a hooker, and I daresay you would have played against him a few times. It is quite funny to me that you mentioned the program and not the player. Conversely, I've never seen a heading say: The BBC is in favour of........

BM: If the claim is correct it must be the case that the greater the disparity in weight and power between packs, the greater the danger. At senior level you rarely get a vast imbalance in size and strength.

ETR: Yes, I agree that the new laws favour bigger packs! You cannot swipe across the board with such a generalization and eliminate the considerations for the safety factor (see alleged safety debate below). You got me confused by switching roles quite rapidly from prosecutor to defence lawyer and judge. Any exception to the rule could be catastrophic. Aren't we all here because of the safety aspect of the scrum?

BM: At lower levels there is often great disparity but no big increase in injuries—the claim is nonsense. This is the crucial point in this alleged safety debate—the full weight of the opposition shove cannot legally come until the ball leaves the scrum-half's hands and referees must make sure that it does not.

ETR: I am in full agreement with you here as per long standing law!

BM: If this is enforced, a hooker's strike takes literally one second and this hooking window allows weaker packs to get the ball away before being shoved off the ball. Now they say they know it is dangerous, are they still going to coach their players to shove early and illegally? Cockerill knows this is disingenuous because he had a long and illustrious career when the laws were applied.

ETR: There is still a greater opportunity for an equal team that pushes with 16 legs instead of 15. This actually increases the danger for the 6 front rowers. I insist that's the reason the referee is there—to penalize them off the park until they learn the correct way.

BM: He managed to strike without difficulty, usually against much bigger and more powerful opponents. Why, then, does he say this? It is because having to time a shove is much more difficult and not always successful as it may come too early and get penalised or too late, by which time the ball is out.

ETR: This is a team's tactical prerogative and as such the referee should not interfere with it.

BM: What he and coaches with powerful scrums want to maintain is their advantage, whereby dominant packs shove illegally on engagement and deny the opposition this crucial hooking window. The elite game could, if it wanted to, help us all by simply teaching players how to hook and scrummage within the laws.

ETR: They will be penalized accordingly and in the past were assisted by the law and the referee.

BM: It would not take long: they all start from the same point and they have all day to practice. That they are determined not to do it is evidenced by Cockerill's uncorroborated claim that "the hooking thing and debate about the feed ... are long gone." Really? When did this take place? When did rugby decide that one level of the game did not have to obey its laws?

ETR: I am in 100% agreement on this one. That's why we have the laws to govern and make the whole world uniform on scrums, and not just a small town hall edict.

BM: If they want this, they should have the courage to propose and persuade the IRB to pass different laws.

ETR: I believe there is an appropriate channel to put forward ideas about modifications and changes, though I can tell you it hasn't been the most accessible one.

BM: They should not seek to force the rest of the game to accept what they want through selfish disobedience. Make no mistake, this is the final battle for the union scrum; if the elite game deliberately sabotages this initiative, the scrum might as well be the same as in league.

ETR: Brian, I'm sorry, I completely disagree. I've already given several pointers here that can and should be addressed. We have not mentioned the referees' performances. Some are great, others average and others very poor.

I believe referees should be given more discretion to prioritise their rulings with outcomes over process and minutiae. They have to change their attitude and become enablers and judges instead of nit-picking constables. The figure of the referee should be elevated and no conversations or direct instructions to players should take place while the game is on only on stoppages should the ref address players and then captains only.

Happy Days! –
Enrique TOPO Rodríguez

2013.09.17 IRB must bring in 'mole' to dig game out of scrum mess.

http://www.independent.ie/sport/rugby/irb-must-bring-in-mole-to-dig-game-out-of-scrum-mess-29584627.html

By TONY WARD

Enrique Rodriguez is one of the front-row legends of World Rugby. Known as 'TOPO' (the Spanish for Mole), he was a scrum technician who played in all three front-row positions for Argentina and Australia in a test career that spanned from 1979-1987. He has spent 17 years researching and writing a thesis on *Rugby—The ART of SCRUMMAGING*.

This is a man who knows his front-row spuds, and here is his recent response to my views on scrummaging:

"I have authored a scrum thesis published in 2012, a full colour book that studies, analyses and proposes solutions to the problem that is the scrum. My book *Rugby—The ART of SCRUMMAGING* (www.talubooks.com) has the opinions of more than 30 expert collaborators (ex-international players and coaches), it proposes a two-step engagement sequence which will simplify this process and will add safety to the spine and neck of players involved.

"The crouch-touch-pause-engage sequence was devised by a bunch of referees doing the dirty work for the IRB who charged that bunch with the job!

"Now do you think I or Phil Vickery or Jeff Probyn or Colin Deans, OBE, or Phil Keith-Roach or any other former internationals or current experts were ever consulted by those law-making referees? Nope. Do you think anyone dared to ask us something about the technique and what it takes to complete a good scrum? Nope. Therefore, I can easily conclude they have picked and selected an inadequate, inept and ill-prepared group of individuals to carry out this important task that has been preoccupying the whole rugby world including players, coaches, referees, administrators, spectators, media supporters and sponsors.

The scrum won't get better to perform efficiently until

(a) the IRB address referees' roles and behavior;

(b) they bring the scrum laws into the 21st century by overhauling them;

(c) players and coaches are given more responsibility for the scrum process;

(d) referees stop talking to the players while the game is on and speak only to the two captains when needs be and the game is stopped;

(e) laws are simplified to make the job easier on referees.

"All of the above requires work, energy and money. Why don't we start tomorrow?"

When a former test player, who so clearly carries the stripes, who is so obviously passionate and willing to get involved but is not, then why not?

To those in power in Huguenot House, the name is Topo. He is offering no quick fix but his input, and that of so many other former specialists (think Paul Wallace , Des Fitzgerald, Phil Orr and Reggie Corrigan on this little island alone) will surely add immeasurably to the process in train.

I won't hold my breath but I'll watch this space with interest.

"Referees determined to revive the scrum"

Following an article by Graham Jenkins (04/09/2013) in ESPNScrum.com Link below:

http://www.espnscrum.com/premiership-2013-14/rugby/story/196807.html

Referees admitting that they are incorrect? May be we are entering into some culture change—I'd love that. However, I'm of the persuasion that it should not be left up to the refs to revive the scrum. The refs' job is to apply the law book! Most of the problems and modifications are technical and that's why it makes some sense when people say: "A referee that has not played in the front row has less chances of understanding all the nuances"!

The set piece is not a farce, but the personnel in charge of administering it and looking after it are! I believe the testing trials were not extensive enough and the protagonists of those trials were substandard and exhibited very poor technique.

As I recently told Brian Moore through an article that appeared in The Telegraph, contrary to his beliefs and public opinions, I'm certain that we have not exhausted all avenues in finding the needed solutions!

It is very easy to focus on the hit, the players, the coaches and other excuses as scapegoats for the many other important issues that went wrong and are not being addressed! I'd be happy to go in detail with the chairman of the Scrum Steering Group.

This is the best example of how wrong things are. In my 42 years of rugby I know by heart that the supreme entity in control is the law and we human beings are the servants of it. Now we hear the referees have taken control of the situation? They are the group of rugby people that has been tinkering with the scrum engagement for good part of 10 years.

From the brilliant C-T-P-E to C-T-E to C-B-S! If you need to change the law 3 times in 10 years, this means you never got it down pat. Coaches dread having to drop players too quickly because the sword of Damocles is hanging over their heads. This is not exclusive to rugby, other sports and corporate life are full of examples of perpetuation for fear of admitting inadequacy. Got to get it right and bite the bullet and if we did neither well, the door is the most honourable option!

This smacks of a PR exercise in massaging egos in wealthy clubs. The decisions have already been made by the SSG chaired by Graham Mourie for 2 ½ years and John Jeffrey who took over 6 months ago!

Because this is not a normal law change, I strongly recommend that evaluations on progress be done every 4 months. This is the livelihood of rugby and if the IRB has already spent £500.000 over 3 years, we might be well served if they spend another £200.000 fine tuning it in the next 24 months. Any large organisation that has a substantial problem surrounded by controversy would set up an ongoing committee in order to stay on top of it. I find it hard to believe that 16 superbly trained professional gladiators about to enter war with the opposition are asked by the referee to stay balanced. How will the referee know if a player is or is not balanced?

I propose that the ideal engagement sequence is: crouch and pack which creates fewer chances of getting it wrong, is faster to complete and has fewer details to police, referee, judge and penalize!

Here is where the farce exists! Only the coach should be telling the players to stay balanced or unbalanced because this is a tactical decision. Referees are inundated with laws and requirements and they keep adding other duties. What the IRB and some professional lawmakers must do is review the law thoroughly and in accordance to 21st century standards; and review referee practices, mannerisms and directions given to them in the last 18 years since the beginning of professional rugby. Every referee's involvement that corresponds to tactics should be abandoned and decisions left to players and coaches.

This is what I refer to when I say referees should be given more discretion to prioritise outcomes over process and must be wholeheartedly supported by their union when a player is sent off. To complement this disciplinary action, I feel that lawyers, QC's and suspended players should not be given "a free fried" on rugby administration and its public. Tough law is a fair law! Please don't tell me that these days loss of income is a major factor in those decisions.

I applaud what Wayne Barnes just said on behalf of himself and the IRB, however I am still a bit skeptical about their ability to properly control this. By the way, there is no hit here; it has been eradicated by having both front rows ear to ear so don't even mention it because it will not be resurrected. And the ball will go in the middle, won't it? And all the scrums will be square and stationary? Good, because we have been told this will be a very successful change, the best and the last (according to Brian Moore) so you will have no problems.

Wayne, you are not policing the scrum, you are adjudicating the ball to one team or the other. This is the best chance the IRB has to succeed! Another technical point that I feel should be implemented is that the referee should give a hand signal to No 9. This way the only opposition players that would be alerted of the signal are No 9 and the particular flanker!

By eliminating the mechanical stratagem of the hit the IRB have also neutralized the negative attitude in players and coaches. We certainly must remain alert because human nature will conduct and deviate frustration beyond the boundaries of common sense, audacity and legality!

Good communication, ongoing reviews and education are the anaesthetics needed for those teething problems and for a long-term peace with the scrum.

I'd like to commend everyone that has stepped into the ring to contribute to this discussion and debate; overall I feel there is plenty of light being shed over the dark corners of the scrum.

Best regards,
Enrique TOPO Rodríguez.

The forthcoming Aviva Premiership season will be the latest testing ground for the global scrum trial — espn, 29/03/2013

ETR: This is a global trial; if you and people around you are not happy, just say it loudly!

ESPN: From the start of the new season next month, referees will instruct players to "Crouch, Bind, Set" at scrum time in a bid to limit the number of resets and in doing so improve player welfare.

ETR: Everybody can try to prevent any accident but nobody can claim or assure you that accidents will not happen!

ESPN: Props will now be expected to crouch on the referee's call, and bind using their outside arm after the referee has called bind. The front rows will maintain the bind until the referee calls set. At that point, the two packs will engage.

Implementation of the new sequence, a revision of the 'Crouch, Touch, Set" sequence that was trialled last season, follows extensive evaluation during the recent IRB Pacific Rugby Cup, which showed the potential for a more stable platform and more successful scrums.

ETR: I don't think the evaluations were extensive enough or qualitative enough; the team that played under those rules were quite substandard. The real test is taking place with the 4N Championship and the Aviva Premiership, not before!

ESPN: The new sequence has since been adopted in the Rugby Championship, South Africa's Currie Cup, New Zealand's ITM Cup and France's Top 14.

ETR: Despite being adopted as part of a global trial it is not yet a final solution!

ESPN: The results of this trial, along with another involving the television match official protocols, will be considered by IRB Council at its annual meeting in 2014 with any law amendments set to be approved next summer to ensure they are in place a year ahead of Rugby World Cup 2015.

IRB chairman Bernard Lapasset said: "The scrum is a fundamental and dynamic part of our game. It is important that we continue to promote the best possible player welfare standards and this trial process is about putting players first and delivering a reduction of the forces on engagement, which could have significant positive effects on long-term player welfare. I would like to thank all unions for their support and enthusiasm throughout this process."

ETR: We hear this safety hobby horse being flogged, but apart from the hit being eliminated, I'm not convinced they are more concerned with player welfare than turnover and popularity stakes!

ESPN: The IRB will also instruct referees to ensure that the ball does not enter the tunnel unless the scrum is square and stationary and that a straight throw-in is strictly policed.

ETR: One can't help but wonder why the referees enforced the law as it was? Square, stationary and in the middle is as old as time!

ESPN: Lapasset added: "The implementation of the revised sequence alone is not about overcoming all the challenges of the scrum but it is a forward step. There is a collective responsibility for   coaches, players and administrators to make the scrum a positive, fair and, above all, safe contest. Match officials will be stricter when refereeing the existing law."

ETR: Here, Monsieur Lapasset is very correct. The responsibility belongs to all stakeholders. I'm glad to hear that match officials will be stricter, but will they really?

ESPN: RFU Community Rugby Medical Director Dr Mike England, a member of the advisory Scrum Steering Group, said: "The RFU puts a high priority on the welfare of our players at all levels of the game. As with our recent Headcase education programme about concussion injuries, this announcement is an excellent example of how our scientific research into injury prevention can help inform developments in the laws of the game in a sensible way - without affecting the spirit in which rugby is played.

"The RFU is proud to be a key part of this work on the scrum engagement technique as part of its wider programme of player welfare and safety initiatives."

ETR: The RFU and WR have no idea about what technique to apply to the new experimental rules?

I have predicted that they will have to go back to the drawing board. I have seen the signs since the Pacific Cup Trials. It's about time to admit the wide consultation has not been wide enough.

Enrique TOPO Rodriguez

My reply to: Nick Cain / The Rugby Paper — 29/08/2013, Enrique TOPO Rodriguez

http://www.therugbypaper.co.uk/features/columnists/nick-cain/10747/nick-cain-joubert-shows-refs-cant-rule-the-scrum/#comment-1760

Hi Nick,

We are on the same page and you have been very polite in suggesting that the IRB got it wrong again! Also you volunteered a simple solution to an unnecessarily complex problem. I'm not 100% in support of your views and solutions but we both have left aside the symptoms of the poor scrummaging to concentrate on the aetiology of the sufferings.

I've been seeing the deterioration of the scrum at the international level since 1995, when professional rugby started and the IRB started to utilise their army of referees as agents for their administration. Since then there has been a marked emphasis on speed of execution of everything at all levels without attention to detail which is paramount in acquiring and consolidating technique.

Year after year we have seen an increase in referee intervention in areas that have never been their domain before: law making; on-field coaching and management of players; talking to TV, other match officials, players and captains; and coach education. Don't you think they are getting a tad busy?

Now that money is the target, the game continues to get faster, stronger, more technically prepared and more intense. I've been saying that the physical and mental capabilities of the referees have not increased at all. So, has anyone thought that top referees are not equipped to professionally handle the game proposed by the IRB, its marketing department, TV executives and so on?

My solutions

The scrum law needs to be thoroughly revised and brought into the 21st century with the conditions we have in 2013, not 1990. A number of things need to be updated and adapted to the vision of rugby in 2020-2030.

Other areas need an intervention. Give the referees more authority and less work. More discretion to prioritise outcomes over processes. No more talking to players during play; their talk must be restricted to the two captains only and only when the game is stopped.

I have proposed a 2-step engagement sequence: crouch and pack. The first step is to be managed by the players themselves and when the referee is happy he or she will proceed to the second step. Referees are the only objective ones on the field that are able to assert whether a scrum is square, stationary and safe for play. Thus, I believe they are the best to give the order for put-in, but not an audible one; just a hand or arm gesture will do the job perfectly!

Quite conveniently all the attention has been on players, coaches and the scrum itself. It's about time that referees and administrators carry their fair share of responsibility in fixing this problem affecting the whole rugby family.

Thanks, Nick, for lifting the lid on this very complex scrum jar.

TOPO

CHAPTER
15

The scrum law overhaul

But rugby, as Haskell will tell you, is not safe. As an activity, it is not quite in the dangerous category, as some forms of extreme sport might be, but it is a good few degrees further along the spectrum of peril than a walk in the park—and well it should be. That's part of its appeal. Yet this new danger to the modern player, of incapacitation by law book, is almost as sickening as some of the worst types of injury by collision. Constantly worrying about putting a foot wrong is not what the rugby player is for.

We should be talking about an exciting weekend of rugby ahead (wait a few more words, and we will), but it seems as if one of those ties, Wasps' adventure to the south of France to take on Toulon, will be compromised by the absence of the visitor's best player.

Rugby is becoming scared of itself. Accidents happen, particularly on a patch of turf hosting 30 behemoths running every which way, smashing into each other.

Players should not be punished for things they didn't mean to do (and we haven't even mentioned the plight of those poor, hapless props who are sent to the sin-bin for not being as good at scrummaging as their opponents).

The mantra "intention is irrelevant" should be dismissed as the fallacy it is, more appropriate to a medieval system of justice, where being seen to do the right thing matters more to the judiciary than the individuals being tried.

When it comes to red cards and bans, intention is the only thing. Hughes's intention was to slow down by flexing his knee. He ended up sent off and banned for it because of the accident that followed. This is not the sort of hazard a rugby player is meant to fear.

End of THE BREAKDOWN article.

Bring the rugby law into the 21st century

We all know and also take pride in the fact that the rugby law is quite complex; you cannot learn it in a 2-hour reading session. Compared to football and rugby league it is chalk and cheese. This fact goes for just about 98% of the planet's population; the other 2% are mad enough to learn it, joke about it and brag about it. So, in these days of economical demands and financial commitments, the paying punter needs to be considered in the law overhaul equation. TV is our new boss, new paymaster and they have been screaming for 20 years now for a simplification of the law, particularly in the scrums!

I'm talking about speedy action. The only way to achieve this needed expediency is by making outcomes more preeminent than process and minutiae. In 2015 we do not have the luxury of time that we used to have in the 1970s for the referee to demand every single point and article from the 16 players on the field. Therefore, how to begin thinking about it and how will it be done? We need open minds and professional lawmakers! Not referees that are only trying to see everything through their whistle. We need a group of smart people that can figure out the conundrums, the changes that occurred in the last 50 years and adapt all of it to the demands of the next 50 years! If we don't at least try, other sports will continue growing and attracting followers and crowds because they will be a healthier, simpler and uncomplicated proposition.

Attention: I'm Not Advocating for Throwing the Law Book Out the Window

First and foremost, let's make it easier for the referee to officiate; let's create the opportunities for them to go through the 80 minutes of play and to feel they are in control of the proceedings. The referee by appointment and by definition already is in the middle of the action and the centre of the attention in a rugby match, and has full authority over both teams!

So, they don't need to become quasi thespians or shock-jocks with a microphone or pose in front of the cameras. They don't need to behave bigger than what they really are. In my opinion, if a referee ever needs to assert him- or herself this means they have lost the plot from before they started? Authority doesn't need to be reinforced or enhanced! With this approach players will not need to worry about the referee and may restrict themselves to playing. The spectators equally will understand, watch and enjoy the spectacle! Last but not least, TV will favour this simplified approach and the rules will be understood by all—even passionate fanatics like me have never understood all the rugby laws.

SOME OBSERVATIONS

» One of the four principles of rugby has been let down by the administrators: continuity! The much needed and craved continuity of the game is in the hands of referees and administrators.

» If rugby wants to be fast and furious, then World Rugby must reinstate the ruck, including some very tough laws and penalties to stamp out foul play and keep player safety first and foremost.

» Adopting these steps and techniques will go a long way toward restoring the advantage of the team in possession and to a certain point protect it for 1 or 2 seconds.

However, some sort of malaise or curse prevents IRB administrators from consulting with experts in the area of scrummaging. I guess it may be because they would have to admit that they were wrong before. Thus, their good reputation and name is more important than fixing the problems affecting contemporary rugby.

Therefore, I strongly recommend an urgent overhaul of the scrum law. This is a 20th century law that needs to accommodate the demands of 21st century rugby with all its ups and downs. We are not questioning progress but asking for a fair and practical adaptation to it.

A big proviso

This process must be in the hands of independent professional lawmakers, not the referees, due to their vested interest. We already had a less than satisfactory experience when the referees came up with the maligned engagement sequence of C-T-P-E (Crouch-Touch-Pause-Engage) in 2005.

Find below my shopping list which is quite reasonable and doable. It requires ample flexibility of mind, a bit of imagination and a true and honest desire to move forward from all stakeholders and for the better of all stakeholders. Above and beyond all of them this is for the improvement of rugby union which needs to become more competitive against many other sports and by the same token easier to understand to its trusted and faithful followers.

1. Referees need to be helped with a simplified and uncomplicated set of minimal laws favouring outcomes over process. An example of what it should look like and with discretion the referee will give priority to the final outcome.

2. The amount of detail about the law was fine back in 1920 when out of the 80 minutes the ball was probably in play for 10-15 minutes. Today the game is about 300% faster and harder but the referee's brain hasn't increased in size.

3. Today we have about half a dozen TV cameras and microphones to go with it; no player can escape scrutiny whether official or public. The public demands fewer

interruptions or scrum collapses in the game because other sports are leading the way in terms of continuity, intensity and duration. These people pay and support rugby (directly or indirectly) so we must listen to their complaints.

4. We need to apply the universal principle of less is more. I advocated for two steps only for the engagement sequence: crouch and pack.

5. I did send my recommendations to Graham Mourie, chair of the IRB SSG (International Rugby Board Scrum Steering Group),supported by another 29 scrum experts members of the Scrum Experts Lobby (SEL).

6. Today, almost 3 years after seeing the continued degeneration of the scrum, some matches are all right but others are unbearable.

I have always been of the idea that the referee should have less technical involvement (e.g., talking and instructing the players on what to do.) This is the job of the coaches and in this professional era there are plenty. Referees must be very definite about the law and at the beginning of the match may need to be a bit more harsh or assertive in order to control the mob.

Only one command from the referee is needed for the proper execution and completion of a scrum

(a) The big secret or remedy here is to take some responsibility off the referee and give it to the 16 players. But how?

(b) When the referee blows the whistle for a scrum, the 16 players know exactly what positions to adopt, where to assemble, to whom to bind, etc. They don't need the referee to reinforce or remind them of anything!

The separation of both packs at the crouched position must be sufficient for both front rowers to uncoil their bodies and to adopt a safe pushing position (i.e., back parallel to the ground, spine fully extended and not ear to ear).

(c) Then referee is free to call "Pack" or other single syllable command.

(d) The half back will introduce the ball when and however he want but it must go straight to the middle.

(e) Because of his or her lesser involvement, the referee can and should be more strict with all those pet peeves such as crooked feed, pushing too early, gamesmanship in between front rowers, etc.

Thus, the attitude and spirit of the law must be of sharing responsibility as follows: arrive to the mark, assemble and set up.

(f) The pushing is allowed only after the ball has gone in.

(g) Referees must understand that they are enablers of the game and not power seekers. Everybody knows that they are the boss for those 80 minutes so over-officiating always complicates things and frustrate players.

(h) The new scrum law as I conceived it gives players more **responsibility and prizes positive attitude and cooperation in keeping the show on the road**.

(i) This is also a big component of safety practices for the 16 players because nobody is off the hook when it comes to risks of accidents.

(j) **The law must eliminate and punish intent but be a bit more lenient with accidents.** This is the cause of scrum collapses or uncompleted scrums more often than not.

(k) When everybody from WR down to a local club follows these steps, safety will increase 200% as will enjoyment and the ability to play rugby union.

(l) When referees talk or give instructions to any player, this gives an unfair advantage to the other team. Referees should only talk when the game is stopped and of course preferably to the captains only. Furthermore, referee should address players by the number on the back of their jumper and not nicknames or first names. The referee must be addressed as Sir or Madam.

(m) Coaches are a special breed, but also stakeholders, and as such they need to be taught the notions of sharing responsibility and to practice adherence to the law.

In summary, the whole scrum succession of steps would look as follows:

**Proposed Ideal Scrum Sequence of events
+ Responsibility for these actions and steps!**

(a) Referee blows the wistle
(b) Player awareness start
(c) Mental preparation starts
(d) Physical approach and presence to the mark
(e) Players go through assembly routine: feet and body position, hips, back and binding, head position

Responsibility: Players 100% (Only)

(f) Readiness for Engagement
(g) Referee ensures both packs are SQUARE & STEADY (Safety 1)
(h) Referee calls: PACK or other single syllable word

Responsibility: Players 50% + Referee 50%

(i) When the scrum is good the Referee lets the half back (without any voices) introduce the ball:
1. On his own time;
2. Straight; and
3. IN THE MIDDLE of the channel. So the ball can be contested by both teams!

Responsibility: Players 50% + Referee 50%

(k) Only after the ball has been put in, both packs may start pushing.

Responsibility: Players 50% + Referee 50%

NOTE

The only call by the referee here is (h) P A C K. Any other calls would be the equivalent of over-officiating.

THE CONCEPT OF RESPONSIBILITY

Any display of a lack of discipline from players in this system must be dealt with swiftly and in a decisive manner. The responsibility approach leaves little room for leniency.

Quite often I socialize in different circles and when somebody recognizes me the rugby subject comes to the fore. Invariably I get asked a flurry of questions and I give my penny's worth depending on my inspiration. When I mention this idea of stakeholder responsibility some people laugh at me and say, "You gotta be kidding; getting coaches to play fair is like wanting to have a swim in the Sahara Desert," "Players couldn't care less so long as they get paid," and "As long as administrators can cross the Ts and dot the Is and have a few bucks left in the club, that's all they want"

Life has changed a lot in many regards; so has sport but the mentality is much slower in adjusting to the different rules or different ways of doing things. I'd like to use the traffic and transit regulations as an analogy. When I arrived in Sydney 31 years ago, the streets in the CBD would have 4 or 5 signs, mostly restrictions; today each street has close to 20 signs! The laws are draconian; we have more cars and people in the streets and something or somebody has to regulate and control it.

Rules, laws and regulations are based on responsibility for our actions. So why not give more responsibility and freedom to the players and more discretion and flexibility to the referees? What is really important here is that the coaches are very clear on what the objective is apart from winning which it should never be number 1.

Just about everyone involved with rugby are employees of a club, a company or a union and need to think with responsibility as an important component of our reasoning. Life in 2015 is very competitive; every industry, job, occupation and company is very demanding. Rugby players, coaches and referees are not exempt from this. Therefore, acting with responsibility is what makes us move forward as a society.

* * *

CHAPTER 16

THE RUGBY SCRUM AND THE REFEREEING

By Enrique TOPO Rodriguez – 12/05/2013

Use it or lose it! Quite often we hear the referee issue this command these days, supposedly directed to the half back at the back of the scrum or whoever the last person in a maul or a ruck might be. This well-intended practice has been slowly adopted and instituted in the last 18 years under the guise of managing the game and the players and perhaps with the intention to speed up the game, but it has gradually evolved into how and when the game should be played.

I'd like to set the record straight from the outset: this is not another referee-bashing article. Quite the contrary! Far too often referees have been the meat in the sandwich. They need lots of assistance from all corners (e.g., administrators, players, coaches, media)

I have huge respect for rugby referees which are in the middle of the general discussions on rugby, scrum and just about any other subject, big and small, official and unofficial. They are and have been for long time under a lot of pressure to deliver the perfect product. It would be fair to say rugby has some antiquated laws but other laws are still very good and current. However, some common practices are questionable. In a game that continues to grow faster and more complex with an increased level of scrutiny (a top game today has at least 6 cameras recording it) this has never been seen before. Thus, there are very high expectations from the man with the whistle, in the middle of the rugby sandwich.

The public, journalists and everybody else expect players will occasionally get a few things wrong but expect referees to be absolutely correct all the time. When correctness doesn't fall into that special place (or team) the wrath comes down from the four corners. So, I take my hat off to all rugby referees for their thankless job and selfless contribution carried out with all passion.

The referee should be the judge of the law, adjudicating on what is correct or incorrect according to the law and nothing else. However, these days referees spend too much time giving directions to players about how and when the game must be played. This managing of the game is taking us into murky waters!

The how and when should be the domain of players and coaches and the referee should remain impartial because any referee intervention in the game **is interference**. By urging the play they could well be seen as favouring one team or the other and could be accused of being biased.

I suspect that referees have been instructed to become nit-picking constables when in reality they should behave like a Supreme Court Judge. It also appears that in recent years referees have been given extended powers and authority which leads to over-officiating. I would even speculate that the majority of referees are struggling to apply: a) the whole law book; b) their interpretation of the law, particularly at scrum time; and c) the special recommendations that they receive from time to time from peers and authorities. Not even a modern computer would be able to do that job correctly all the time.

These days a referee's job should be that of an enabler, facilitating two very important aspects: a) the game for the players; and b) the spectacle for the audience. They cannot and must not control everything regarding the how and when to play the ball on the field. This is the players' role and something the players should be given the responsibility to uphold and be accountable for. Referees may address the captains for any special requirements and utilise them as another two enablers but refereeing should take place without the talk and instructions to players during the game.

In this era of professionalism all stakeholders must be involved and contribute to the smooth and effective running of three aspects: a) the game; b) the spectacle; and c) the business. We all have a role of responsibility to the game and neither wringing our hands nor sleeping on our laurels will fix the problem. Therefore, I propose that we collectively express our opinions while looking for solutions to these not-so-little problems.

If I were playing opposite to the team in possession of the ball (i.e., defending), the referee's call to use it or lose it is a signal to my team that the ball is about to go out somewhere and this is the moment to stop pushing.

Any warnings or even **positive management instructions** given by the referee are heard by sides as well as TV viewers and spectators too. TV is a huge influence on many of the conversations and decisions made. These factors may or may not generate a perception of biased refereeing, which is always very hard to erase.

An incentive should be provided for forwards to push more and to play a tighter game in reduced spaces, directly opposed to other sports shown on TV such as AFL, NFL, football or even basketball. This will go a long way to preserve the inherent and highly distinctive all-body-shapes attraction, characteristic and intrigue that rugby has.

The backs would love the extra space given. In the early 2000s the Australian forwards were distinctively fanning out in defence, thus the pack tightness was eroded and almost lost. This bad habit also translated into the scrummaging department where the Wallabies have struggled on and off particularly in the last 15 years.

For some reasons people want to see 15 hares running and dodging obstacles around the field while also ready to morph into 15 bulls tackling, pushing, shoving and jumping. There is no doubt that any coach would love to see his forwards arriving all together to the wing or point of contact with the opposition. But the moment we want to do everything as jacks of all trades and masters of none, we lose our specialty and the uniqueness of our roles. Another very important fact is that specific fitness for every position is not something you can acquire or just switch on and off. Go and ask any back that gets caught in 2 or 3 mauls too often!

On the other hand, we have the old trusty rucking which is bordering on extinction because is too physical and too dangerous. We need an international edict to resurrect it. This is the best way to speed up the game without tampering with or affecting its fabric, the tradition or the spirit. Reinstating vigorous rucking will also help the referee by spitting out the offside bodies. Any normal human being that has been rucked out a couple of times will think more than twice about doing it again. **This has always been the spirit of the game.**

Therefore in concluding two immediate problems we face and have been facing for a while:

(a) The referee's voice regarding technical or tactical matters is a source of distraction. In this case the 16 forwards and the 2 half backs are affected by it. Ask professional tennis players if they like the umpires talking while they try to serve or play out a point.

(b) Referees should only be heard when ruling and explaining their rulings. Players are guilty or not guilty. Any grey area becomes a problem that needs management.

(c) Referees have no time for management; they need to administer the law.

What do you think?

Enrique TOPO Rodriguez

* * *

Following reply by Mr. Malcolm Lewis (17th May 2013) [Cardiff Society of Welsh Rugby Union Referees. Worked with Ray Williams and John Dawes for more than 20 years in the WRU]

Hi Topo-

Some thoughts after reading your paper:

This is an excellent qualitative analysis of the problem facing the scrum and, even more so, facing the game today. I believe we—being the stakeholders having some kind of input outside refereeing, coaching and playing—should have great concern for the way the game is evolving. The scrum has received, quite rightly, much criticism and coverage recently, to the extent that the IRB has been forced into introducing a change in the scrum law for next season.

Your paper "The Rugby Scrum and the Refereeing" is an excellent paper. Did you send it to the IRB? It has repercussions on other aspects of the game to which you briefly refer.

As a result I am attaching a paper for your thoughts which I presented to our Referees Society in 2010. It was passed to the Referees Parent Body and then to the WRU. Unfortunately the WRU just made the glib remark that no amendments to the laws would be addressed until after the World Cup! They did not even make any specific remarks regarding the paper—good or bad! Disappointing. But now the IRB, quite rightly, have listened to the huge amount of criticism on the scrum and have acted.

The breakdown (T/R/M) has had an enormous effect on the game in the past few years to the extent that it has become the battleground on which teams must win. Enough said. Read the paper. Since 2010 the number of breakdowns has increased further.

Regarding your paper:

As I said, excellent. I totally agree with all your comments, particularly regarding managing the game by referees. Totally unnecessary. They should apply the laws fairly— their sole job. The amount of talking and shouting they do is not necessary. They have taken over a huge coaching role in the game—without the necessary qualifications—and now more than ever have a huge effect on the outcome of the game. I do sympathise with them to some degree but they have brought it on themselves by becoming the major instigators of factual change; ignoring many laws with the mistaken belief that they are doing the game a huge service; and believing that they now are the sole judges and juries.

The game has changed—unfortunately for the worse. Fewer players playing, fewer spectators, a worse shop window (unattractive game), more disciplinary problems, more injuries and a worse legacy.

I'm afraid it has become a really negative picture. It does seem as if money is ruling the world of rugby and it has become a game for the wealthy. How much are tickets for the Lions v Australia?!

I'm getting carried away, so I'll stop.

Again, a great paper, Topo.

Regards
Malcolm.

I have the pleasure of including the 2010 paper Malcolm Lewis sent to me. It was prepared by the Cardiff Society of Welsh Rugby Union Referees which in fact supports many of my claims before and after.

At this juncture, it is worth noting the interrelation of the positions and phases of rugby union whereby the outcomes of the scrum may influence the ruck or maul and, quite obviously, the development of the line out.

Simply speaking if your pack is forced to push extra to compensate for some technical inadequacies, more than likely your legs will be gone by the time you have to jump or lift in the next line out. Hence the importance of getting it right at scrum time and making sure that you are the giver and not the taker of the pressure.

Refereeing the 'breakdown' — A position statement

1) Summary

(a) The failure of referees to apply some of the Laws vigorously and consistently has resulted in an increasing number of 'breakdowns' in the game.

(b) There are now so many that the game has been affected adversely.

(c) One partial solution is that referees are directed to adopt a 'zero tolerance' approach to players who willfully go to ground after a tackle situation.

2) Introduction – the 'breakdown'

(a) The 'breakdown' is that aspect of rugby union football when the progress of play has stopped and continuity interrupted. It is characterized by a 'contact area' in open play when neither a ruck nor a maul have been formed.

(b) It often follows a tackle and other players are also on the ground (i.e., 'off their feet').

(c) It is also known as a 'pile-up' and occasionally a 'mess'.

3) Background

(a) The 'breakdown' is becoming an area of increasing controversy resulting in inconsistent refereeing both in and between games.

(b) It is an aspect of the game that has caused confusion, frustration and even anger amongst coaches and players and disappointment and rejection with the game amongst spectators.

(c) It is now so prevalent that the game is in danger of losing some of its appeal and popularity – if it hasn't already done so.

(d) 'Breakdowns' have become a physical battle for possession on the ground and referees are becoming more and more lenient towards players 'going to ground'. They have become a tactical battleground with the possibility of a 'turnover'.

(e) In turn, this has led to kicking duels (many of them purposeless) because teams are reluctant to risk conceding possession in their own half.

(f)　Recent comments about the elite level of the game in the UK illuminate the thinking:

    I.　Matt O'Connor (Leicester Coach) 'Risk outweighs the Reward" – i.e., teams are afraid to attack.

    II.　Mark Cueto (Sale & England) "The Breakdown was a lottery- we lived in fear of getting turned over".

    III.　Rob Andrew (RFU) "Players being allowed to rest their body weight on the bodies of other players on the floor – creating more people off their feet than we've ever seen."

    IV.　Mike Ruddock- (Worcester Coach) "We've gone from 130 years of clarity where at the Ruck you can't use your hands and the Maul where you can to a hybrid which is confusing to everyone."

    V.　Steve Bale (Daily Express) "One man tackles another – and loads of others then dive in – perfectly reflects rugby union's horror stories."

(g)　In view of this weight of overwhelming opinion, it is therefore timely to address this serious shortcoming.

4) The nature of the problem

(a)　The success of the game as a sport for participants (at all levels) and for spectators (live and via broadcast media) is predicated on letter and spirit of Law 14: "The Game is to be played by players who are on their feet. The player must not make the ball unplayable by falling down. Unplayable means that the ball is not immediately available to either team so that play can continue" (emphasis added).

(b)　Importantly too, a Welsh Rugby Union 'Performance Chart for Referees' issued to Advisors requires an evaluation of referee compliance to "... [ensure] that arriving players stayed on their feet".

(c)　Other Laws pertaining to the 'tackle – ruck – breakdown' include:

    I.　15.6(a) "Players are on their feet if no other part of their body is supported by the ground or players on the ground";

    II.　15.7(c) "no player may fall on or over a tackled player";

    III.　15.7(d) "No player may fall on or over the players lying on the ground after a tackle with the ball between or near to them";

    IV.　16.2(a) "---must have their head and shoulders no lower than their hips" and

V.   16.3(a) "Players in a ruck must endeavor to stay on their feet".

(d)   In recent years it is evident that referees have become increasingly tolerant of the failure of players to remain on their feet – especially the players arriving at a tackle situation.

(e)   So embedded in the fabric of the game has this become that the term 'breakdown' has entered the vocabulary of players, coaches, commentators and media analysts.

(f)   This is an accurate of the situation: play has broken down and it has been suspended for a period of time.

(g)   At the highest level there are, on average, 160 'breakdowns'.

(h)   This has significant implications for the amount of 'ball in play time' when the ball is actually playable and being played.

(i)   There are three further consequences of the 'breakdown' situation:

   I.   It is a facet of the game in which there is no 'fair contest' for possession. This represents a further departure from the aims and spirits of the game.
   II.   The natural 'ebb and flow' of the well-played game is compromised because additional time is provided for defences to (re)align, and attacking facets of play are negated.
   III.   This has shifted the fine balance between defence and attack in favour of the former.
   IV.   Hence, the game is impoverished as a spectacle
   V.   Moreover, because fewer options are available for the attacking team to attack, there has been a tendency to revert to a series of 'pick and drive' movements close to the breakdown – often in the hope that the defending team will commit illegalities and be penalised. As a consequence attacking play is stifled.

(j)   As an aside, the ensuing 'breakdowns' are often violations of Law 15.6(f): "Any player who first gains possessions of the ball must not go to the ground at the tackle or near to it unless tackled by an opposition player".

(k)   Indeed, it is not uncommon to see a team seeking to do no more than maintain possession towards the end of the game by attempting to "run down the clock" in this way.

(l)   More positively, it is a tactic that is now relied upon by some teams when close to their opponents' goal line. In a recent game one team retained uninterrupted possession for approximately whilst (apparently) striving to score a try from only a short distance.

(m) Notwithstanding the technical accomplishments of players in maintaining possession in this way, the possibility to do so has cultivated a lack of ambition.

5) Refereeing the 'breakdown'

(a)   It has become customary (and accepted) that 'breakdowns' are refereed as though they are rucks.

(b)   Rucking was first introduced into the game as a coaching term where the feet were used to win the ball – this seldom exists in the modern game.

(c)   The ruck has a very precise definition: "A ruck is a phase of play where one or more players from each team, who are on their feet, in physical contact, close around the ball on the ground. Open play has ended" (IRB, 2009: p. 94).

(d)   Yet in spite of this clarity, a situation whereby a team contests possession for the ball whilst on their feet is very rare indeed.

(e)   With referees encouraged to provide preventative advice to players, the word 'ruck' is being called to convey to the players that whether or not a ruck has been identified, the referee is seeking to bring orderliness to the 'mess'.

(f)   This has meant that there are (many) instances when laws pertaining to the ruck are being applied inappropriately – that is to say, the application of the laws has become blurred and/or neglected.

(g)   Consequences of this include:

    I.   The absence of rucks (as defined in the Laws) in the modern game;

    II. 'Sealing off' the ball at so-called rucks thus preventing fair contests for possession at those phases of the game

    III. Referees accepting actions deemed positive (i.e., keeping the ball alive and preventing opposing players from slowing up and/or 'killing' possession) whether or not they are within the Laws.

6) (Some of) the possible ways forward

(a) There are alternatives for how the game moves forward with regard to this particular issue. These include:

I.   Status quo – the game is constantly evolving, and this is part of its evolution. This has the virtue of being what all stake-holders are familiar with in 2009/10.

II. Amend the law(s) that are concerned with this facet of play. This has the virtue of being a 'clean start' for all stake-holders when implemented. In the interim, the status quo remains.

III. For refereed to receive a directive to 'police' this facet of play more vigorously and to adopt a 'zero tolerance' approach to players wilfully going to ground at the tackle situation. This in turn requires the support of referee coaches, advisors, assessors, national refereeing bodies and the International Rugby Board. This has the virtue of being merely a change in emphasis (not in Law) and addresses the cause of the current problem, not the symptom(s) of it.

7) Recommendation

(a) Option 6) a) iii) above to be pursued through the appropriate procedural channels with immediate effect. That is to say, for referees to receive a directive to 'police' this facet of play more vigorously and to adopt a 'zero tolerance' approach to players wilfully going to ground at the tackle situation.

(b) This requires that the matter is:

I.   presented to the Welsh Society of Rugby Union Referees (the 'parent body') for discussion amongst the constituent societies;

II. if adopted, presented to the Welsh Rugby Union for consideration; and

III. if supported, advanced to the International Rugby Board for consideration and further action.

Cardiff Society of Welsh Rugby Union Referees

January 2010

Reference

International Rugby Board (2009) Laws of the Game – Rugby Union. Dublin: International Rugby Board.

The following are my additional comments to Malcolm Lewis' paper on points (3), (4) and (7).

(18/05/2013)

3) BACKGROUND

(d) It also diverts the attention and focus of the real game, switching into a new dimension which is accepted based on perceived assiduity.

(e) It is very easy to obtain or recover the ball in breakdowns therefore teams squander their possession knowing they will scrap possession back quite easily.

When we reverse the situation removing that opportunity and possession becomes harder to secure from the breakdowns, teams will be more judicious and will discriminate and select more carefully when and where to kick.

Obviously, these days the money factor has made just about everyone more conservative, risk averse and devoid of initiative.

4) THE NATURE OF THE PROBLEM

(d) Since 1995 with the advent of professionalism and also previously with the commercialisation of rugby–including shamateurism–the intrusion and influence of media has been very pernicious. Money has changed the priorities, objectives and type of outcomes of the game. In short we are now serving different masters.

Any new culture requires a smooth transition from the old to the new. The laws, operational procedures, human resources, strategic plans and stakeholders commitment need to be involved in some sort of representation with the decision makers. I doubt that this was the case with the IRB declaration in 1995 that rugby is no longer amateur. As a whole, rugby has been more reactive than proactive. The IRB was reluctantly pushed by the World Rugby Corporation to make fast decisions and take a plunge into the unknown.

This has also been enabled by the obsession of giving rugby some artificial continuity by referees and IRB directives on interpretations of the law. This silly idea that the ball has to fly at all times? I advocate for a mixture of all the elements rugby has and only captain or coach should decide on changing tactics and strategy.

The four principles of rugby union remain:

1. Go forward
2. Support
3. Continuity
4. Apply pressure (to recover the ball in defence)

These four principles must be at all times the domain of the players not the referee, because very simply he or she is refereeing both teams and must not take sides while play is on.

(i) Be it negative, speculative or conservative rugby, this has developed through the years and it has become part of the rugby fabric. Rugby may be an intelligent game but is played by people of different capabilities, virtues and skills and it should be inclusive, providing opportunities for everyone.

Therefore, we must not stop this rugby trait. The IRB need to educate players and coaches on the virtues of perhaps approaching the game differently with the aim at engaging the crowds.

(j) Maybe introduce a new rule that after 60 seconds of not using possession it becomes a turnover to the opposite team. Of course it would be very hard to define when a team is or is not using the ball.

(k) I feel the laws shouldn't stifle tactical initiatives—no matter how obscure or conservative they might be—through technical law manoeuvring because this would be akin to killing coaches' and captains' brains and with it the ability to play a thinking game. It's got to be an incentive for creativity. This point is one of the rare beauties of rugby where two teams trying to outsmart or outmanoeuvre each other provides a great spectacle of the unexpected. Other times they may display the too obvious and boring, but this is the price to pay. This should occur regardless of how ugly it might look.

On the other hand, the opposite would result in a stereotyped, artificial and stifled game. Rugby is a fairly regimented game as it is, thus it doesn't need any more programming. We must preserve the human input, player interaction, creativity and flexibility. Those qualities combined with education to the spectators will produce a spectacle to be envied by all other sports.

7) RECOMMENDATIONS

I would use a different word in place of police. Referees are and must be enablers and facilitators of the game. This job is more about catching people doing things right than doing things wrong.

Malcom, I think your paper is worth updating and recycling!

Good luck with it,
TOPO

CHAPTER 17

BBC5 radio interview

BBC5 RADIO INTERVIEW – "THE SCRUM" PROGRAM

BBC 5 Radio Interview: "THE SCRUM" , 29/03/13 (07.30 AM, Sydney - 28/03/13, UK)

PRESENTER: Eleanour Oldroyd

INTERVIWEE: Enrique TOPO Rodríguez

SUBJECT: Four questions on the current state of the Rugby Scrum

PREPARATION QUESTIONS:

1) IN YOUR OPINION, WHAT HAVE BEEN THE KEY CHANGES IN SCRUMMAGING?
In my view the influencing factors were:

(a) The advent of the power scrum. In the early 1970s, the biomechanics of it changed dramatically, packed down approximately 40 cm lower than the traditional pre-70s scrum. This trend gradually made life very difficult for hookers. The Argentine-coordinated push (e.g., Pumas, San Isidro Club) dominated Wales, France, South Africa, Australia, etc.

In 1980, Carlos "Veco" Villegas was invited to the Welsh RU Centenary Congress to give a dissertation on how to coach the scrum. The scrum then shifted from being mainly a means to restart the game with the focus on an upper-body wrestle to lower body work which later became known as the power scrum. This substantially modified the position of the front row and made it very difficult for traditional hookers to hook for the ball.

(b) The advent of professionalism. This renewed attention to strength training and fitness, and advances of technology accentuated the previous changes.

Coaching specialisation created a success-obsessed culture when before competing and participating was the thing. Nowadays it's all or nothing.

In my view, players became faster, stronger and richer but not smarter!

Scrums became very well-drilled units with plenty of technique, fitness and strength focus, mental concentration, attitude and timing but they were still not a thinking unit. Hooking was a secondary or even tertiary concern because it was deemed that pushing was more efficient.

(c) The 2004 ELV's promise to overhaul the law. The idea was to adjust the law because infringements often halted the contest for the ball. However, ELVs did not address the scrum problems and failed in their   primary objective.

(d) The 2005 decision by the IRB to take control of the dangerous scrum. Following the pressure by some insurance assessors, the IRB wanted to fix the problems experienced with the scrum but engaged the referees to do their dirty job. Therefore they organised for a large group of referees to assemble at the Lensbury Club. Brian Moore was invited to attend as a journo but was not allowed to speak up. Here they conceived and introduced the maligned crouch-touch-pause-engage sequence which complicated and endangered the whole process. This became a way for referees to acquire political and on-field power. Now that the players were restricted by referees, the only option was to transfer all the emphasis and power onto the hit.

Forwards, while being restricted by the C-T-P-E, waited for the engagement and then unleashed their weight as soon as they went crashing onto the opposition. This became a competition in and of itself, with both packs trying to win the hit. Hooking is definitely disappearing and hookers are getting bigger!

This sequence allowed referees to misinterpret and mismanage the whole process by manipulating or anticipating the timings of the steps of one another. Players unaware of what the referee will do next was something never seen before in any sports. Thus, players also decided to take advantage of the confusion and cheat when possible. The 4 steps each of 16 players can take equal 64 mini steps which provide more margin of error due to different brains and different reaction times.

2) IS THERE A PROBLEM WITH THE SCRUM NOW?

Don't think the scrum today is safe, more efficient or more effective than it was 6 years ago. If anything, it is more unpredictable, a bit of a lottery. The fact we are still investing this time into discussing it is because it is not functioning properly. More leadership is needed in order to prevent more losses (e.g., of players, public defecting to other sports, disenchanted sponsors pulling out of rugby).

Coaches, players, spectators, sponsors, media and, I daresay, referees also are not happy with the level of confusion and discontentment produced by the time wasted with collapses and restarts. Currently it is used as a weapon to gain penalties. The proper way within the spirit of rugby is to use it to restart the game through an even and fair contest.

3) ARE SOME OF THE NUANCES OF THE SCRUM BEING LOST?

»   Hooking as an option has almost disappeared which is a real shame. It needs to be resurrected!

»   The scrum must be steady and square before the ball goes in.

»   Ball in the middle needs to be enforced; for far too long this has been left as a last priority.

»   Pushing must only be allowed after the ball is introduced.

»   It concerns me greatly that the current dialogue and commentary of some allegedly knowledgeable rugby people consists of saying that the scrum is just a way of restarting the game and shouldn't be that difficult to fix. Dannie Craven and Ray Williams, OBE, would be spinning in their graves and cringing at the lack of understanding. The scrum is not only a way to restart the game of rugby but also the foundation from which we start building our attack or our defence with the aim of dominating the adversary.

»   The scrum is meant to be a formation where many skills are displayed for a short time. It also allows for players of all different shapes to take part in the action. The scrum is the epitome of teamwork and discipline, mental concentration and winning attitude.

4) WHAT WOULD YOU CHANGE OR ENFORCE?

» The IRB urgently need to simplify the laws to encourage a better understanding of all stakeholders. The law needs to be less prescriptive! It must be written by lawmakers, not referees or insurance assessors.

» **Referees should:**

  » Be like a Supreme Court judge not a nit-picking constable.
  » Be given more discretion so they can judge and focus more on outcomes and less on technicalities of process.
  » Call players by their last names. Familiarity does not help here!
  » Not talk or interfere with the tactics of the game. No coaching either!
  » Focus on refereeing the game instead of managing the game!
  » Enforce two very old laws:
    » **The ball put-in must be in the middle (and controlled just like in the lineout).**
    » **Packs can only push once the ball has been introduced.**

» Use a 2-step controlled engagement: Crouch and pack. They should also ensure there is more distance between packs so the front rows can uncoil their bodies to a safe and strong position.

» Assume responsibility for the current main objectives of the game and up keeping of it.

5. WHY ARE THERE STILL SCRUM COLLAPSES?

1. Not putting the ball in straight
2. The C-T-P-E is a poorly constructed engagement sequence
3. Front rows too close (not enough time and space to uncoil bodies)
4. Too much emphasis on the power of the hit and engagement
5. Lacking togetherness and common purpose
6. Poor grips between both front rows
7. Poor grips in second row and back row
8. Poor technique
9. Skin-tight jumpers impeding early and secure grips for the whole pack

CURRENT (3) STEPS ENGAGEMENT SEQUENCE ANALYSIS

1. Too time consuming
2. Difficult to synchronise
3. Involves too much guessing
4. Mentally and physically taxing on players
5. More steps equals more margin of error
6. Weakens the scrum structure

NEW (2) STEP PROPOSED ENGAGEMENT SEQUENCE ANALYSIS

1. Time efficient and effective
2. Easier to synchronise and referee
3. Less strenuous on players and more definite
4. Fewer steps equals less margin of error
5. Responsible approach is safer
6. No guess work, standardised, uniformed

Scrum and rugby law must be abided to by all and sundry. There cannot be different shades of grey or different interpretations for different hemispheres. It's either black or white. Responsibility also applies to everybody involved in rugby, both on and off the field.

14th May 2013
Jeff Probyn's Column in The Rugby Paper, UK

This week saw the IRB announce its latest incarnation of the scrum engagement sequence that incorporates pre-binding and the need to put the ball in straight.

I have to say that I honestly don't think the IRB are truly interested in sorting out the mess that they have created at the scrum and although they have commissioned trials and testing, they have not asked for or taken any advice or comment from those with direct experience of the changes that have been made.

This despite an almost continuous deluge of negative comments from all sections of the media (particularly my old mate, Brian Moore) and public over what most see as an avoidable problem were the IRB to react quickly and tell referees to enforce the laws of the game as written.

Former Australian and Argentinean international prop Enrique (Topo) Rodriguez was so worried about the current situation at the scrum he contacted a number of former players and coaches and formed the Scrum Experts Lobby (SEL), a group of 19 ex-international players and coaches with more than 500 front row caps from 8 countries to gather opinions and offer recommendations to the IRB's Scrum Steering Group.

That group presented a paper to the IRB making 5 recommendations. The following is a consensus of philosophies which embraces the need to re-establish the rugby union scrum as a safe, fair, physical, mental and attitudinal contest for possession, meaning that it is a means of bringing the ball back into play following a contest conducted to the letter of the law and in the spirit of the game.

This would be received by the rugby community with a sense of relief as the scrum is currently viewed with ambivalence by rugby people, detestation by the uninitiated and concern by the stakeholders, particularly the media.

1) Safety first

»   The scrummaging contest for possession must take place within the stipulation of the laws of the game.

»   All the laws relating to the scrum should be respected and enforced by officials, administrators, referees, players and coaches.

2) Features that need to be eradicated

»   The use of the word hit by the referee

»   A crooked feed, in either direction to the scrum

Both the above are flagrant infringements of the laws of Rugby Union Football

3) Role of the referees

»   The referee is in charge of the match and is the ultimate authority within the 80 minutes of play.

» Refereeing is not to be confused with coaching, or giving tactical orders. This means referees need to restrict themselves to the book of the laws. This will give them more time to concentrate on many other facets of the play.

» Referees, apart from refereeing, should assume a neutral role which is impossible once they start to perceive one scrum or the other as being the dominant scrum.

» Referees are technical arbiters of the laws of the game and not self-appointed (or institutionally appointed) managers who control the players, tactical aspects of the game or its nature. Refereeing and management are two completely different activities with utterly different motivations, aspirations and skill sets.

» Referees must be given more discretion to be able to interpret the technical minutiae, so as to favour outcomes over process.

4) Summary of scrums

» Stationary before the ball is put into the scrum

» Steady and square

» Both packs must not push before the ball is put in

» The ball must go into the scrum straight along the middle line between the two front rows thus making hooking by either front row (once it has passed the line of the first foot) a viable option and thus should be reinstated as a tactical option.

» Both packs may push as little or as much as they wish after the ball has been put in.

» Wheeling is a very destructive and negative tactic. It should be completely outlawed (perhaps allowing a tolerance of 45° degree for accidental wheeling).

All the above points are based upon the notion that the scrum is not only a way to restart the game of rugby but also a foundation from which teams start building their attack and their defence; it is also reiterating the laws as written.

5) Engagement sequence

» A two-step engagement sequence ('Crouch! Pack!' or 'Ready! Set!') would reduce margins of error and preparation time.

» The referee will strictly control both steps, giving his or her directions when he or she considers both packs to be in readiness mode (i.e., safe and stable).

» A pre-bind (currently on trial) seems to be favoured in order to eradicate the hit.

» If the pre-bind regulation is adopted, the pre-engagement distance between front rows should be within binding (gripping) distance.

The pre-bind will come into practice at the start of next season, but I think that it has many potential dangers that have been overlooked by the SSG which doesn't have enough front row players amongst its membership.

When the IRB first introduced referee-led engagement with the Crouch, Touch, Pause, Engage call in 2007, it became obvious to all that it did not work as they had hoped despite a lengthy trial before its introduction. However, it took 5 years before they revised the call.

There have been two more attempts at trying to sort out the mess but they too have failed so we have now arrived at what the SSG call a tested solution that will permanently fix the situation.

We can only hope for the sake of the scrum and the game that they are right and the scrum experts are wrong.

BBC5 radio program – The Scrum, 28/03/2013

INTERVIEWER/MODERATOR: Eleanour Oldroyd

INTERVIEWED AND TELEPHONE HOOK-UP: Brian Moore, Phil Vickery, Matt Stevens, Phil Keith-Roach, Nigel Owens, John Jeffrey (IRB), Ed Morrison (RFU), Sean Fitzpatrick, Mike Cron, Enrique TOPO Rodriguez.

THE COMMENTS
You may follow the program through the enclosed link:

http://www.bbc.co.uk/iplayer/episode/b01rxp8z/5_live_Sport_5_live_Rugby_The_Scrum/

MIKE CRON

The South Pacific Cup trials are currently being played in NZ and AUS. They have so far reflected that the new scrum laws have reduced speed and acceleration of the engagement and ironically generated more power from feet base (i.e., more solid base).

The new sequence will be: Crouch – Firm Bind – Set (after packing, the binding can be adjusted).

The Bath University study has established that through this method it will be a reduction of 25% of forces and power on the hit.

The professional era has brought bigger and stronger front rowers and forwards; in some cases the average weight is around 115 kg/player. Twenty years ago it may have been 105 kg average per player.

The following statements in capitals are those of Mike Cron; I have added my comments below them.

(a) THE LAW NEEDS TO ADAPT TO THE MODERN ATHLETE.
   ETR: Somehow I do not agree with this point of view. I'm of the view that the athletes must adapt to the systems and the laws.

(b) THE LAW HAS TO EVOLVE.
   ETR: Absolutely yes, and I am calling for a scrum law overhaul.

(c) WITH THE NEW LAWS, REFEREES FEEL MORE RELAXED.
   ETR: This is relative to the person, the match and the pressures of the particular game they are refereeing.

(d) THE REFEREES ARE ABLE TO RULE EASILY AND PICK UP FAULTS BETTER.
   ETR: I don't know about that. It is still a complicated and cumbersome engagement sequence with complex additional steps that require full attention from the referee. Sometimes it is not enough.

(e) THIS IS A SOMEHOW ELONGATED PROCESS.

ETR: Yes, indeed. It is too elongated and involves too much rigmarole. We need to simplify things and make everything much easier to digest for all involved.

PHIL VICKERY:

A combination of technique versus power and the combinations of different players need to be considered by the coaches. The northern hemisphere tends to play to gain penalties with the scrum. This is very different to the southern hemisphere where they play just at completing scrums ASAP to restart the game.

SANZAR scrum coaches got together in 2010 to address technical problems with elite players. One important initiative at Super 15 was to provide feedback to elite front rowers, ringing them on Monday when the coaches considered the players were experiencing technical or fitness problems.

NIGEL OWENS

Called for more responsibility from players and coaches. Also that they targeted negativity. He felt referees have too many things to control and check on, so the crooked feed generally comes at the bottom of their list and priorities. He didn't see many problems at club level, but elite levels are completely the opposite, very difficult with the professional group.

JOHN JEFFREY

After discussions with the majority of premiership coaches in UK, discovered that coaches did not want a straight feed, preferred to secure their ball. Insisted that the IRB felt compelled to get the buy-in from different stakeholders and that at times felt could not enforce the law book as is. IRB is going through the trial process with 18 franchises in the South Pacific region (Australia, New Zealand, Tonga, Fiji and Japan) at a level below Super 15 to put in practice the pre-bind engagement modifications. They are forced to go through a lengthy process because of the possible legal ramifications if they don't. Therefore the global trials will take place so they get the buy-in from all main influential rugby playing countries. These changes must be in place two years before the RWC. Therefore the IRB aims to arrive to the 2015 RWC achieving a scrum completion success rate of 80% in its matches.

PHIL VICKERY + BRIAN MOORE + PHIL KEITH-ROCHE

Cannot have a referee saying "Please guys, do it right" or "Just get it right." The law must be enforced as is. Is it a generational difference? Scrum must be steady and square and the ball must be put in the middle with the pushing coming after the ball has been introduced. No pushing before the ball goes in otherwise penalty. It is a belief that Northern Hemisphere plays scrum to milk penalties and win games. Southern Hemisphere plays the scrum just to restart the game (common misconception but true in many places). They want to reinstate the hooking!

I would like to add that I want to see referees coming out with an attitude of catching people doing things right. More positivity is needed to counter negativity!

TOPO

CHAPTER
18

Technical considerations and recommendations

TECHNICAL CONSIDERATIONS AND RECOMMENDATIONS

A reminder to the Scrum Steering Group [SSG/IRB] — March/April 2013

Scrummaging should be a seamless transition of multiple interconnected steps executed by the sixteen men actively playing the game, all in unison. Far-fetched? That is my own definition of the ideal scrum. For this to happen, each one of those sixteen players need to

(a) understand it;

(b) believe it;

(c) commit to it;

(d) prepare for it physically, mentally and attitude wise;

(e) embrace the concept of togetherness;

(f) execute skills as trained and train as you play;

(g) pay attention to implementation, the domain of coaches;

(h) continually review; and

(i) remember that scrums are imperfect and vary depending on the strength of the opposition or how tired our players are.

I suggest that a good scrum has the following components:

» 20% technique

» 20% fitness preparation

» 20% organised teamwork

» 20% individual initiative and attitude
» 20% unmitigated passion

THINGS A COACH MUST NOT DO

1. Don't neglect to practice scrums! The players need to feel the physical workout in training, so they feel confident during the game.

2. Don't practice scrums too close to the match! For example, if you play on Saturday and want to do a heavy scrum session, plan it for the Wednesday before. On Thursday, do only a light one. This is pure physiology and planning for sufficient rest after strength and scrum work.

3. Don't conduct long (i.e., 20+ minutes) **pack against pack sessions**. This will avoid unnecessary injuries.

The Bath University scrum measurements research project (2011)

A study was commissioned and funded by the IRB in 2011. This was conducted by the Sport and Science Department of Bath University and some players from the King Edward's School 1st XV participated in it. Senior lecturer Dr. Grant Trewartha was in charge of looking at the forces and loads the body was subjected to during scrummaging sessions. Furthermore, some senior club players, representatives and internationals were considered during the measurements. Several Scottish club were also involved in trials and measurements to complement the Bath University work.

To condense the final findings of the study, it was concluded that the force at engagement time could be reduced up to 25% by changing it to a pre-bind routine. I consider this one of the greatest driving forces which eliminated the hit, quite rightly so. This hit doesn't exist in the law or any coaching manual either. In my view it was a development (an overcompensation) in response to the restrictiveness of the crouch-touch-pause-engage sequence. If we try to be too draconian, the players unwittingly will develop ways to overcome the shackles. That's why I strongly believe that less is more. We must simplify the processes in rugby favouring outcome.

INSURANCE INDUSTRY INFLUENCE?

If you don't believe that insurance and insurance assessors have had a big influence in the way the laws and the scrum have developed, have I got some news for you!

I am not saying that this is bad or good; I'm just indicating that this is one of the main additional driving forces in the rugby scrum equation.

Like anything else in life, if we get too much influence from one extreme, we need to balance it. This balancing act could be a very difficult job for a person that is not prepared for it, or that has neither the desire nor the resources for it. Just beware!

NZ's Accident Compensation Corporation (ACC) to play key role in trial of new rugby scrum law

http://www.voxy.co.nz/sport/acc-play-key-role-trial-new-rugby-scrum-law/5/164901

Monday, 19 August, 2013 - 12:14

New Zealand's ACC Scheme will play a pivotal role in helping the International Rugby Board (IRB) assess the effectiveness of its new scrum engagement law.

The law change, which aims to improve player safety and reduce frustrating scrum collapses, is gradually being phased in on the world stage—but for many Kiwis, their first glimpse of the new law in action would have been during Saturday's Bledisloe Cup match between the All Blacks and Wallabies in Sydney.

ACC's role will be to help the IRB assess how well the new law improves player safety.

ACC was approached by the IRB because of a previous study ACC carried out into scrum safety, as part of its rugby-focused injury prevention work. In tandem with the New Zealand Rugby Union (NZRU), ACC has developed a world-leading injury prevention programme called RugbySmart. This has been instrumental in reducing serious injuries, particularly those sustained by front row players at all levels of the game.

ACC is uniquely positioned to assess the safety aspect of interventions such as law changes because of the comprehensive data it collects about injuries through its claims process. Everyone who sees a doctor or other health professional in New Zealand because of a rugby injury automatically has an ACC claim lodged on their behalf.

"The real test will be when the new law takes effect in the amateur game next season," says ACC's Programme Manager Sport, Isaac Carlson. "We'll analyse all the rugby-related claims we receive in New Zealand throughout the season, and that will give us a picture of how well the new law is working in terms of improving player safety."

The law change is expected to enhance player safety because props in the scrum will be required to bind their arms before the rest of the players engage or come together in the scrum.

"The consensus is that this should help prevent collapses of the scrum, which is where a lot of serious injuries can happen. The new law is also expected to reduce impact on engagement, and if you hit something with less force, that will potentially reduce both the likelihood and severity of injury."

The IRB has said it plans to assess the scrum engagement trial next year, with the aim of having approved amendments in place a year ahead of Rugby World Cup 2015.

For many rugby fans, their focus will be less on safety and more on whether the new law delivers a more enjoyable spectacle, but Mr Carlson says a better game and a safer game can be one and the same thing.

"A key insight we promote through RugbySmart is that correct technique is also winning technique, so you don't compromise your ability as a player in any way by playing safely."

Scrum Experts Lobby (SEL)

A Set of Recommendations for the Consideration of the SSG/IRB

The Scrum Experts Lobby (SEL) is a group of like-minded former international players and coaches that share a passion for rugby and, more specifically, scrummaging.

Having had the benefit of consulting with close to 40 scrum experts in the preparation of this book, I invited a number of individuals that have already expressed concerns and interest to contribute to this discussion.

We do have at heart the health and existence of the rugby union scrum that sadly has been subjected to attacks and misunderstandings from all possible angles in the last 10 years. We also understand that it is very difficult, though not impossible, to learn and understand the nuances of scrummaging if a person has not had first-hand experience. Moreover, we fully appreciate and respect the positions and responsibilities within the administration of global rugby.

It is for those very reason that we sympathise with referees, coaches and administrators as this job is not an easy one. I would like to leave this presentation in your capable hands with only one request: to be informed of the outcomes of your discussions.

The Scrum Experts Lobby was comprised of (in alphabetical order)

Diego Cash	Argentina
Pieter De Villiers	South Africa
Colin Deans MBE	Scotland
Andrew Hopper	England
Peter Horton	Australia
Jake Howard	Australia
Philip Keith-Roach	England
Tom Lawton	Australia
Clive Norling	Wales
Marcos Ocampo	Argentina
Philip Orr	Ireland
Fred Paoli	USA
Emilio Perasso	Argentina
Graham Price	Wales
Jeff Probyn	England
Heinrich Rodgers	South Africa
Enrique TOPO Rodriguez	Argentina/Australia
Cobus Visagie	South Africa
Ray Williams OBE	Wales

The following MyoQuip document was sent to the SSG as part of our submission, as a reminder of the necessary techniques and physical demands, particularly for front rowers.

Body height in the rugby scrum:
the value of equal hip and knee joint angles

by Bruce Ross, MyoQuip (November 2006)

Introduction

Despite the undoubted importance of efficient force delivery in the scrum, there is very limited published material addressing the actual dynamics of force delivery.

Powerful scrummaging is dependent on appropriate body position and limb alignment, not just in the relatively static situation immediately after engagement but throughout the entire contest of the scrum. Much of what passes for best practice in scrum formation reflects a failure to critically examine the actual geometry and mechanics of body position and how these change during the scrum contest.

I believe that an optimal configuaration of body position and limb alignment on engagement involves hop and knee angles each set at 90° with both trunk and shank being parallel to the ground. During the scrum, hip and knee joints should move synchronously so that their angles remain equal. The hips may sink slightly relative to the shoulders but trunk and shank should remain parallel.

Body height and joint angles – what the experts advocate

Modern thinking on scrummaging usually advocates consistency of body shape for all participants regardless of position, with the feet approximately shoulder width apart and toes level. There also seems to be general agreement on the need for the trunk to be horizontal or for the shoulders to be slightly higher than the hips. (Greenwood, 1978; Smith, 2000; : NSWRU, 2004; Vickery;O'Shea, 2004; Argentinian Bajada method)

However, when joint angles are discussed there is substantial divergence of opinion on the appropriate angle at the knee joint:

Jim Greenwood, *Total Rugby,* 1978

More than three decades on Greenwood's book, though overtaken by a succession of Law changes, remains a rugby classic. Its underlying logic is compelling. Figure 1 summarises his views on body position:

The above notes were included in the SEL submission with recommendations and suggestions as follows.

Recommendations and suggestions submitted to the Scrum Steering Group (SSG/IRB)

TO: IRB Law Committee and Scrum Steering Group
         Mr. Graham Mourie, Mr. John Jeffrey, Mr. Mike Hawker, Mr. Brian O'Shea,
         Mr. Mike Cron, Mr. Didier Retiere,
FROM: Enrique TOPO Rodriguez
DATE: April 10th, 2013
SUBJECT: Pre-bind modifications Trials, South Pacific Cup,
         March/April 2013 – Review of YouTube videos

Dear Graham,

Many thanks for asking me to have a look at the recent modifications applied to the scrum engagement law during the South Pacific Cup trials. As you may appreciate, this subject being a passion of mine, I have taken your request with all due seriousness and professionalism.

In recent times I had some contact with the other listed gentlemen, mostly to do with my book, *Rugby–The ART of SCRUMMAGING*, but on other matters too. Thus, since we all have the scrum as a common interest, I thought this would be a good opportunity to communicate with all of you after I watched and reviewed the 17 matches through the YouTube links.

As you may appreciate, I do have the benefit of consulting and discussing the scrum subject and current issues with a wide group of experts, several of whom have more than 50 years committed to rugby and scrummaging.

In defence of these scrum law modifications, I'd like to add that, due to the complexity of scrummaging, it might take 2 to 3 years for full adaptation and understanding of the general objectives and particular tasks by referees, coaches and players. It has been proposed that the scrum will morph into a different structure and this is no mean feat.

It has been claimed that, by altering the biomechanics of the engagement, it has achieved a 25% reduction on the forces that generally develop at the front row assembly point during this phase of the scrum. At this juncture a reduction of a quarter of the forces and a reduction of potential risks is not an insignificant amount—well done!

To facilitate our observations, I would like to establish that in scrummaging there are three intimately and inter-connected (nonetheless different) phases to contend with: a) preparation; b) engagement; and c) ball put-in and push. It is extremely important than the three are completed successfully in order to attain what I call the top trilogy: a safe, successful and efficient scrum. The first is, and should be, solely domain of the players. However, the other two require the combined commitment and right attitude of players and referee; both parties must share responsibility for the outcomes. To utilise an orchestra as a metaphor, the referee should operate as the conductor during steps b and c, and the players should be in charge of fine tuning their instruments (bodies) in step a as well as executing steps b and c.

Have watched the SP Cup trials videos, even though the problematic hit has been eradicated, other problems and side effects are developing. This comes as no surprise to me because we have a very well compressed and competitive structure with super-fit and competitive athletes, and we have squeezed or restricted it in one particular point, without adjusting the whole structure. The scrum will accordingly react and try to compensate for those restrictions by creating advantages even at their own detriment.

I have detected a number of technical and physical deficiencies surfacing that, in my opinion, compromise player safety and technique. Hence, you will have to evaluate whether taking the risk of 2 to 3 years adaptation is worth the risk.

Following are my observation in regards to the different anatomical areas compromised:

1. Spinal Cord and Neck are compromised by being unnecessarily flexed or extended (see hyper-flexion and hyper-extension) in three vital areas: a) cervical; b) dorsal; and c) lumbar. The safest and most efficient spine position for front rowers in the

scrum is the equivalent to the squat, with the back straight and head in alignment with the spine.

2. When the legs of both front rows are overextended there is no transfer of their own weight or the weight of the back five. Thus the emphasis and critical area has transferred onto the upper body and neck muscles of the front row players. To support this view, when forces are projected forward toward the opposition there are only three possible directions to go: forward; upward; or downward. I see in these trials a marked tendency to go upwards which is very risky indeed.

3. The scrum formation is too loose, lacking cohesion and togetherness. This generates extra risks, particularly for the tight five, not just the front row alone. The back rows, by merit of being semi-detached, are not exposed to these forces as much as the rest.

4. It was quite noticeable that the heavier packs have easily asserted s u p r e m a c y by generating momentum from the beginning. Conversely, the lighter or weaker packs, when stationary, are in the receiving end like targets. Lighter packs have no defence against that initial impulse or shove.

5. Moreover, when the lighter or weaker pack wants to contest or counter that supremacy, invariably they resort to two tactical initiatives: speed of execution or anticipation and getting lower than the opposed pack. This sometimes works but other times it is counter-productive, favouring the heavier pack that is able to wrestle its way down on to them

6. The results in these situations are mixed but it is obvious that once the initial resistance is broken, inertia takes over and makes the winning pack push its opposition pretty fast and unusually long distances. This is also a situation of increased risks!

7. Having noticed an accentuated use of the wheel to destabilise the opposition, which in my opinion is even more dangerous than the hit because the receiving side is neither aware of nor prepared for these twisting forces, I recommend the wheel must be completely outlawed or have a maximum tolerance 45 degrees.

8. The call often appeared inconsistent (e.g., crouch too long but other times too short, ball goes in too quick, touch really means bind).

9. Front rows tend to be too high. Sometimes they start from a good position (i.e., backs parallel to the ground and legs flexed) but as scrum progresses they degenerate into an upright position. A domino effect results in the second rowers also getting very high as they have no choice but to follow their front row!

10. Competitiveness and aggression have not diminished with these modifications but the structure of the scrum looks very fragile and vulnerable to several different forces and influences. The scrummaging technique has deteriorated and the functionality of the eight positions has been compromised.

11. The pre-bind law appears to protect the weak packs and it may be so on paper, but on the field, the bigger and stronger packs are able to establish ascendency much quicker. So, it may be a question of whether we are equalising upward or downward.

12. Between 1984 and 1985 several spinal injuries occurred in Australia at school level including two catastrophic. As a preventative measure the ARU introduced the Under 19's Laws Package which was also adopted by New Zealand and by the IRB. Obviously the mandate was to de-power the scrum at school levels. Thus the first reaction of the smart coaches was to pick flankers as props; because it was not required to push, they selected runners instead. It probably worked for 2 or 3 years although the level of scrum expertise for grass roots for senior levels was depleted.

13. It can also be concluded that Australia has been sporadically performing in scrummaging for the last 20-25 years. This type of regression or involution could well occur with the introduction of the pre-bind initiative that reduces the need for technique,   conditioning and attitude. I strongly believe that raising the levels of coaches' technical expertise and increasing the numbers of dedicated coaches will improve the whole of scrummaging.

14. We need to consider that initiative is a very good thing but initiative without technical knowledge could be very detrimental. I refer to enthusiastic coaches, players and   referees that go into problem-solving mode without considering the repercussions to the whole scrum.

15. It appears to me and my colleagues that professionalism in rugby has brought increased skill to all areas of the game except to the scrum.

16. In my estimation, long-term injuries that may be sustained under the present scrum laws and the associated consequences may take 3-5 years to be apparent. Furthermore, in some cases, it could be only after retirement (15-20 years) that real repercussions could be researched, detected and accounted for.

Technical Recommendations for Consideration

(a) Crouch is almost a given. Therefore, why not use just 2 calls? This will simplify everything and it will provide more time and control to the referees. For example:

"Crouch" with a good pause and then "Bind;" or
"Bind," a pause and then "Pack;" or
"Bind", a pause and then "Set."

(b) The second row has one knee on the ground which takes the majority of their weight off the front row before engagement.

(c) The ball put-in must be strictly in the middle.

(d) Pushing starts with the ball coming in.

(e) Outlaw the wheels. This is a very destructive and dangerous practice that contradicts all the precautions and safety measures taken by the IRB.
Find enclosed technical data and support information from MyoQuip
http://www.myoquip.com.au/Scrum_equal_joint_article.htm

I'd also like to quote two well-known specialist front rowers and very successful coaches.

1. **Topo, Pre-bind allows players to pull other players out of position and could be dangerous. It is the shirt that causes binding problems as too tight to grab. Regards, Jeff Probyn – England, 37 caps, 1988-1993**

2. **Excerpts from The Rugby Paper, UK (article by Paul Eddison, 7/04/2013) - Comments by Philip Keith-Roach, Former England, Scrum Coach 2003 RWC (also Member of the SEL)**

First the scrums are brought together as per law 20.1 (j) which says that the scrum must be stationary until the referee gives the order or signal for the scrum-half to put the ball in. Shoving can only start after the ball is put in.

Lawmakers need to draw their attention to law 20.5 and cross out the first sentence which says that "the scrum-half should put the ball in without delay."

As per the second part of the law, it's the referee who must decide when the ball is put in, and he or she should be able to check the scrum is steady before letting the scrum-half get involved.

Only then, in that second part of the process, would the pushing contest begin after the referee has checked the scrum is stable. When law 20.5 is changed, it would entirely remove the incentive of charging in for the hit and there will be no illegal gains because you couldn't get that edge before the referee has checked the binding and ensured that the scrum is stable.

It would also make it much easier for the officials to check on crooked feeds which, by the way, is one of most widely unpopular and sore points within the rugby family.

When lawmakers do that, then there will be no more early engagements. I still do a lot of work with top level clubs and we do live scrummaging sessions with a two-step process (first the engage, and then the push once everything is stable). I can say there are almost no collapses, the concussive nature of the hit is completely removed, and you are able to put teams on the back foot and go for pushover tries all legally.

Yours faithfully
Enrique TOPO Rodriguez

Reply from the SSG (IRB)

A very brief response was received on 10/04/2013, just shy of 8 hours after I sent the recommendations. One can easily assume that not a lot of internal analysis and consultation took place throughout the SSG as its members are from all over the world! The response from SSG member Brian O'Shea (delegate from Australia) stated that:

» Our points of view and solutions were "based on opinion rather than evidence."
» The SSG were waiting for "a tested solution that will permanently fix the situation."
» **The decision was "too important for the future of the game to get even partly wrong."**

Well, today is Easter Monday (06/04/2015) and instead of seeing a permanent fix in place, it's getting messier and messier week by week. Let's combine academia, common sense and common knowledge, plus dedicated practitioners that know what they are talking about.

Following this email exchange I also had several meetings with Mike Hawker, chairman, ARU and member of the SSG, but no receptiveness was forthcoming. We, the SEL Group of 29 scrum experts were on the outer without having been in the inner circle, not even a single discussion!

Andrew Hopper, English referee and former hooker from Somerset, UK, also member of the Scrum Experts Lobby, wrote to me with the following comments and copies of letters he sent to the Chairman of IRB/WR. Since 2005, the whole scrum law review and changes process has been a very expensive guessing exercise with very poor results! It is hard to imagine that this was conducted by professional personnel.

Monsieur Lapasset,
Or whoever may be in your position of influence after the 2015 RWC, when WR is likely to revise the efficiency of the law and the game, please reconsider your internal protocols, examine carefully the consultants you hire and look for people that are really committed to rugby.

Topo, my frustration with scrum dysfunction got to the point where I wrote WR/IRB another firmly worded letter. Having watched 6N games where early push and abject bent feeding were being ignored, I couldn't help myself and got to pounding out a letter. It had to be done.

Monsieur Bernard Lapasset,
World Rugby
Pembroke House
8-10 Pembroke Street Lower
Dublin 2

Wednesday 18th February 2015

Dear Monsieur Lapasset

I write as a lifelong and passionate rugby enthusiast, deeply concerned about a key aspect of our game. I refer of course to the set scrum.

Our scrum is the very foundation of our game; it is a part of rugby's soul, its very identity and DNA. Ask people in the street what they associate with rugby, they'll say, 'Big blokes, singing, drinking, passing backwards...and scrums!'

Yet, despite the new engage process, apparent adherence to the two key laws and CBS commands, our scrum is once again on the slippery slope toward abject dysfunction. Those two key laws are:

» Straight feed
» No pushing before the ball goes in

Inexorably, due to the sloth of elite level referees and the failure of WR to correct this, bent feeding is now the norm again. Witness the actions of replacement Welsh scrum half Mike Phillips in the 6N. He clearly sees the straight feed law as something beneath his station. So blatant is his bent feeding he is showing open contempt for the straight feed law, knowing that he will get away with it.

Please explain why a law breach that is so clear and obvious is being ignored.

Then there's pushing before the ball comes in—the only difference from the previous deeply embarrassing mess during the CTPE era is that pre-bind has shortened the gap. Teams are hitting and driving more and more before the most obvious bent feeding puts the ball into the second row.

RWC 15 is only 7 months away. Our game will not just be in the shop window of the world it will, for 5 weeks, be in the spotlight of the world. The way things are currently, the scrums in the world cup will be an excruciating embarrassment of collapses, re-sets, penalties, free kicks and unpoliced bent feeding. It is simply not acceptable.

As it is, we have massively excessive and unnecessary referee interference with the scrum on form up. The deeply tedious trend of referees lecturing front rows for 20 or 30 seconds, then taking 9 or 10 seconds to voice the CBS commands–an eternity for loaded packs to be kept waiting–then finally the referee telling the 9 when to put the ball in. It's a joke, quite frankly, a very bad, deeply embarrassing joke. Then when we've been through all that agony, we see the scrum collapse, or if it does stay up, the most blatant bent feed into the second row. What on earth is going on?

Two words appropriately describe this, words you will know well; they're French words.

Ridicule and debacle.

Pre-bind should all but eliminate scrum collapses. The reason it doesn't is that teams, denied the opportunity to contest the ball due to bent feeding, find other ways to contest. The result? Collapses, resets and penalty after penalty after penalty. Such a turn off. The problem is so acute that coaches are actually coaching their teams to see scrums as a source of penalties and nothing else. So they coach their packs to force penalties or, all too often, to hoodwink the referee into awarding one. And don't kid yourself, Monsieur, most elite referees are hoodwinked constantly.

Unequivocal and consistent enforcement of the straight feed and no push laws would force teams to concentrate on winning their own ball instead of relying on penalties. Scrums would stay up! The raison d'etre of a loose head prop on his team's ball is to keep the opposition tight head up and the tunnel open so the hooker can see and strike the ball. None of that applies when bent feeding rolls the ball straight to the number 8, so what incentive is there for that loose head to keep the scrum up? None. Possession of the ball is a foregone conclusion, so the props find other ways to contest with each other and yet more collapses with tedious whistling occur. This results in more expressions and sighs of dismay, annoyance, irritation and despair from those watching. What an abject dysfunctional nightmare and an acute embarrassment.

Please understand that despite my clear annoyance at the desperately poor management of scrums by WR and referees, my motivation in writing to you is genuine concern for our game.

The question is now, will you bother replying? I don't expect you will, will you, Monsieur? Whether you do or you don't, you will be hearing from me again and again and again until this intolerable nonsense is dealt with. Just so you know.

With respect
Yours sincerely
Andrew T Hopper
18-02-15

Are we witnessing the death of the hooker in rugby union?

To finish this chapter on technical considerations, why not look at the perils of hookers and how their position has regressed? In the following article, Dave Nicoll explains it very well, so I decided to copy it in full for your enjoyment! Of course good old hooking hookers would cringe but this is the reality of today's scrums. The IRB has failed to protect this position and specialized skill.

By Dave Nicoll - 17 October 2014

Much has been made of the death of the traditional number 7 in recent seasons, but it seems the issue is more prevalent in the position of hooker.

It seems long gone are the days of players such as Brian Moore, John Smith and Sean Fitzpatrick who have been replaced by, well, nobody really. Scanning the international landscape you'd struggle to pinpoint almost any hooker who could hold a candle to the aforementioned trio.

If pushed you could maybe argue Bismarck du Plessis is of true international class, in the traditional sense of a hooker, however even he has been somewhat struggling for form in recent months. Behind him you could maybe look to the likes of Dylan Hartley and Richard Hibbard, but you could hardly argue they would be considered amongst the all-time greats.

Even the All Blacks seem to be struggling in the hooker department with an over-the-hill Keven Mealamu backing a competent if unspectacular Dane Coles. Even worse the Wallabies find themselves scraping the hooker's barrel with the likes of Polota-Nau, Hanson and Fainga'a all failing to fully establish themselves.

In the Northern Hemisphere the situation isn't much better with the French having failed to settle on a hooker for much of the past couple of seasons whilst Scotland's continued selection of Ross Ford shows just how bare their cupboard is.

The issue here appears to be that coaches are favouring hookers who are considered to have more rounded skills in favour of those who perform the basics well. Given the mess the scrum has become it seems a hooker is no longer required to actually hook the ball meaning this art has been all but lost in favour of crooked out ins.

This is obviously hugely regrettable, but it is the loss of hooker's abilities to throw the ball in at the line-out that we must truly mourn. The failure of so many supposedly international class hookers to perform this most basic of tasks must be considered a true travesty in the modern game.

What this basically boils down to is modern coaches preferring a hooker who is more akin to a back rower than a front rower. There is an increasing trend in the modern game for coaches to select athletic hookers who are able to carry the ball in the loose, make numerous tackles and win turnovers. Whilst these are all attributes any coach would wish for in a hooker, they should not be preferred to the position's core skills such as line-out throwing.

The best example of this erosion of the traditional hooker is Leicester Tigers and England player Tom Youngs who spent the first 17 years of his rugby career as a centre. It was only at the age of 22 that coaches decided Youngs had some of the necessary attributes to play in the front row, and therefore set about converting him.

Now this shouldn't detract from the incredible things Youngs has already achieved as a hooker, nor should it detract from the fact he is clearly an excellent footballer; what it should highlight however is the rapidly declining expectations placed on hookers, even at an international level.

Youngs clearly has the attributes necessary to be an effective rugby player, but you only have to look at how England's line-out fell to pieces when he replaced Dylan Hartley during the Six Nations and Autumn Internationals. This isn't just an issue with Youngs, however; it is more one across the whole of professional rugby where skills such as this are being devalued immensely.

This trend looks set to continue with back row players continually being converted into hookers in a bid to give a team more options in the loose. It seems modern coaches are putting much more emphasis on the breakdown rather than the set piece. Maybe I'm wrong but to me there seems at least as much value in being able to retain your own ball during line-outs and scrums, or maybe teams these days are happy to just make do?

Do you think we are witnessing the death of the hooker in modern rugby?

* * *

CHAPTER
19

Stop press

STOP PRESS

My silver bullets for an ailing scrum

A substantial attitudinal shift combined with a necessary law update

Introduction

It is my intention to briefly describe previous scrums experimentations, results, consequences and developments in order to build my case on what solutions may be advisable to consider when creating a long lasting positive solution. I will briefly describe common practices permitted and encouraged by the law in the last decade or so, in regards to the scrum engagement laws.

Origins

I) CTPE Engagement Sequence (2005-2013)

The crouch-touch-pause-engage sequence was conceived by a group of referees appointed by the IRB to come up with solutions to control the engagement hit in scrums. They met at the Lensbury Club (Shell Staff Club) in London in 2005 and came up with the CTPE engagement sequence. All that was needed was to maintain the scrum SQUARE and STEADY as the law requires. These problems lasted 8 years and the subsequent considerable damage exerted onto the scrum, players and public opinion was done. In my opinion, the lesson here would be to give the law-making to professional law makers.

II) PRE-BIND Engagement Sequence (2013-2015)

In 2013 the IRB, through the recommendations of their Scrum Steering Group, came up with the current pre-bind engagement sequence and introduced it to international rugby in August 2013 for the 4N championship. This sequence stopped both front rows charging, but oddly enough the HIT/charge development was never part of any law book or coaching manual. However, this engagement sequence favours older and stronger players over younger ones. Furthermore, over time it seems to have nullified much of the hooking skills and hooker specialists. In my opinion it doesn't provide a safe platform for all because the closeness of both front rows doesn't allow players to properly stretch the back and spine into a safe pushing position.

By definition younger, inexperienced players may suffer more the consequences of this law. Coincidentally, it is now very hard to find quality competitive props. So I assert that the IRB should give the law-making to professional law makers.

CLARIFICATION: When I started writing the manuscript for *Rugby—The ART of SCRUMMAGING* in 2014, I supported a two-step/two-call sequence. However, after reviewing the developments of last 12 months and consulting various world opinions, I now propose a new, more radical attitude and law change and strongly recommend a one-step/one-call sequence from the refs.

Introduction

The last 28 months of Crouch-Bind-Set sequence law experimentation have yielded mixed and varied reviews. Rugby enthusiasts are not happy with the inordinate amount of time spent in packing down scrums (quite often unsuccessfully) and are increasingly frustrated by a penalty going to one side or the other with everybody clueless as to what went on. (I must confess that not even I can see at the distance what the infraction was.) Some referees seem happy with the control they exert on the match, forgetting that their main objective is to enable the 30 players to play for 80 minutes.

I don't think anyone would disagree with me. Today's big rugby partners and stakeholders are TV and the media. I'm sure they would much prefer an easy flow-through match and that spectators understand what's going on. Rugby 2015 is seriously competing for TV air space, sponsors' money and spectators' participation. In my modest opinion there are two base points for them to improve: the attractiveness of the game and an understanding of its laws, interpretations, strategies and tactics.

Rugby doesn't need to be too complicated

Through the years many coaches and rugby experts have said that rugby is a simple game, so let's make it even simpler so we can compete successfully with other sports while we are enjoying the beauties and benefits of rugby. Rugby needs more supporters.

I'd like to propose that World Rugby consider trialing the following suggestions as many law variations have been trialed to date. A holistic and integral long-lasting solution to reaffirm the rugby scrum is needed. This will be a complex re-education process and a two-point platform to guide the rationale seems to me the best way to start in order to fully comprehend any changes and ramifications. We must keep in mind the acceptance, repercussions and satisfaction of all sectors involving referees, officials, players, coaches and spectators.

Therefore, I propose a substantial attitudinal shift and a necessary law update.

Some explanations

Our complex rugby scrum is again on its knees, improving occasionally and worsening more often. Discussions have been very divisive as indicated above. I recently decided to do a bit of a technical audit of the international scrummaging status quo, consulting with a few experts.

Here is a simple, systematic, step-by-step proposed guideline of what we would like to see reflected in the scrum law.

It is a given that at school and club levels there isn't that much intensity or speed of execution and there is a lot of supervision so the preventable is prevented. There may be some exceptions but in general we would say it is under control and on the safer side, particularly now that the British Medical Association has intervened in the UK sports education system.

However, when we jump on the global elite scrum circus, it is a different story. I believe in the last 28 months (since the introduction of the pre-bind engagement law), the attention to detail has been gradually lost and, slowly but surely, the scrum is deteriorating even more.

In the last 20 years, with the help of financial affordability, technology and increased communications (internet), rugby has become a fast and furious proposition. It is also more intense and more demanding on everyone involved these days. Players are faster, stronger and better prepared. This may carry moments of exhaustion and lack of attention because for some it's just too much to handle.

I also argue that referees' jobs have become more complex and that some of them have not kept up with these developments and demands. I'm sure referees train professionally but the game of rugby union, pushed by TV and other external factors of professional life, has surpassed the physical and mental capabilities of human referees. A simplification of the laws would make their decisions more accurate, reduce or eliminate the margins of error, and improve the chances of getting it right first time.

I argue that until such time that World Rugby overhauls the scrum law, we will continue to have problems with referees, players, coaches, spectators and the media.

Tenets

The fundamental tenets for my proposed scrum law reform are separated in the three main areas of responsibility:

I) The Law
» An unambiguous leadership is needed from World Rugby administration in the process of updating the law.

» The scrum law needs to be simplified for the sake of safety, referees' support, players, spectator's benefits and rugby itself.

» Any over-officious mentality must be recognized as a negative attitude and neutralised with added player responsibility and discretion given to referees.

» Less is more. A simplified procedure that saves time and adds continuity translates to happier spectators!

» Speed up the whole process by simplifying it and eliminating unnecessary time-consuming steps.

» Eliminate the cheap technical penalties from scrummaging. Re-education is needed in regards to the scrum objectives.

» A positive attitude must prevail in players, coaches and referees, all operating within the traditional sportsmanship and spirit of the game. Money doesn't cause these problems but the mind does! A good tune-up is needed.

II) The Referees

» Reduce excessive referee involvement and intervention in the game. Referees must be enablers or facilitators of the game, not policemen, coaches or managers. Conversely, referees must be assured that they are the supreme judges for the 80 minutes of the match.

» Provide the referee with more discretion to decide when scrum development is good enough and must continue on.

» Technical strictness is essential for a sound scrum formation. However, that technical strictness is less necessary for the outcome when the scrum is almost completed. This is NOT to be interpreted as free license for players to do as they please (e.g., many times the ball is about to come out of No. 8's feet). It would be at the referee's discretion to enforce an infringement occurred earlier in the front row. Again, this is at the referee's discretion, particularly in regards to player and scrum safety

» Referees must be very strict when enforcing the general points of the scrum laws, particularly the three vital points that are essential to the upkeep of safety and game fairness: scrum square and steady; ball in straight; and no push until the ball is inside the scrum.

III) The Players

» Players must be given more responsibility and accountability for the technical procedure of scrum setup. The iconic rugby scrum will be preserved and enhanced by its own participants' responsibility.

» Players must learn that rugby is not just a sport but a profession and a source of employment for many people. Responsibility toward protecting the integrity of the game and the opponents should be of utmost importance when it comes to misbehavior, sportsmanship and any other acts that may jeopardise the proposed and agreed terms and outcomes.

Furthermore, in providing a certain spectacle to paying viewers and spectators, players also have an obligation to the standard and quality promised by the responsible organisation. The idea of giving more responsibility to players is complex and outreaching.

The above added responsibility and accountability will increase safety, game continuity and manageability, public appeal and broadcast ability and media attention. It would also reduce unnecessary stoppages and the frustration of participants and followers.

Thus, the philosophical silver-bullet solution I am proposing here is to embrace the following specific guiding rules or steps and to articulate them within the scrum law.

» Be less PROCESS MINDED and more OUTCOME MINDED.

» More DISCRETION applied in refereeing the formation of both packs.

» Simplify this PROCESS and look for specific positive OUTCOMES when possible

» REFEREE WHISTLES FOR SCRUM and 16 players run to the mark. ALL THE PLAYERS KNOW WHAT TO DO!

» NO CROUCH call is needed; THEY ARRIVE in A CROUCHED POSITION and wait.

» Both packs must be given approximately 5 seconds to get ready. Exceeding the time would be an infringement, left at referee's discretion to decide.

» Referees should be given the necessary discretion (and obligation) to look, assess and ensure the following general points: scrum is square and steady; feet are firmly planted on the ground; backs are straight and parallel to the ground on and after the engagement; players are bound; both packs are still, steady and square before engagement; and both packs are separated by 80 cm to 100 cm at shoulders.

ALL of THE ABOVE MUST HAPPEN WITHOUT THE REFs INTERVENING OR GIVING ANY VOICES. Every player knows very well what to do and must be held fully responsible for it.

» Referee must not manage or coach players. Their job is to control the game like a judge according to the law book and penalise whoever is infringing the law!

» Referee must not talk to anyone while the game is ON. (Talking to one team is also alerting the other, telegraphing his instructions.)

» They should talk only after the whistle and not give instructions to anyone about when or how to play! These are tactics or strategies and are the sole domain of one team or the other.

ONE CALL ONLY FROM THE REFEREE: PACK!

Referees should love this approach because they don't have to intervene until both packs are ready. This gives them more time to observe other parts and fewer minutiae to control. Only on engagement they will need to concentrate on technical matters, such as body shapes, togetherness, height, ball in straight, scrum square, scrum steadiness and other technical rigmarole.

Conclusion and closing

I hope World Rugby considers a wider practical vision when investigating alternative avenues to fix this problem. It's been 10 years since the experimentation of the engagement sequence Crouch-Touch-Pause-Engage, then in 2013 onto Crouch-Bind-Set and today, July 2015, some of us are still scratching our heads in disbelief, perhaps looking for divine intervention to finally get it right and other times disappointed with the loss of time, uncertainty and unfulfilled opportunities. Soon the 2015 Rugby World Cup showpiece will be on, a good opportunity for checks and balances. Therefore, I invite and propose herewith these new ideas for investigation and consideration of World Rugby. I sincerely hope all scrum things will go well and improve, yet if nothing is done we can not expect improvement. I strongly believe that if all stakeholders are asked to take more responsibility in their roles, the greater good will prevail.

I'd like to thank all the rugby enthusiasts that have collaborated in the making of this book. Including Meyer & Meyer Sports for the wonderful job done in presenting all these ideas and materials in a user-friendly format.

To the readership, I sympathise with all of you, scrummaging is not a "light meal", nor should it be. Thus, I would like to thank you most sincerely for your keen following, patience, and wholehearted support.

At this juncture in parting, I'd like to reiterate my priorities for rugby (scrummaging being an important component) but just one of them): Therefore, I will always advocate for: SAFETY, EFFICIENCY, and ENJOYMENT of all people involved with it and supporting it.

Thank you.

Enrique TOPO Rodriguez - 29/06/2015

Credits

Cover Illustration:	Victoria Rodriguez
Cover Picture:	© Thinkstock, iStock, robertsrob
Copyediting:	Anne Rumery
Layout, Typesetting, Jacket & Cover:	Eva Feldmann
Photos:	Unless credited otherwise, photos are taken from TOPO's personal collection.